Introduction to Marketing

Introduction to Marketing

Marjorie J. Cooper, Ph.D.
Baylor University, USA

Charles Madden, Ph.D.
Baylor University, USA

Elaine O'Brien
Strathclyde University, UK
(adapting author)

HarperCollins*Publishers*

658.8

This edition first published in 1995 by
HarperCollins College Division
An imprint of HarperCollinsPublishers Ltd, UK
77–85 Fulham Palace Road
Hammersmith
London
W6 8JB

British Library Cataloguing in Publication Data
A catalogue record for this book is available from the British Library

ISBN 0-00-4990019-6

Typeset by Harper Phototypesetters Ltd, Northampton, England
Printed and bound by Scotprint Ltd, Musselburgh, Scotland
Cover design: The Senate

Contents

International Edition Preface

The subject of marketing is now firmly established as a major academic discipline. This subject has its origins in psychology, sociology and economics, but one would be wrong to suggest that it is merely a product of these. Marketing has now come of age.

Over the last decade educational institutions across Europe have been expanding their provision of marketing teaching not only at undergraduate but also postgraduate level, with many new dedicated MSc programmes being launched to meet the increased demand for the subject. As well as students, business in general has been more proactive in adopting the marketing concept; even governments have recognised the need to train their industrialists in this area in an attempt to increase their level of international competitiveness.

In the academic arena interest in the marketing subject has increased dramatically. The Marketing Education Group, which encompasses all UK marketing academics has a current membership of more than 750, this figure being only 250 ten years ago. With all these academics dedicated to both furthering teaching and research in the area, the future looks promising.

This introductory text is designed for the student or business person new to the subject to establish a good understanding of the basic principles of marketing, how it operates within society and how marketing should be managed within the company. The Marketing Mix elements of price, place, promotion and product are all covered in great detail and these are then linked into the crucial area of marketing planning. There are also chapters dedicated to the areas of Non-profit Marketing and Ethics in Marketing, which are two of the newer areas of importance to emerge.

Throughout, the text has a series of both European and US examples, giving it further international appeal. Whatever your background or interest in the subject, I hope you enjoy marketing since it is a challenging and exciting subject.

Elaine O'Brien
University of Strathclyde, Scotland (June 1995)

An Overview of Marketing

Marketing has led to the development of wonderful products, such as television, microwave ovens, refrigerators, air conditioning, personal computers, cordless telephones and bottled soft drinks. Also, marketing has been responsible for bringing those products to you at prices you can afford. Marketing provides the means for you to find those products in nearby stores or order them by telephone or post, because part of marketing is distribution – getting those products to you. Marketing gives you information about new products and about new versions of old products through advertising and selling. Market research helps manufacturers and retailers know when you are dissatisfied and what you would like done to improve their services. And there is much more. Marketing touches nearly all aspects of our lives today and makes them better.

The focus of this chapter is to introduce you to the study of marketing, beginning with how, exactly, marketing is defined and the importance of studying it. The discussion of the different eras of modern business will help you understand how the practice of marketing has evolved during the last century. Finally, an explanation of the marketing concept will give you a foundation for evaluating the kinds of marketing activities you may encounter.

Why Study Marketing?

One of the problems related to learning marketing is that we see so much of it (television ads, stores, etc.) that we feel we have nothing left to learn. Nevertheless, there are several good reasons to study marketing.

First, anyone who is even mildly interested in the world as a businessperson or as a consumer, needs to understand marketing. Marketing is the focus of most business activity today.

Second, marketing represents a substantial cost to society. Studies indicate that for every pound spent in the marketplace, half goes to cover the cost of bringing a product or service to the customer. That may seem extravagant, until you consider the variety of products, the convenience of locations, and the types of services that you usually receive along with the goods themselves. In other words, you are also paying for choice and convenience.

Marketing pervades our society. It pays for much of our culture and affects our thinking, both directly and indirectly. For example, large contributions from a number of companies helped the American team participate in the Olympic Games recently. Not only did these companies purchase large blocks of advertising on television and around the Olympic area, but they also contributed directly to the team's expenses.

Finally, marketing is responsible for generating revenue, and without that contribution employees would be without jobs and customers would be without products and services.

This chapter introduces some of the marketing basics that will be used throughout this book: what marketing is, the forms it takes, and how marketing is carried out in today's business world.

Marketing Defined

What, exactly, is marketing? If you ask a group of people you will get a variety of answers, but there are some fairly typical responses. Many people think that marketing is advertising, some that it is selling, and still others that it is retailing. Marketing is all these things, but also much more.

Let's start with two formal definitions. The Chartered Institute of Marketing defines marketing as:

> "The management process responsible for identifying, anticipating and satisfying customers' requirements profitably."

Ideally, a more global one according to the American Marketing Association:

> "Marketing is the process of planning and executing the conception, pricing, promotion, and distribution of ideas, goods, and services to create exchanges that will satisfy individual and organisational objectives."

Dividing this definition into four parts will make it easier to understand:

1 Marketing is a process, and that process involves both the planning and execution of the marketing programme. In the planning stages, many decisions must be made: What product shall we offer? Who should it be marketed to? Which intermediaries should be involved in the distribution of the product? How shall we promote the product? What price shall we charge?
2 The marketing process consists of four elements called 'the marketing mix'. These four elements are product, price, promotion and distribution. ('Distribution' is sometimes called 'place', so that we have the 'Four Ps of Marketing'.) Think of your last purchase. What did you buy? What was the price and the means you used to pay for the item? How did you hear about the product or brand? Remember the answers to these questions and you will have one marketing mix in mind. Each element in the marketing mix will be discussed later in more detail.
3 Ideas, goods and services can all be marketed. All three fall under the designation 'product'. And most products are a combination of these three.

For example, a new car consists not only of the good (tangible), the car itself, but also the dealer service (intangible) that the customer will get with the car. Political candidates market ideas, and the price they 'charge' for the opportunity to implement those ideas is your vote. Churches offer ideological services in exchange for participation and voluntary giving.

4 The focus of marketing is to facilitate exchanges. An exchange takes place when one individual or organisation offers something of value to another individual or organisation in return for another something of value. In the former instance the something of value is the product; in the latter instance it is the price.

Usually the price involves some form of money, but it could be votes (already mentioned), other goods, donations of various kinds, or simply time. The marketer's role in the exchange is to find ways to add value to the product offered, so that customers are satisfied with the outcome of the exchange. That is, customers believe that the cost to them is less than the value of the product and services that they have received. The value added to an exchange by marketers can be couched in terms of 'utilities'.

Marketers Create Utilities

Marketers create what economists call utility. Utility is the want-satisfying power of a product or service; 'utility' and 'usefulness' mean the same thing. There are four basic types of utility.

Form utility is the result of converting raw materials, components, and parts into finished products. Plastic casings, electronic circuit boards, microchips and electrical wiring are converted into computers. Leather, thread, support materials and metal buckles are made into Ferragamo sandals. Similarly, music, orchestra, conductor, dance troupe, scenery, and choreography are made into Royal Ballet performances.

Time and place utility means that products and services are available to customers when and where they want to purchase them, respectively. For example, when a child has the flu, his/her mother wants the prescription immediately at the nearest pharmacy – not three days later or a hundred miles away. Seville oranges are a treat when purchased at your local grocery store; they would not be such a bargain if you had to drive to Seville to get them.

Ownership utility is created when ownership of the product may be transferred at the time of purchase. If you buy a new car, you want to assume ownership; you do not want to go down to the dealership and sign the car out every time you want to use it.

The Marketing Concept

To understand the practice of marketing today, it is necessary to review the stages through which modern marketing has evolved. The marketing concept, which we shall examine in more detail presently, reflects the development of the marketing profession. Marketing historians generally recognize three distinct eras in the evolution of the marketing concept.

The Production Era

The Industrial Revolution ushered in the production era. During the last half of the nineteenth century, dramatic changes occurred in technology and transportation. Electricity was 'tamed', rail transportation became prevalent, and the assembly line and mass production were introduced into manufacturing. Products could now be made in a fraction of the time – and for a fraction of the price – that it had formerly taken in cottage industries. And consumers perceived that many mass-produced products were superior to 'homemade' ones. Encouraged by the scientific management movement – epitomised by Frederick W. Taylor and his *Principles of Scientific Management* – businesses found that they could sell everything they could produce. Product shortages and high consumer demand were the order of the day.

While marketing practice was known, the emphasis remained on production until the mid 1920s. During this time Henry Ford made his famous statement so often quoted to exemplify the production orientation: 'They [customers] can have any colour they want, as long as it's black.' So much for customer satisfaction!

With customer demand seemingly insatiable, we can perhaps forgive the philosopher Ralph Waldo Emerson for observing: 'If a man writes a better book, preaches a better sermon, or makes a better mousetrap than his neighbour, though he builds his house in the woods, the world will make a beaten path to his door.' Unfortunately, Emerson made a better philosopher than marketer. Chester M. Woolworth built a better mousetrap, one that was appealing to mice, sanitary to use, priced only a little higher than the wooden variety, and one that never missed. But housewives were reluctant to throw it out with the dead mice because it looked more expensive than the old traps. They were also reluctant to remove the rodents and clean up the trap to re-use. Consequently, they eventually refused to buy the new mousetraps.

This example is only one of many that illustrate the fallacy of the production orientation to doing business. First, a production orientation assumes that customers will interpret 'new and improved' in the same light as the engineers who designed the product, a patronising attitude that assumes business knows what is best for the customer. Next, this philosophy assumes that what the buyers want is a mousetrap. They may want a different solution, like a poison or an exterminating service. Good engineering and production quality may produce a better product, but it takes more than form utility to create success in the marketplace.

The Sales Era

From the mid 1920s to the 1950s, manufacturers became so effective at producing goods that consumer demand began to wane. Businesses began to focus on activities to sell the product, primarily personal selling and advertising. During this era the stereotype emerged of the salesperson delivering a 'hard sell' to the customer. Hard sell techniques, and a general lack of training, led to selling taking on an undesirable image in the minds of the general public. For example, many unemployed farmers and factory workers were sold 'sample cases' and sent door to door with no training at all. Sales professionals continue to struggle with the negative image that is a legacy of this period.

During this period, it also became more important for businesses to promote their products to wholesalers and retailers, thus encouraging them to stock more of the product. Marketing departments were subordinate to finance, production and engineering, and heads of marketing were often designated as 'sales managers'. While selling and advertising are important components of marketing, they are not the entire picture. Yet we still see many companies today who are stuck in their development at either the production or the sales stage.

The Marketing Era

After World War II, factories stopped producing tanks and artillery and again began producing consumer goods in greater quantities than ever before. It was a shift from a sellers' market to a buyers' market, and some businesspeople began to realise that large production quantities and extensive promotion did not ensure that consumers would purchase their products. In fact, a radical change in business philosophy was needed. Businesses must first determine what customers want and then produce it, rather than the other way around.

This change in thinking led to the formulation of the marketing concept. The marketing concept is a philosophy of doing business in which the goals of the organisation are best realised by offering products that the customer wants and by providing customer satisfaction. The development from production orientation to marketing orientation or concept would look something like this:

- Production orientation: our function is to produce the best quality products available and find a way to get them to the customer.
- Sales orientation: our function is to persuade customers that our products are the best and to get those customers to buy our products.
- Marketing orientation: our function is to find out what the customer wants and then produce it and market it in such a way as to maximise customer satisfaction with the purchase.

Both the production and selling orientations are inside-out approaches to doing business. A company looks at itself first, what it does and what it wants to do. Then it tries to make customers conform to the company's way of doing business. A marketing-oriented company employs an outside-in approach. This company gathers information from the marketplace and tailors its way of doing business to match the needs and wants of customers.

Implementing the Marketing Concept

Many successful companies have adopted the marketing concept. These include McDonald's, IBM, Procter & Gamble and Apple Computer. For example, the

Apple Macintosh™ was a direct answer to consumers who complained that existing personal computers were not user friendly and were totally unsuitable for an educational environment. The 'Mac' introduced simple pull down menus that could be manipulated with a mouse. Easy to use and easy to understand for schoolchildren and adults alike, the successful 'Mac' made marketing history.

No matter how good an idea sounds on paper, it is only useful if it can be put into practice. Many companies give lip service to the marketing concept. They claim to be 'market-driven', but a slogan is not enough to change the way customers perceive a company. The marketing concept must permeate the thinking of employees in all areas of the company.

Some common modifications that suggest a marketing orientation are a vice president of marketing at the same organisational level as the VP of finance and the VP of production, the use of product/brand managers, marketing plans and marketing research.

However, sometimes these trappings are merely superficial. Levi Strauss got into a lot of trouble a few years ago trying to market three piece men's suits in department stores. The company got off to a good start. They did extensive research among men who represented the proposed market for the suits, and their respondents gave the Levi Strauss management team excellent feedback: the suits should be carried by specialty retailers, not department stores; alterations were important, because each man wanted his suit tailored just for him; the Levi name was a stumbling block for this market because people just did not identify Levi with three piece suits. A new name was recommended for the line.

The company proceeded to market the suits through department stores under the Levi name as separates in order to rule out alterations. Not surprisingly, the entire line was a colossal failure. It lasted only one season and was quickly dropped. The company had not implemented its own market research. It had asked prospective customers what they wanted, but had not listened effectively to the answers!

For the marketing concept to be successfully implemented, it must be adopted from the top down in an organisation. If top management does not make the commitment to running the company according to the marketing concept, there is very little that other members of the organisation can do.

But commitment from top management is not enough. The marketing concept must also be adopted across functional areas. That is, these changes must include finance, production and engineering as well as personnel and customer service departments. Policies that relate to credit, service, and returned merchandise are just some examples of areas that must be sensitive to a customer orientation.

Of course, there are limits to implementing the marketing concept. A company has to pay its bills, stay in business and make a profit. It can only go so far in satisfying customers. And sometimes if a firm satisfies one group, it may alienate another. Likewise, non-profit organisations must also act within the scope of their goals and ideals. So executives and managers must recognise realistic limitations while still maintaining an overall commitment to satisfying customer wants and needs.

Broadening the Marketing Concept

Since the 1960s, the marketing concept and marketing practice have gone beyond traditional marketing of goods and services. It has become apparent that organisations in the non-profit sector can use marketing tools very successfully. Thus the marketing concept has broadened to include non traditional transactions, such as Army recruitment, universities throughout the UK utilising the media to market their courses, and private hospitals promoting their facilities as would any profit-led organisation.

It is now common for companies in the non-profit sector to make extensive use of marketing to reach and serve their publics. Colleges and universities, hospitals, political candidates, the Rotary Club and local churches all practise marketing techniques. The chapters that follow are filled with powerful ideas that can help you make a living. These ideas can also be used if you wish to make valuable contributions to non-profit organisations by helping them employ marketing techniques to achieve their goals.

SUMMARY

This chapter discussed some of the reasons for studying marketing and how the practice of marketing is so pervasive in our society. The American Marketing Association's definition of marketing, and that of the UK Chartered Institute of Marketing, gave us an opportunity to carefully examine the various components of marketing, particularly the marketing mix. An important aspect of the marketing mix is its ability to create utilities for customers, and it is in this context that marketing practices should be evaluated.

The evolution of the marketing concept further emphasised how business has moved from focusing on itself to focusing on customers and on meeting their needs. While many companies still show some residual influences from those earlier eras, we can be confident that the most successful companies will be carefully implementing the marketing concept as we know it today.

The need to broaden the marketing concept to include non-traditional organisations was examined. While it is obvious that businesses cannot survive without pleasing their customers, it has not always been so obvious that non-profit organisations also have constituencies to serve. The broadening of the marketing concept has led in recent years to the implementation of marketing practices in these non-business organisations.

FURTHER READING

Assael, Henry. 1985. *Marketing Management*. Boston: Kent Publishing Readings Co., Chapter 1.

Baker, M.J. 1991. *An Introductory Text*, 5th ed. MacMillan, Chapter 1.

Boone, Louis E. and Kurtz, David L. 1992. *Contemporary Marketing*, 7th ed. Ft. Worth, Texas: Dryden Press, Chapter 1.

Crosier, K. 1975. 'What Exactly is Marketing?' *Quarterly Review of Marketing* (Winter).

Fullerton, Ronald A. 1988. 'How Modern Is Modern Marketing? Marketing's Evaluation and the Myth of the "Production Era".' *Journal of Marketing* (Jan.): 108-125.

Guiltiman, Joseph P. and Paul, Gordon W. 1988. *Marketing Management*, 3rd ed. New York: McGraw Hill Book Co., Chapter 1.

Hunt, Sharyn and Cooke, Ernest F. 1990. 'It's Basic but Necessary: Listen to the Customer.' *The Marketing News* (5 Mar.): 23.

Kotler, Philip. 1991. *Marketing Management*, 7th ed. New Jersey: Prentice Hall, Chapter 1.

Kotler, Philip and Levy, Sidney J. 1969. 'Broadening the Concept of Marketing.' *Journal of Marketing* (Jan.): 10-15.

Lamb, Jr., Charles W., Hair, Jr., Joseph F. and McDaniel, Carl. 1992. *Principles of Marketing*. Cincinnati: South-Western Publishing Co., Chapter 1.

Pope, N.W. 1979. 'More Mickey Mouse Marketing.' *American Banker* (12 Sept.): 54.

Pride, William M., Dibb, S., Simkin, L. and Ferrell, O.C. 1994. *Marketing, European,* 2nd ed. Boston: Houghton Mifflin Co., Chapter 1.

2 Marketing Management

The practice of marketing is complex. It requires in-depth knowledge of all aspects of marketing, research on customers and on the environment as it relates to marketing, and the discipline of applying sound management principles to marketing problems. Good marketing is partly art, partly intuition and partly genius. These aspects are very difficult to convey in a textbook; therefore, we will focus on those aspects that can be studied.

One of the most basic aspects of successful marketing is the management of the marketing function itself. Marketing managers set goals, develop marketing plans and direct the implementation of those plans to create profitable transactions for the firm. Without skilful marketing it is virtually impossible for a company to survive in today's highly competitive environment. That fact alone makes marketing extremely critical in the business world today.

This chapter includes an expanded discussion of the marketing mix and considerations in putting together a marketing plan.

Managing Reebok

Reebok International sounds like a worldwide enterprise; in fact, it is a US company that distributes a British-made product named after an African antelope. Reebok is a well-known, successful brand in the US today; in 1979, when Reebok was eager to enter the American market, it was virtually unknown.

Reebok teamed up with Paul Fireman, who had experience in the camping and sporting goods industry. While Reebok was looking for marketing assistance, Fireman was looking for a new, exciting product. But entering the athletic shoe market was a tough proposition. Sales in that market were $1 billion in the early 1980s, and competition was strong. Nike held a 35 per cent share of the market, with Converse, Adidas, and others also holding large pieces of the pie.

Reebok needed an innovative and aggressive marketing strategy to break into the market. But Reebok already had some advantages: production capabilities and the experience in marketing athletic shoes in Britain. Plus Reebok had some unique features: attractive styling, soft leather uppers, a range of colours, a tradition of Olympic running shoes, the trade-marked Foster Heel Cradle, cooling mesh toe, air-breathing Gore Tex inner liner and a dual density midsole.

Realising that Reebok could not successfully appeal to everybody, Fireman wisely decided to try to appeal to a segment of the market on the basis of some trends that he observed in the athletic shoe market. First, different shoes were being used for different kinds of sport: tennis, basketball, jogging, etc. Second, few options were then available for women. Third, the aerobics market was just emerging.

By targeting the aerobics market and women in particular, Reebok identified an as yet untapped market segment. By 1986 Reebok was the leader, with a 31.2 per cent share of the athletic shoe market.

The Marketing Mix

In the hierarchy of marketing decision-making, strategies are supportive of objectives and goals, and tactics are supportive of strategies that have been selected. In marketing, the areas of greatest tactical control are the marketing mix elements. Marketing mix elements that are selected for a particular tactic must be consistent with, and supportive of, the proposed objective of a particular strategy. As mentioned in the first chapter, the marketing mix is composed of four variables: product, price, promotion and distribution (place).

Product mix management offers the marketing decision-maker a number of tools with which to differentiate a product. Such attributes as the physical product itself, features and benefits, services associated with the product, level of quality, installation, instructions, packaging, branding and accessories are all tools in making the product suitable for a particular target market. As mentioned earlier, dozens of product styles with differing benefits are now produced by Reebok.

Price management, sometimes called 'terms of sale', offers such tools as basic price, price flexibility, discounts, allowances, rebates and geographic terms. A car manufacturer, such as Vauxhall, may offer both rebates and zero per cent financing to new car buyers to increase the number of cars sold.

Distribution management tools that are available to a marketing manager are the type of channel, types of middlemen, kinds and locations of stores, transportation, storage, service levels in the channel, and overall objectives of the distribution mix. Maytag washers are sold through their own dealers, while Hotpoint sells washing machines through a variety of discount, appliance and department stores.

Promotion management offers advertising, including audience, media, copy and source; salesforce, including number, selection, training, motivation and location; sales promotion, including point of purchase displays, coupons, contests and premiums; and publicity, including news releases, news conferences and grand openings. Although both 7-Up and Sprite sell a lemon-lime carbonated soft drink, each brand has targeted a different audience for its commercials.

Unlike the environment, which we shall look at in the next chapter, the marketing mix consists of variables that marketers can control and adjust to fit the demands of their customers. Decisions about the marketing mix should be made with the customer's wants and needs foremost, enabling the marketer to initiate satisfying exchanges. Each element in the mix represents a nearly infinite variety of options from which to choose, and the various combinations of those four elements add even more complexity to marketing mix decisions.

To better illustrate each element in the marketing mix, let's examine them individually.

Product

As noted in the American Marketing Association's definition of marketing, 'product' is an umbrella term. It can be a good (tangible), a service (intangible) or an idea (also intangible). For example, a new computer is a good, a haircut is a service, and inalienable human rights is an idea. Most products have service components (a McDonald's hamburger has a convenience component), and most services have product components (a hotel room rental may include toilet articles).

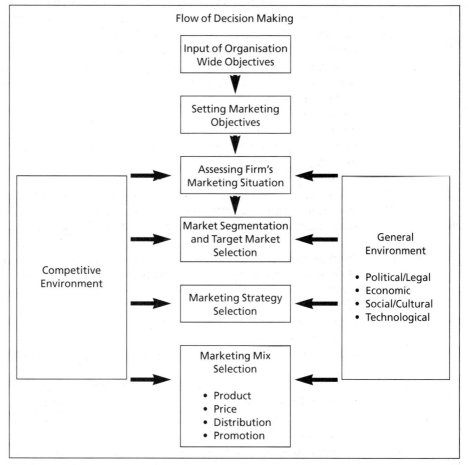

Figure 2.1 Marketing Strategy Formulation Process

Companies should research their customers, find out what they want, and produce a product with the desired characteristics. The product also includes appropriate packaging, brand name, warranty, and, if necessary, the service agreement. The actual design and manufacturing of the product are not marketing activities, but the decisions concerning which product attributes to offer and how the product should be constructed affect the want-satisfying ability of the product. Thus even engineering and production departments need to recognise and observe the marketing concept.

Consider the introduction in the spring of 1992 of a new chocolate bar from M&M Mars: the Milky Way II. Milky Way II was designed and marketed to satisfy consumers' needs for taste, reduced calories and reduced fat. Although sugar-free sweets had been around for some time, this was the first chocolate bar to be made from caprenin, a reduced-calorie fat developed by Procter & Gamble. While it was necessary for chemists, engineers and production personnel to be involved in physically making the new product, it was marketing that determined the need for the product and the want-satisfying attributes that would make Milky Way II attractive to consumers.

Price

In some ways price is the most difficult to manage of the four marketing mix elements. Price must be high enough to cover costs and make the company profitable but not so high that customers refuse to buy. It must be high enough to reflect real quality and enhance the product's image, but must not convey the impression that the seller is trying to take advantage of the consumer.

Price is usually money, but it can be anything of value that the customer is willing to give up and the seller is willing to accept. Price is often the basis for competitive advantage when product offerings are otherwise perceived by the market as identical. However, heavy discount pricing can lead to price wars, which may force some firms out of business.

In spite of the obvious disadvantages of competing solely on the basis of price, this practice continues to be a popular strategy. A recent development of marketing tabloid newspapers in the UK has been to focus primarily on the price component of the mix. This has resulted in a price war which may, in the long term, be damaging for the industry.

Promotion

Promotion is marketing's communication with the company's various publics, with special emphasis on its customers. Promotion informs people about the company, its products and product attributes. The company may announce a new product or new features on an old product. Special interest groups may urge the public to take a particular position on a political or social issue.

Promotion can be broken down into several areas. One is personal selling, which uses face-to-face communication between buyers and sellers. Other forms of promotion involve mass communication: the use of impersonal, mass media, such as television, newspapers and magazines. Mass communication can be further subdivided into advertising, public relations and sales promotion. Advertising is a paid form of communication with an identified sponsor. Public relations involves events, press conferences, community and charitable sponsorships, and publicity releases. Sales promotion generally refers to devices that entice customers to take immediate action, such as coupons, point-of-purchase displays,money-off offers, premiums, samples and demonstrations.

Distribution

Distribution means getting the product from the producer to the consumer in the quantities desirable and at a convenient time and location. It may be very simple as when the producer markets directly to a consumer. When you buy tomatoes from a farmer by the roadside, you are taking advantage of a very short channel of distribution (sometimes called the marketing channel).

Most distribution channels are more complicated and involve such intermediaries as wholesalers, warehousers, distributors, brokers and retailers. These intermediaries perform a variety of marketing functions, including storage, transportation, inventory control and credit management; they also provide marketing research and promotion assistance to other members of the channel.

Managing the Marketing Function

Marketing management consists of two very broad objectives:

1 To analyse the marketplace for opportunities and appropriate target markets.
2 To put together a marketing mix that will be both satisfying to customers and profitable for the company.

A key element in these objectives is the identification of desirable target markets. A target market is a group of customers with fairly homogeneous needs and wants that can be served by the company's products. Keep in mind that the entire focus of the management process should be the development of satisfying and profitable marketing mixes for the right target markets.

Marketing managers are responsible for planning, implementing and controlling marketing activities. Sometimes this responsibility is referred to as 'marketing strategy planning', sometimes as 'strategic planning' and sometimes as simply 'marketing management'. The term 'marketing management' seems more comprehensive, since planning, implementing and controlling are well recognised as separate management activities; thus 'marketing management' will be the designated umbrella term in this book.

This chapter and Chapter 19 will focus on the planning process. Implementing and controlling the plan will be the focus of Chapter 20.

Opportunity Analysis

Planning starts with an analysis of market opportunities. The business environment is complex and dynamic; nothing stays the same. Products that sold yesterday may be left on the shelf tomorrow. Witness the demise of British Caledonian Airlines and the Clydesdale department stores.

Companies are frequently guilty of two opposite errors of judgment. One extreme is to try to be all things to all people. Some companies, in the attempt to find new markets, diversify without the technical know-how, experience or distribution channels needed to serve these new markets. On the other hand, some companies define their businesses so narrowly that they miss many outstanding opportunities. The latter mistake has been labelled 'marketing myopia', the inability to define one's business in such a way as to allow the company to take advantage of legitimate openings. Good examples of avoiding marketing myopia are AT&T, which defines itself broadly as being in the communications business rather than, narrowly, as in the telephone business. Kodak says it is in the 'imaging' business.

Setting Objectives

After an analysis of market opportunities, planning moves to understanding the organisational objectives that have been set by the company or the non-profit organisation. Top management sets these objectives, which include implications not only for marketing but also for production, finance, research and development and other areas. Yet if we keep the marketing concept in mind, we recognise that even objectives for other functional areas should be market-oriented.

For example, if top management wants to develop a presence in Europe, an obvious implication for marketing would be to analyse those European markets. Even if production and engineering can make the product, that does not guarantee that the product will satisfy European customers.

Next, the marketing manager must set marketing objectives that are in keeping with the company's overall objectives. It is crucial that top management and marketing work very closely together to prevent conflicting strategies. This is one of the roles of marketing research: to assist management in identifying new, potentially profitable markets that are a good fit with the company's make-up. Not all opportunities will work well for a particular company. Home healthcare, cellular telephones and waste disposal management are growing areas, but entry into these markets would probably spell disaster for McDonald's or General Foods. They do not have the technical expertise, the distribution channels or the experience in these markets to be successful.

Strategy Selection

This step consists of identifying and evaluating alternative strategies. This is a complex process and should be further broken down into the following:

segmenting markets, identifying target markets and choosing marketing strategies.

Segmenting Markets

Market segmentation is a process that marketers go through to divide a mass market into groups that have relatively homogeneous needs or wants for a given product or service. In the case of our Reebok example, the segment that spawned Reebok's success was women who bought the shoes for aerobics.

There are a variety of ways in which market segments can be identified. For example, geographic divisions can be used. Pasta and fresh herbs are more commonly eaten in the Southern countries in Europe, whereas more Northern countries tend to eat more hearty stews and cooked as opposed to fresh vegetables.

Demographic segmentation is very commonly used. Such variables as age, gender, race or ethnic background, income and education can be used to differentiate the preferences and behaviours that a market segment might exhibit. For example, in comparing black consumers with white, we find that black people spend proportionately more than white people on clothing, personal care and home furnishings. White people spend more on medical care, food and transportation. Black people buy twice as many record albums as white people and significantly more orange juice, rice, soft drinks and instant potatoes.

Psychographic segmentation divides potential buyers into certain lifestyle and values categories. The original concept of the yuppie was coined to designate 'young, upwardly mobile professionals'. Psychographic segmentation assumes that lifestyle patterns are associated with particular patterns of consumption. For example, General Electric discovered through marketing research that consumers associated its GE brand with conservative, older business types. To change that image, and thereby appeal to a broader range of customers, GE adopted its now-famous slogan, 'We Bring Good Things To Life'.

Finally, segmentation can be based on situational usage or the benefits that individuals derive from a particular product. For example, customers may want a van for 'hunting and hauling' and a family car for everyday use. Certainly the people who buy cars for basic transportation and economy differ greatly from those who buy cars for prestige, speed, or performance.

Heavy, medium and light users of a particular product can also be differentiated. 'Lite' beer is actually aimed at the 'heavy user' segment of beer-drinkers. Research shows that this group wants to be able to drink more beer without filling up!

It should now be obvious that specially tailored marketing mixes must be developed with specific segments in mind. Reebok used special product features, such as a variety of colours, to appeal to women. They used the cushioned heel and dual-density midsole to appeal to aerobics participants. They chose premium pricing to reflect product quality, and they advertised in women's magazines to reach their target market. They also offered samples to aerobics instructors, direct selling to dealers by Reebok's sales staff, and advertising in trade magazines to move the product through the distribution channel.

Identifying Target Markets

Simply segmenting markets is not enough. Companies should then determine which target markets to pursue. Members of a viable or potentially successful target market should have the following characteristics:

1 A need or desire for the product.
2 The ability to pay for the product.
3 The authority to purchase (for example, minors cannot purchase alcohol).
4 The willingness to buy.

An analysis of the various target markets should be carried out to assess the degree of fit between these four characteristics and the firm's resources and expertise. Those markets or market segments that offer the best fit are the ones to pursue. If any of these four factors is lacking, marketers should look elsewhere.

Choosing Marketing Strategies

The three major classes of marketing strategies are *undifferentiated* strategies, *differentiated* strategies and *concentrated* strategies. Sometimes firms do not need to segment a market but to develop a single marketing mix for the entire mass market. An undifferentiated strategy means that a particular product and marketing mix are equally desirable and suitable for everyone in that population. Marketers use this strategy infrequently today because it results in so much wasted coverage. It can also be pre-empted by competitors who offer specialised versions to smaller segments of the total market.

A major benefit of this strategy is that a company can save resources in terms of production efficiency. A single version of a product is less expensive to produce than multiple versions with varying colours, styles and features. A company can also concentrate on doing an in-depth analysis of a particular market with each element in the marketing mix finely tuned to this market.

An example of an undifferentiated strategy is Heinz Baked Beans. It is mass-marketed through supermarkets. The generic nature of the product (it is used in the same way by virtually everyone) makes it a good candidate for undifferentiated marketing.

A differentiated strategy is one in which marketers design different marketing mixes to satisfy smaller segments of the total market. A differentiated strategy works very well because it recognises that products or services can have different bundles of desirable features. Those different bundles can be matched to consumer tastes and needs.

A good example would be some changes that Reebok has made since its initial entry into the US market. Reebok now offers the 'Fitness Walker' for casual walking, the 'Power Trainer' for workouts, professional racing shoes for speed walking and the 'Rugged Walker' for hiking.

One drawback is that the more differentiated the strategies become, the less cost-effective the entire approach becomes. Inventory costs will rise because retailers need to maintain a selection in a variety of styles. Production costs will rise because the manufacturer must produce different forms of the product.

Concentrated marketing is a frequently used subset of differentiated marketing.

This occurs when a firm decides to focus its efforts on profitably satisfying a smaller segment of the target market. As already mentioned, a concentrated strategy can be an effective enemy of the undifferentiated strategy.

The US Time Company became the world's largest watch company by developing a reliable, reasonably priced watch for people who just want to tell time. The watch, Timex, completely upset the watch industry, which had previously focused almost exclusively on watches as high-priced, high-quality symbols to commemorate special events, such as Christmas, graduation or retirement. Timex was not only a good product, it was offered at a lower price. It was also distributed in department stores, discount houses and many other retail stores, rather than in expensive jewellery stores, as had been the case with other watch brands.

Market Position Strategy Alternatives

While choosing among undifferentiated, differentiated and concentrated market strategies represents one type of strategy decision, a company must also consider its position in each of its competitive markets. Companies usually fall into one of these four categories: market leader, market follower, market challenger and market nicher.

Market leaders are those who clearly dominate their markets. When they make changes in their products, others will follow or be forced to respond in some way. Examples include IBM (computers) and Xerox (copiers).

Market challengers are those firms that aggressively attempt to move up in their competitive position and aspire to become market leaders, or at least influential followers. Avis's 'We Try Harder' advertising campaign has allowed it to successfully challenge Hertz for domination of the car rental market.

Market followers imitate market leaders but from a distance. They are most successful in stable, profitable markets where there is plenty of business to go round. They can be more profitable than the market leaders simply because they assume none of the risk of innovation. They implement a new idea once it has been proven to work.

Market nichers are small or large firms that specialise in serving smaller segments ignored by major competitors. The Pierre Victoire chain of restaurants is an example of focusing on a particular market segment to gain a differential advantage. This chain specialises in offering good quality French style country cooking, but at an affordable price and has extended throughout the UK by using franchise agreements.

The Importance of Strategic Planning

The very heart of marketing is the process of strategically approaching markets in such a way as to enhance the long-term growth and profitability of the firm. Marketers want to make their companies more responsive to customer demands and more flexible in meeting changes in the environment. The process outlined above (or something very similar) is used by every sophisticated marketing organisation for identifying potential markets and developing targeted marketing mixes.

SUMMARY

Managing the marketing mix involves setting objectives, developing strategies to meet those objectives and finding suitable tactics for carrying out the marketing plan. Each of the four elements of the marketing mix – product, price, promotion, and distribution – must be planned and carefully executed to accomplish a firm's objectives. Each of these elements involves a variety of dimensions that will affect a marketer's overall success. For example, promotion involves advertising, public relations, sales promotion and personal selling. Each of these areas requires expert advice for a marketing manager to be effective.

The process for managing marketing requires an analysis of the marketing situation, including the target market. The second requirement is that a satisfying marketing mix be developed and maintained with ongoing adjustments to the dynamic marketplace. Specifically, marketing management includes opportunity analysis, setting objectives and strategy selection. Marketers can then select their target markets and implement the appropriate strategies to reach those markets.

FURTHER READING

Baker, M.J. 1992. *Marketing Strategy & Management*, 2nd ed. MacMillan.

Boone, Louis E. and Kurtz, David L. 1992. *Contemporary Marketing*, 7th ed. Ft. Worth, Texas: Dryden Press, Chapter 2.

Geneen, Harold. 1984. *Managing*. New York: Doubleday.

Guiltiman, Joseph P. and Paul, Gordon W. 1988. *Marketing Management*, 3rd ed. New York: McGraw Hill Book Co.,Chapter 1.

Hutt, Michael D. and Speh, Thomas W. 1989. *Business Marketing Management*, 3rd ed. Hinsdale, Illinois: Dryden Press.

'International Newsletter.' 1987. *Sales and Marketing Management* (Apr.): 86.

Kotler, Philip. 1991. *Marketing Management*, 7th ed. Englewood Cliffs, New Jersey: Prentice Hall, Chapter 1.

Neidell, Lester A. 1983. *Strategic Marketing Management*. Tulsa, Oklahoma: PennWell Books.

Norgan, S. 1994. *Marketing Management – A European Perspective*. Addison Wesley.

Pride, William M. and Ferrell, O.C. 1991. *Marketing*, 7th ed. Boston: Houghton Mifflin Co., Chapter 1.

3 The Marketing Environment

How does the environment affect marketers? Social, economic and environmental trends, are just some of the factors which may affect a company's operations. In Germany, for example the introduction of the Blue Angel label to denote environmentally friendly products gave some companies an overnight competitive advantage. The environmental movement has grown in strength throughout Europe, and now most companies offer bio-degradable packaging as standard, e.g., McDonald's.

Social trends and changes in lifestyles have also presented both opportunities and threats to companies. The 'fitness fad' of the 1990s has presented opportunities not only to the sports industry, but also to the food industry. A case in point is that of the soft drink Lucozade, previously positioned as a drink to take to an ailing friend or relative. It has now been completely repositioned, due to its high sugar content, as an energy-booster to be consumed after partaking in sports.

Changes in the economic environment can either result in an industry being forced to cut margins, in order to offer a more competitive price to consumers with reduced buying power, or being able to invest in new plant and machinery, since long-term income is assured. In recent years Eastern Europe has undergone some radical changes, with companies eliminating jobs to adapt to a market environment. Although this is an extreme situation, the development has had a direct and lasting effect on the way business is conducted.

As you can see from these few examples, marketing managers are continually called upon to respond to elements in the environment that affect the way a company does business. Although marketers can control the elements of the marketing mix, it is virtually impossible to control the elements of the environment. But it is equally certain that marketers must find successful means to deal with the environment, to cope with the negatives and take advantage of promising developments. This chapter deals with the various aspects of the environment and examines ways in which marketing decision-makers can use information from the environment to their benefit.

Micro Environment Versus Macro Environment

The environment within which a company manages its marketing plan is composed of two parts. The micro environment is the sum total of forces and parties close to the firm that affect its ability to satisfy its objectives, including its marketing objectives. These forces include the company itself, members of its marketing channels, customers, competitors, and other relevant publics, such as stockholders. The macro environment consists of those larger forces in society that affect all of society's micro environments. Legal, economic, political, social, and technological forces in the environment affect any company's decisions and ability to successfully compete in the marketplace.

Analysing and Responding to the Environment

The environment offers both opportunities and threats to an individual firm. Threats often come in the form of changes that catch a company off-guard. For example, how could Johnson & Johnson have anticipated the cyanide-laced Tylenol capsules that confronted them in the early 1980s and again in 1986?

Other threats that often appear are changes in the economy that make less money available for spending, make money more difficult to borrow, or make revenue less valuable through inflation. Consumer concerns may cause law-makers and regulators to take action against a given company or an entire industry. In the wake of Heileman's withdrawal in the US of PowerMaster Malt Liquor from the marketplace, the Federal Bureau of Alcohol, Tobacco and Firearms began examining other brewer advertising as well, and additional regulation is anticipated by the drinks industry.

Equally likely, however, is that opportunities will arise in the form of changes that match the strengths and capabilities of the firm. For example, AT&T, Sharp, and Canon are only a few of the companies that are targeting the burgeoning home office market. According to research findings, 34.4 million US households currently have a home-office, and 59 per cent of those generate income. Consequently, spending for home-office equipment and services now exceeds $15 billion and is expected to grow. Home office buyers need reliable products, low prices, and more post-sale support than corporate customers. No single competitor could have forced this market to emerge, but many businesses will enjoy the opportunities that it presents.

An example of changing social sensitivity by marketers can be demonstrated by the company Robertson's, producers of jam and marmalade. This company had a logo of a Golliwog on their jars and since this may be considered offensive by some racial groups, the packaging was adjusted.

Many of the sports traditionally dominated by men have become popular with women and have presented opportunities to diversify in the clothing range. Hill walking in the UK is being enjoyed by an increasing number of women. Companies like Rohan, Wild Rover and Berghaus are now offering a much more extensive range of colours than the traditional blue and red worn by men.

The above examples illustrate the impact that social, economic and technological changes can have on business. Regardless of the form the environment takes, it is comparable to the weather in that every competitor has to live with it.

Reacting to Versus Controlling the Environment

Much has been written in recent years about the ability of a firm, through lobbying and other proactive techniques, to exercise some control over the environment. Examples include lobbying for changes in the regulatory environment of a business (such as direct marketers do with respect to postal rate increases) and adopting ideas that lead to the increased consumption of a particular product.

Another option is to assume a leadership role in research and development, thereby affecting the overall technological environment. For instance, DuPont developed an amazingly strong fibre called 'Kevlar' in the early 1980s. Today Kevlar can be found in army helmets and flak jackets, tennis rackets, golf clubs, gloves, aeroplanes, motorcycles and thousands of other products. This product has been extremely profitable for DuPont.

Political and Legal Environment

While each of the macro environmental elements stands alone, there is some flow and overlap among them. For example, the social environment frequently flows into issues that become political in nature. Governmental bodies that either make laws or regulate business often take social issues quite seriously.

In recent years the question of nationalism has been a significant social issue in many countries. With countries becoming involved in block trade agreements, individual countries are becoming increasingly aware of such things as tariffs on imports. Some countries apply a law of no foreign ownership, which may be a deterrent to exporting to that country. Many global companies have focused their production in countries where the cost of labour is considerably lower than elsewhere, so reducing their manufacturing costs.

Consumerism, another social trend that often feeds increased regulation, arises from the belief that consumers must be protected from illegal and unethical business activity. In the United States the Food and Drug Administration's (FDA) investigation of Ortho Pharmaceutical Corporation's Retin A is a case in point. Approved by the FDA as an anti-acne prescription cream, the product was subsequently promoted as an anti-aging treatment. The FDA objected and has begun to take a more active role in the marketing of many other pharmaceutical products.

Firms in a particular industry may respond to counter actions taken against them. These same FDA investigative tactics prompted the formation of the Coalition of Healthcare Communicators, which includes the American Association of Advertising Agencies, the Pharmaceutical Advertising Council, and other health, media and pharmaceutical companies. The group develops strategies to deal with the FDA, and increasing pressure from the pharmaceutical industry appears to have caused the FDA to back off in some respects.

In the case of Europe, individual companies are governed initially by their own national governments and secondly by the EC regulations. Larger companies, like the car manufacturers tend to come under European scrutiny. Consumer activists in Europe have for a long time been campaigning to have some of the basic safety equipment included in the US models as standard, for the European models as well. The case of airbags in cars is one example which is still not resolved, with many car manufacturers still being allowed to offer these as an 'optional extra'. Activists' campaigning can make a difference and has led to many changes in the laws affecting consumers, especially in the area of safer products.

Laws that Affect Marketing

These laws can be roughly divided into two broad areas for which the laws were enacted. The first area deals with anti-monopolistic laws designed to protect companies from each other and to preserve competition among businesses.

Table 3.1 lists major laws passed in the UK this century, which affect how marketing can operate. The laws fall into two main categories: pro-competition and consumer protection. The first set of laws is to ensure that no one company or consortium of companies can restrict others from operating in a chosen market, by erecting barriers to entry. The second set of laws was introduced to ensure that companies produce safe products that perform as promised and that they do not practise fraudulent advertising or selling.

TABLE 3.1 Major Laws Affecting Marketers

Pro-Competitive Legislation	Consumer Protection Legislation
Monopolies & Mergers Commission Prevents companies from operating in any way which may distort, prevent or restrict competition.	*The Fair Trading Act 1973* Provides a framework for continuously reviewing any practices which may not be in the consumer's best interest.
Financial Services Act 1986 This act ensures that competition is not threatened in any way by the practices of regulatory bodies, investment exchanges or clearing houses.	*The Food Act 1984* *The Medicines Act 1968* *The Misrepresentations Act 1967* *The Trade Descriptions Act 1968* *The Prices Act 1974* *The Unfair Contract*
Restrictive Trade Practices Act 1976 This act is designed to investigate any circumstances in which two or more people who produce a good enter into an agreement to either restrict the conditions of sale or the price set. The agreement will be investigated by the Office of Fair Trading to see if it is in the best public interest or not.	*Terms Act 1977* *The Sale of Goods Act 1979* *The Supply of Goods and Services Act 1982* *The Consumer Protection Act 1987* All of the above-listed acts ensure that consumers' interests with regard to the good quality of food, pricing details and description and performance of goods are safeguarded.
Treaty of Rome This is a European Community Treaty which seeks to dismantle government trade barriers, at the same time ensuring that they are not replaced by private barriers, which may in some way fragment the Common Market. The Treaty aims to prevent restriction of competition, whilst also prohibiting any practices which may affect trade between member states.	*The Consumer Credit Act 1974* Ensures the protection of consumers who enter into hire purchase or credit agreements. *The Weights & Measures Act 1985* Regulates the marking and accuracy of quantities included in products.

Many companies encounter problems when interpreting laws applicable to them, since parameters can be rather vague. In order to avoid breaking the law many companies use the most recent court rulings to give them clearer guidelines as to what is and is not acceptable practice.

Regulatory Forces

Regulatory bodies can be run either by government or by the industry itself. Government-run agencies tend to be a little stricter and in the case of industry self-regulation not all companies in the industry decide to take part. Many self-regulatory bodies started in an effort to prevent government from becoming directly involved, with companies establishing codes of ethics for their industry. One example is that of advertising where the ITC Code of Advertising Standards and Practices aims to keep broadcast advertising 'legal, decent, honest and truthful'.

Some UK government regulatory bodies and their responsibilities are listed in Table 3.2.

TABLE 3.2

Regulatory Agency	Responsibility
Department for Trade and Industry	This body has a wide remit focusing on the promotion of competition and enterprise in the UK on both a national and a regional level and anything related to business development, e.g., grants for educational training of managers.
Ministry of Agriculture, Fisheries and Food	This body develops policies for these industries and has responsibility for environmental issues, rural issues and policies relating to the food industry.
Department of the Environment	This department is responsible for practices which can directly affect the environment, both at a national and local level, e.g., town planning, environmental protection, inner city issues.
Department of Employment	Deals with such things as equal opportunities, industrial relations and legislation relating to health and safety at work.
Export Credit Guarantee Department	This body acts as an insurance system for exporters against the risk of non-payment and insurance for new investment abroad.
Central Statistical Office	This department co-ordinates the statistical work of other departments and provides advice on central economic and social policies.
Department of Transport	This department deals with all areas related to transport, from motorway road safety to regulations for the coast guard.

State and local agencies also regulate the behaviour of firms with respect to their marketing activities. Historically, abuses or suspected abuses of the public good led to regulatory constraints on business.

Self-regulation frequently forestalls governmental intervention by giving the business community an opportunity to take responsibility for problems before they become large enough to require regulation. The drawback of this approach is that there are non-subscribing businesses and non-compliant businesses. Unfortunately, apart from informal sanctions, nothing can be done legally to compel these businesses to abide by the other companies' codes.

In recent years there has been a general move towards deregulation of a variety of regulated industries, such as the airlines, banking and public utilities. During periods of deregulation or declining regulation, many opportunities develop for innovative behaviour. At the same time, the lack of regulation often allows increased levels of competition or near-predatory levels of pricing, which eventually results in some firms leaving the industry.

Economic Environment

The economic environment is one of the most volatile and rapidly changing aspects of the marketing environment. The money supply, inflation rate, interest rates, and consumer expectations can make what would otherwise be a successful marketing plan a failure or may save what is basically a flawed strategy.

In the UK throughout the 1980s, the Government ran a monetary-based policy, the driving force of which was to reduce the level of inflation. Countries throughout Europe employ different methods to control inflation, but most countries in the European Union now have fairly stable rates.

When money is tight and consumers' incomes drop, they will decide to do without some products. Businesses will put off major expenditures for capital equipment and will postpone research and development of new, risky products. Companies often reduce their marketing budgets during hard times; it is common to see promotional budgets, for example, cut dramatically.

Interest rates are a particularly critical factor in determining economic direction. If interest rates are dropping or stable, consumers tend to respond with purchases. If interest rates are rising, consumption tends to be restricted in the long run. That is, people are reluctant to make major commitments, and that circumstance has a domino effect throughout the economy, impacting on businesses as well as individuals.

Inflation also tends to have a disrupting impact on the economy. Inflation means that prices rise faster than consumers' spending power. Some countries in the world experience annual inflation rates as high as 25 to 100 per cent.

A major problem in responding to economic conditions is to be able to manage the real value of your money. This problem is no less real for businesses than it is for individual consumers. The cost of living index, which is keyed to commonly-purchased goods and services, is computed periodically to give marketers and consumers a basis for comparing costs across the whole economy. This one indicator tells marketers much about how to plan their future production and marketing strategies. Over several years, inflation may be falling or low and stable; at such a time consumers may grow confident that inflation has been eradicated. Nevertheless, inflation is part of a cycle that continues to change on a regular basis.

Business Cycle

While the economic environment changes constantly, it tends to change in predictable ways, although the length of business cycles is difficult to predict. The typical business cycle starts with a period of prosperity: high availability of money with low unemployment and high total income for consumers. This period is then followed by a rise in unemployment and a fall in overall buying power that characterises a recession. A temporary decline in the rate of growth in the economy may not qualify as an official recession, but if the condition persists for a longer time, generally three quarters of a year or more, economists declare a recession. If a recession lasts a long time, unemployment becomes extremely high, wages decline and consumer spending drops dramatically, experts will announce a depression. Monetary policies during a recession or depression are very restrictive, and businesses usually respond with defensive strategic moves. Inventories are cut, marketing efforts are reduced, and plans are made to control damage rather than try to build market share.

The final stage of the business cycle is referred to as recovery. It occurs when the economy moves from depression or recession back towards prosperity. During this time, the rate of unemployment begins to drop, disposable income rises and consumer expectations become more optimistic. Marketers cannot control the stage of the business cycle, but the way they respond determines how profitable the period will be or how they may minimise loss in a period of economic distress.

Consumer Demand

Chapter 5 will explain how consumers make individual choices; here we simply note that marketers must understand the underlying reasons for consumer demand. Determinants of consumer buying power, which underlie consumer demand for goods and services, include total income, disposable income, discretionary income and wealth.

Total income is the amount of money received by an individual, including wages, rents, investments, pensions and subsidy payments for any given period of time. Disposable income is the money left after taxes have been taken out. Discretionary income is what an individual has left after purchasing basic necessities such as food, clothing and shelter. Discretionary income is the income on which marketers of non-essentials base their market measurements and estimates. Changes in discretionary income might affect the purchase of a new car, holiday or household appliance.

Credit enables one to expand discretionary income in the short run while impairing it in the long run. It further expands the options available to a consumer by enabling him or her to obtain high-cost items before having saved the money to buy them. Wealth is the accumulation of past income and other financial resources into various forms: savings, securities, retirement funds, jewellery, real estate, antiques and any other investments.

In addition to these measures of consumer spending power, there are some derived indices that help marketers estimate demand for specific products. A commonly-used measure is the effective buying index (EBI). This index is published by *Sales and Marketing Management,* a trade publication widely read by marketers. EBI is similar to disposable income because it is based on salaries, wages, dividends, interests, profits and rents, less national and local taxes. A related measure, called the buying power index (BPI), is a weighted index of population, effective buying income and retail sales history. The higher the index number, the greater the potential for consumer spending. The index can be used for a variety of purposes, from planning sales territories to evaluating whether markets should be expanded into new geographic areas.

International Economy

The European economy is tied more than ever before to the world economy. In fact, this is true for every industrialised country in the world. Interest rates, availability of capital, and other economic factors cut across international boundaries. The reason is the vast increase in international trade in the past decade and the level at which international trade continues.

For example, the pound is impacted by the exchange rate; that is, how much the pound is worth in a foreign currency. When the pound is worth less, we pay more for imported products. When the pound rises against foreign currency, we pay less for the same products.

Marketing managers are not insulated from these forces, even if their companies do not engage in foreign trade. For example, the influx of Japanese-made products, as well as those of some excellent European competitors, into the United States has contributed to the demise of some American businesses. This points to the severe penalties of being unable to compete in a world market, even if you are a domestic producer!

Some countries do not allow movement of profits out of their countries. In the early 1980s, it was illegal for multinational firms to expropriate, or take profits out of Greece. Kodak Corporation had a very profitable subsidiary in Greece but was unable to transfer those profits out of the country. Kodak continued to operate there in the expectation that under a more liberal regime that law would be repealed and monies could be repatriated to their headquarters.

Competitive Environment

There are really two approaches to the competitive environment that can be considered by marketers. One, the approach taken by economists, assumes certain model characteristics for industries or firms. The second, a strategic view of competition, is that there is a constant interaction among firms in an industry and firms outside the industry who are all competing for a limited amount of disposable or discretionary income.

Economic View of Competition

Economists recognise four theoretical models of competitive structure: monopolies, oligopolies, monopolistic competition and perfect competition. Monopolies contain one dominant company with many barriers to entry into the market. Because of the high cost of investment, the low profit margins, or other factors, it is virtually impossible for new companies to break into the industry. Thus one firm dominates.

Under a monopoly, the product has few or no substitutes, and it is assumed that monopolists have perfect knowledge, and therefore perfect control, of the market. Public utilities are a good example of monopolies.

Oligopolistic competitive structures contain few competitors, and prospective entrants into the market find some barriers to entry. The firms in the industry tend to be homogeneous, although attempts are made to differentiate on the basis of real or perceived variations in the marketing mix. Market knowledge is assumed to be imperfect. Examples include car manufacturers and cigarette companies.

Monopolistic competition involves many competitors with relatively few barriers to entry into the market. Products made by monopolistic competitors are differentiated and have many substitutes. Product differentiation is frequently based on branding and advertising. Knowledge of the market is assumed to be greater than an oligopoly but less than a monopoly. Such products as toothpaste and refuse bags are examples of monopolistically competitive industries.

Perfect competition is characterised by an unlimited number of competitors with no barriers to entry into the market. The products are homogeneous and frequently standardised. Knowledge of the market tends to be near perfect because of the way channels of distribution are set up. Examples are commodity markets, such as peaches or cotton.

Strategic Competition

Marketers who represent oligopolies or monopolistic competitors view their industries as venues for developing strategic plans. Competitors are seen not only in the direct sense but also indirectly. For example, manufacturers of televisions must consider films and other forms of recreation as indirect competitors. Much of this book will be devoted to how strategic competitors obtain or retain competitive advantage.

Social Environment

A more difficult environment to measure, but as important as the economy for marketers, is the social environment. Social trends tend to develop rather slowly and often seem more ambiguous when they are measured. Social environmental trends arise out of factors as deep-seated as cultural values and aspirations and take the form of measures such as 'standard of living' and 'quality of life'. Trends change and marketers must decide which trends to serve or whether they are only passing and insignificant.

Some recent social trends include the consumer movement, green marketing, nationalism, and health and fitness.

The consumer movement has been active in the United States for well over a hundred years. It has taken a variety of forms, including pressures leading to many laws. A book by Upton Sinclair, *The Jungle*, chronicled the lack of health standards in the meat-packing industry during the first part of this century and led to legislation that made food, drug and cosmetic products much safer. More recent consumer movements have included pressure for safer cars and pressure to control prices during periods of high inflation.

Green marketing, which is the marketing version of the environmental movement, has become popular. It is characterised by a growing awareness of the environmental damage going on around us. Environmentalists spearheaded the movement to raise public support for recycling, pollution control and other environmentally sensitive issues. Some products are now marketed as having been manufactured with recyclable materials. Other products are sold with directions on how to responsibly dispose of them and their containers after use. The fact that our landfills are being used up indicates that recycling will continue to be a major consumer issue in the future. Likewise, marketers who have developed strategies to address green marketing are already finding rewards, both in profitability and positive attitudes toward the firm's social responsibility.

Nationalism has grown in recent years, aided by the resurgence of patriotism during the time of the Persian Gulf War. With many companies now operating in a global marketplace, there is a growing concern over the fate of the small domestic firm. Many companies have adopted a nationalistic approach to marketing, encouraging people to buy home produce; even larger companies like British Airways recently ran a campaign with the slogan 'Fly the Flag'. In the UK not many consumers have been greatly influenced by these campaigns. In France, however, the nationalistic feelings are much stronger, with French farmers and fishermen regularly undertaking violent protests against the import of foreign goods. This has led to a resurgence of some very nationalistic policies by government, which many would argue contravene the wider agreements of the European Community. Finding the balance between protecting national interests, whilst being part of a wider trading block is a problem faced by all members of the Community.

Health and fitness as a social trend has been with us for some time now. The demands for healthcare, preventive healthcare and various forms of exercise have expanded. Sports equipment, health clubs and a variety of other goods and services have proliferated as a result. The marketing implications of this trend extend even to food marketing, product safety and such diverse areas as music volume and the amount of time people devote to sleeping.

Technological Environment

The technological environment is often paired with the economic environment because technology so heavily influences competition and the ability of an industry to be profitable. But technology is a specialised area that must be given high priority for marketers and deserves separate consideration. Historical comparisons that liken obsolete consumer products to buggy whips and slide rules can be interesting, but most technological changes occur in much more subtle ways.

Marketers now recognise that the life of a given product is getting shorter all the time as companies try to maintain cutting-edge technological features in the products they bring to the marketplace. For example, developments in personal computers are making the large mainframes less and less practical except for specialised projects. The expectation that we will develop highspeed rails based on superconductive materials now threatens to make obsolete a great deal of conventional rail and air travel. Possibilities based on solar technology have threatened for a number of years to change the competitive mix for public utilities that sell gas and electricity services.

Marketers must be aware of major breakthrough technology and be willing to invest in using that technology for new product development, for improving customer service, for shortening the distribution channel and for achieving better marketing mixes for individual market segments.

SUMMARY

The environment in which marketing operates has a tremendous effect on what strategic and tactical decisions marketers must make. The environment also has a bearing on how successful a marketing programme will be. Some environmental variables are controllable, or at least they can be influenced. Other factors are simply constraints with which marketers must learn to operate.

The political and legal environment creates legislation that marketers must take into account in producing and marketing their products. Much of the existing legislation is actually designed to preserve competition in the marketplace.

Economic variables affect marketing by enhancing or detracting from the willingness of customers to make purchases and by influencing the timing of those purchases. By studying these factors, including the business cycle of the industry in which one is attempting to operate, it is possible to find better ways to meet customers' needs and still make a profit. Competitors, of course, are also a factor; they can be counted on to increase the uncertainties that marketers face.

Finally, the social environment often dictates the types of products, the styles, flavours, colours, etc. that consumers are willing to purchase. Social trends, coupled with new and evolving technology, often create new oppportunities in the marketplace, as well as making some older industries obsolete.

FURTHER READING

Godiwalla, Yezdi M., Meinhart, Wayne A. and Warde, William D. 1980. 'Environmental Scanning – Does It Help the Chief Executive?' *Long Range Planning* (Oct.): 87-99.

Jain, Subhash C. 1984. 'Environmental Scanning – How the Best Companies Do It.' *Long Range Planning* (Apr.): 117-128.

Lazer, William. 1984. 'How Rising Affluence Will Reshape Markets.' *American Demographics* (Feb.): 17-21.

Menendez, Teresa and Yow, John. 1989. 'The Hispanic Target: An Overview of the Major Markets.' *Marketing Research* (Jun.): 11-15.

Palmer, A. and Worthington, I. 1992. *The Business and Marketing Environment*. McGraw Hill.

Pride, William M. and Ferrell, O. C. 1991. *Marketing,* 7th ed. Boston: Houghton Mifflin Co. Chapter 2.

'Research: A Potent Factor in Reaching the "Macho Market".' 1988. *Marketing News* (26 Sept.): 12-13.

'Smith Corona's Market Is Tapping Out.' 1990. *Business Week* (16 Jul.): 31.

Smith, D., (Ed.) 1993. *Business and the Environment, Implications of the New Environmentalism*. Paul Chapman Publishing Ltd.

Zeithaml, Carl and Zeithaml, Valarie. 1984. 'Environmental Management: Revising the Marketing Perspective.' *Journal of Marketing* (Spring): 46-53.

Zeithaml, Valarie. 1985. 'The New Demographics and Market Fragmentation.' *Journal of Marketing* (Summer): 64-75.

4 Finding and Selecting Markets

Sergeant David Currie, a UN Army recruiter, discussed the interesting problem faced by people with his assignment: 'While almost any secondary school leaver could join the Army, l can spot the ones who are likely prospects just by chatting with them. If they are driven by needs for educational opportunity, adventure, money or security, I can usually put them in the Army. If they need education and can achieve this through scholarships or loans, [the situation] is less likely to lead to my swearing them in.'

Sergeant Currie, who based his description of the various 'markets' and 'non-markets' for UN recruiting on more than 20 years of experience, gave a good explanation of market segments and how to qualify them without ever using standard business terminology. Nevertheless, Sergeant Currie clearly understands his 'markets'.

The focal point for all marketing activity is the potential market for any product. Therefore it is important to understand the composition and characteristics of markets before you will be able to design satisfying marketing mixes for them. As we said in Chapter 2, a market is a group of people who satisfy four criteria:

1 They need or want the product.
2 They have the ability to pay.
3 They have the authority to buy.
4 They are willing to buy.

Large numbers of decision-makers who select products for themselves and/or family members characterise consumer markets. Business markets (or industrial markets) are often represented by purchasing agents and committee buying groups. Many marketing professionals believe that business buying decisions are more rational and are based more on economic factors than are consumer buying decisions.

This chapter examines how marketers take broad consumer markets or industrial markets and break them into manageable units for targeting with specific marketing mixes. Usually markets will be broken into segments, because very few products can be sold the same way to everyone. Most effective marketing strategies are based on the notion that a particular market segment with particular needs and characteristics can be identified and addressed as an individual audience, a 'rifle' rather than a 'shotgun' approach.

Market Segmentation

Markets for goods and services tend to occur in heterogeneous aggregates. That is, different people have different needs and wants. For example, everyone does not want the same kind of car. Some people are looking for sportiness and performance; some look for luxury and comfort; some are concerned with having enough room for the children when they travel; and some have entirely different needs from any of these. Markets are segmented, or broken down, to a level at which their needs or characteristics become more homogeneous. At this point marketers can devise a marketing mix to appeal to this homogeneous group.

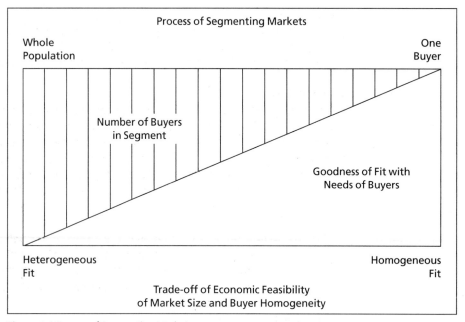

Figure 4.1 Process of Segmenting Markets

As illustrated in Figure 4.1, we could carry this process to its logical extreme and conclude that the most homogeneous segment is an individual. After all, no one is exactly like someone else. Individuals, however, rarely constitute enough demand to make it profitable for businesses to serve each person with a unique marketing mix. Thus marketing managers segment markets to a size somewhere between the level of the individual and the level of the total market, in which needs are so diverse that no single marketing mix could satisfy everyone.

The economic feasibility of serving a market is an important consideration in making segmentation decisions. If markets are segmented to too small a size, then the resources necessary to communicate with them become wasted. Consider the cost of trying to design a unique car for every single driver in Europe! Market segmentation, then, becomes a process of trading off market segment size against homogeneity of preference.

Criteria for Effective Segmentation

Obviously, there are many ways to segment a market. You might, for example, develop a product that appeals to cautious people. But how would you identify and reach only those who exhibit the characteristic of cautiousness? How many of those people are there? We don't know because we have no means of tabulating such a trait.

Since there are far more ways to segment a market than we can possibly use, we must examine the standard criteria for evaluating market segments. The four criteria that tell us whether a market segment is viable include the following:

Measurability

The purchasing power of the market segment that wishes to own a business some day is not really measurable. However, the number of people who have, for example, a home office for which they make purchases *is* measurable.

Accessibility

It is one thing to be able to measure a segment; it is another to be able to reach that segment. An example is the group of secondary school leavers who are positively disposed to a career in the military. While they may be somehow identifiable, it would be difficult to find a means of communicating with them separately from the general population. Any media that will reach them will incur a lot of wasted coverage by also communicating with uninterested individuals.

Substantiality

As already mentioned, market segments must be large enough to be economically feasible. A company would probably not find it profitable to develop a line of footwear for marathon runners over the age of 75: while they exist, they may not exist in numbers large enough to pay for a specialised marketing mix.

Actionability

This criterion is the degree to which programmes can be designed and maintained for serving segments that are identified. No one business can be all things to all potential customers; this limitation often keeps businesses from serving marginal segments. A good marketing manager will prioritise targeted segments and only go after those that are profitable, meet the company's objectives, and can be served with the company's resources and expertise.

Segmenting Consumer Markets

Segmentation variables are the groups of characteristics that are selected for dividing a total market into segments. As we shall see, there are many possible variables for segmenting a market, but it is only practical to use a few of these in any given situation.

Variables that are selected to be used in segmenting a market should be tied to the behaviour, attitudes and product usage of the market. Keep in mind that these decisions will be different for each business, each market and each product involved. It should be clear that variables for segmenting the breakfast cereal market would not necessarily be useful for segmenting the car or travel markets. In fact, even within a broad market, such as the travel market, the variables for segmenting business travellers may differ from those used to break holidaying families into segments.

There are four broad classes of variables used to segment consumer markets: geographic, demographic, psychographic and behavioural.

Geographic Variables

Geographic variables divide markets into units based on countries, states, regions, counties, cities or neighbourhoods. This type of segmentation is based on the differences among people who live in different places. Market research has shown that people who live in different areas of the country come to prefer different types of sports clothes, car equipment, and even recreation.

Sometimes these differences are linked to climate: snow shovels and car-tyre chains are sold more in the North than in the South. Most homes in Northern Europe have central heating fitted as standard; whereas in the south of Spain air conditioning is the priority. Tastes in food also vary on a geographic basis, with those in Southern Europe consuming a larger proportion of fresh fruit and vegetables. Northern European countries, however, have traditionally based their cuisine around ready-cooked as opposed to fresh dishes.

Geographic variables may include population density. Population centres are important for some businesses. One major department-store chain defines its markets as urban areas with populations of 500,000+. Many specialised companies require a certain critical mass before they can expect to operate profitably.

Demographic Variables

Demographic variables are probably the most frequently used class of segmentation variables for consumer markets. These variables represent objective information that can be counted; thus it is often called quantifiable data. Demographics include variables such as age, gender, family size, stage in the family life cycle, income, education, race, occupation, religion and nationality.

Some demographic measures, such as age, tend to fall into standardised categories. A typical age grouping for adults might be 20–34, 35–49, 50–64, and 65 and over. Educational groups would include primary school, secondary school, school-leavers, graduates and post-graduates. Many of these categories are derived from the census; however, others are a function of the special needs of the business doing the segmenting.

Age can be used to segment markets for toy manufacturers, book publishers and clothing manufacturers. Some book publishers are now marketing large-print editions for the over-50 age group.

Gender accounts for differences in purchasing behaviour with respect to some health and beauty aids and some recreation equipment.

Income produces differences in the types of products consumed, as well as in proportions of income spent on various product categories. For example, as income rises a smaller percentage of total income is spent on food, and the percentages spent on recreation and education increase.

Japanese tourists to the UK have increased dramatically in number over the last decade This has led to many tourist destinations extending their promotional material to include Japanese as one of their mainstream languages.

Psychographic Variables

Psychographic segmentation includes measures of social class and lifestyle. Psychographics can be more difficult for marketers to use because they are not standardised and are not easily quantifiable. Generally psychographic profiles of groups are obtained by asking consumers to agree or disagree with a series of statements that represent activities, interests, preferences and opinions.

Social class is usually represented by six distinct classifications: upper-upper, lower-upper, upper-middle, lower-middle, upper-lower and lower-lower. These categories, which came into widespread use during the 1950s, have traditionally been linked to some distinctive behaviours. For example, the upper-upper class is composed of 'bluebloods', people who are born rich. These people typically disdain conspicuous consumption, are heavily involved in community service and charitable endeavours, and, surprisingly, take a fairly conservative approach to spending.

In contrast, the lower-upper class is composed of the 'nouveau riche', the newly wealthy, who often exhibit their newfound wealth in purchasing products that announce their success. Highly-paid executives, successful entrepreneurs, and some professionals – doctors and lawyers especially – fall into this class.

The upper-middle class is made up of upper-level white-collar managers, professionals and 'smaller' entrepreneurs. Like the upper classes, they are typically college-educated. In fact, the upper-middle class places a great premium on education and spends a large proportion of its income on it. The upper-middle class has incomes well above the national average – ideally at least twice the national average. Members of this group often aspire to reach the lower-upper class and many do eventually.

The lower-middle class is made up of lower-level white-collar workers and upper-level blue-collar workers. This group's income and education runs at or slightly below the national average. They purchase many appliances, electronics and tools. There is a strong emphasis on family ties, and this group seems to have a local rather than a cosmopolitan view of life.

The upper-lower class consists of lower-paid workers, with some secondary education or maybe a diploma. Their jobs are usually unskilled or semi-skilled, and their incomes are slightly below the national average.

The lower-lower class has the highest unemployment rate; its members are often on welfare and at or below the poverty level in terms of income. Characterised by poor health and shorter life spans, this group also has the highest rates of illiteracy and the least formal education.

Although the distinctions between classes were more clear cut in the past, many of the differences remain. These differences can be important to marketers who are trying to effectively segment markets. For example, the lower classes tend to take holidays fairly close to home. If they do travel long distances, it is usually to see relatives. Also, lower classes tend to prefer the local news, while the upper classes are more likely to watch the national news.

While social class is rather standardised, there are hundreds of lifestyle measures. Rarely will two lifestyle scales be alike in naming any particular category, since each measure is generally developed for a specific company and purpose. However, there is a commonly-used lifestyle measure called 'VALS', for values and life styles. Introduced in 1978 by SRI International, VALS was updated and refined for release in 1989. The VALS system categorises people into three major groups: people who are principle-oriented, status-oriented and action-oriented. (These are further subdivided into eight segments.) Principle-oriented consumers, for example, seek to behave in ways consistent with their moral and ethical beliefs; status-oriented people are looking for a secure social position; action-oriented individuals like to have an impact on their environment and the rest of the world around them.

Many advertising agencies claim to have used these VALS categories to create successful campaigns for their clients. However, VALS and other psychographic systems are not without their critics. First, it is argued that a standardised system like VALS cannot possibly provide the insight that a customised study can give a marketer. Second, while knowing that a market segment is made up of successful, take-charge people who are active, sophisticated and self-confident may help a copy-writer write an ad, such information will not tell you whether the market segment is profitable. Finally, VALS has been criticised as too simplistic and generalised to be useful for specific marketing problems.

Behavioural Variables

Behavioural bases for segmentation include such variables as benefits sought, user status, usage rate, loyalty status, readiness status, and attitude towards the product. User status, for example, could be further broken down into non-users, potential users, first-time users, regular users and ex-users. Readiness status can be subdivided into no awareness, awareness, informed, interested, desirous, and intending to purchase. These kinds of behavioural segmentation variables have been very useful in gaining insight into buying habits as well as in differentiating how buyers might respond to various marketing efforts. For example, the 'frequent-flyer' programmes offered by many airlines are targeted towards the heavy-user segment of airline services, generally business travellers.

Benefit segmentation occurs when the market is segmented directly according to the various benefits that are sought from the product. For example, the tooth-paste market is made up of those who want cavity prevention, those who seek fresh breath and whiter teeth, the hedonistic element desiring good taste, and the economic group, who will buy the brand with the lowest price.

Recently Healthy Choice introduced eight varieties of lean meats, plus 21 other varieties of thin-sliced lunchmeats and hot dogs under the Healthy Choice name. These, along with Weight Watchers lunchmeat line, are designed to turn light users of lunchmeats into medium or heavy users. Here a new product is introduced to expand sales of an existing category, lunchmeats, on the basis of a benefit that has been proven desirable in other food categories: lower calories. Thus new lunchmeat segments are targeted: the weight-conscious/healthy-eaters segments.

Segmenting Business Markets

Industrial markets differ somewhat from consumer markets in the way markets' segmentation variables are chosen. While demographic factors such as industry, company size and location might be used, other variables can also be effective means of segmentation. These include purchasing approaches, operating variables, situational factors and personal characteristics. Industrial markets tend to have more standardised – thus more identifiable – buying procedures than do consumers. Industrial buyers also tend to be more rational in their decision-making process.

Industry often determines the geographic location of a market segment. The City of London has a large concentration of financial institutions, whereas the Central Belt of Scotland has many computer-servicing firms. A given product may also be targeted toward several kinds of industries. A ceramic-tile producer may identify as possible target markets swimming-pool and hot-tub manufacturers, residential-home builders and commercial construction companies.

Size can be a factor in segmenting an organisational market. Larger customers who account for a much larger percentage of a marketer's revenue may receive volume discounts and special service.

Single-Variable or Multi-Variable Segmentation

At this point in our discussion, you may be wondering whether to use only one variable in segmenting your market or more than one. The answer in this case, as in so many cases, is 'It depends'. Single-variable segmentation is certainly easier and simpler than multi-variable segmentation. But the real question is 'What does it take to clearly identify your target market?' Use only those variables that differentiate behaviour and/or call for a differentiated marketing mix.

Certainly multi-variable segmentation allows you to be more precise in your definition of the target; however, for each segmentation variable you add, you will cut your total market into smaller and smaller pieces.

Let's look at an easy example. Suppose you have a total market of 100 people, of whom half are male. Your product is designed strictly for females, so you cut your market in half with one segmentation variable – gender. Now suppose that this product is fairly expensive, so you further define your market as those with incomes of £40,000 or more. If only 20 per cent of this group have incomes of £40,000 or more, you now have only ten people left in your target market. And so on. So beware of using multiple segmentation variables unless they are clearly called for by the nature of the product and the market.

Steps in Market Segmentation

The process of segmenting markets can be done by following a general procedure. The following steps show the order of the decisions that must be made in segmenting markets:

1 Select the basis for segmentation.
2 Profile possible segments.
3 Forecast market potential by segment.
4 Forecast probable market share of segment.
5 Choose market segments.

Much has already been said with respect to selecting the bases (or variables) for segmentation. Marketers must determine one or more characteristics of potential buyers that classify them into various segments. Once these segments are identified, then they must be analysed further to determine other chacteristics, particularly those on which a marketer could base marketing mix decisions. For example, Levi Strauss realised that every American male adolescent needs one pair of casual cotton trousers smart enough to wear when meeting his girlfriend's parents. Thus were born Levi Dockers, a dramatic marketplace success not only with adolescents but with parents too!

Forecasting market potential and market share by segment is done to determine sales potential and, more important, potential profitability. Some segments will be eliminated on the basis of insufficient sales and/or profit to justify the effort and expense they would require.

Finally, choosing market segments includes taking into account the previous analysis as well as the firm's overriding goals, the company's resources and expertise, and the feasibility of serving a given market segment effectively and profitably. This final decision is not a simple one. To make good decisions, marketing managers must do their homework. For example, accurate sales forecasts depend on correctly reading and interpreting economic and environmental trends. Analysis of potential market segments depends on solid demographic, psychographic and behavioural research. Because much of what we have talked about here is time-consuming and expensive, we often find marketing managers making 'seat-of-the-pants' decisions, that is, decisions based on intuition and experience. While we understand that 'real world' decisions must be made without perfect information, we also caution against relying too much on personal judgment in a marketplace as competitive as ours has become.

Market Targeting

Although the notion of undifferentiated markets may, as already discussed, have many drawbacks, this approach has worked fairly well in some select product categories. For example, some snack foods, such as potato crisps or pretzels, cut across a wide variety of market segments and require little differentiation. This strategy offers some obvious advantages. It is cost-effective and allows for economies of scale if a sufficient level of sales is generated.

The problem with this strategy is that when one approaches markets from an undifferentiated standpoint, the heterogeneity of the market makes any given appeal less effective. Consequently, less impact results from the marketing effort and fewer prospects are persuaded to buy.

The alternative, differentiated marketing, is the process of targeting several market segments and designing a separate offering for each. Effective market segmentation contributes to the ability of the firm to find such markets and serve them in ways tailored to specific needs. Here, multiple marketing mixes may be developed and implemented for various segments.

The third approach, concentrated marketing, is simply seeking one market segment and focusing most or all attention on that segment. For example, while Porsche has a research facility that builds engines for most of the car-makers in the world, this company has chosen to concentrate on the upscale, general-purpose sports car market. This has resulted in Porsche 'giving away' a lot of segments outside of sports cars; however, the company remains a major player in the segment chosen.

Choosing among these strategies in general should be based on the same criteria that we have discussed with respect to selecting market segments. What segments, if any, are appropriate targets for your firm's marketing mix or mixes? By looking at sales forecasts, you will get some idea of sales potential. You should also look at profitability, however, because a high level of sales does not necessarily ensure that you will make any money. Also, by looking internally at your company's objectives and resources, you can determine whether an interesting market opportunity is right for your company. As we have already pointed out, your company, like Porsche, may prefer to pass up some opportunities in order to concentrate on what you do best.

Positioning for Marketing

While a product, brand or company has objective characteristics, any of these may also possess perceived characteristics in the customer's mind. For example, in the minds of most people, IBM means computers, Xerox means office copiers, and Hertz means rental cars. Each of these companies is perceived as the market leader in each of their respective product categories.

The position a product, brand or company holds has to do with how customers view it relative to its competition. This view may be based on product attributes. For example, one brand of toothpaste is positioned as the 'freshest'. The Pot Noodles snack is positioned as a 'fun' product.

Another basis for positioning is the price-quality relationship. Tiffany's is positioned as a premier source for high-quality jewellery and gemstones. You may pay more, but you get the assurance of the highest quality.

An example of the success of positioning was the introduction of the Mars Ice Cream Bar. This did not compete directly with traditional ice-cream products, nor with standard chocolate bars. A new product category was created and many chocolate bar manufacturers followed the example.

SUMMARY

The ability of a marketer to find some area of perception that is not fully claimed by competitors and for which there are significant numbers of customers available is a constant challenge. Consumers are increasingly overwhelmed with choices of products and services that have never been available before. More and more, a differentiated position with respect to others in the category becomes very important to compete effectively – in fact, to even receive passing notice.

Positioning strategies should be selected very carefully, with full awareness of target market characteristics, needs and attitudes. Ideally the choice of a positioning strategy should lead to gaining and maintaining a competitive advantage. The task today for marketing professionals is to discover and develop a niche in the market wherein a product can be differentiated and defended against competitors.

Market segmentation enables a firm to take a focused approach to marketing. Rather than scattering resources randomly, a company should segment the market to find identifiable, profitable and reachable groups that have a need for the product and are willing and able to buy. Not all variables for segmenting the market are useful. We have many choices: geographic, demographic, psychographic and behavioural variables. Markets should be segmented on the basis of variables that represent differential purchasing behaviour on the part of customers.

Furthermore, the results of segmentation should be the basis for a unified marketing effort targeted toward each segment. Thus a single marketing mix should be effective for individual market segments; otherwise the segmentation process is faulty.

In the process of putting together a firm's marketing strategy, it is also important to consider forecasted revenues and profits. Unprofitable segments should be eliminated from consideration, as well as segments that require a radical departure from the organisation's customary expertise and pool of resources. These are often long-shots that backfire and cost the organisation dearly.

Positioning is a critical issue. Because customers act on what they believe, the crucial element is how the product, brand and/or company are perceived. Success or failure can often be attributed solely to the effects of the positioning strategy. Companies who think through this question very carefully stand a much better chance of seeing a project come to a profitable fruition.

FURTHER READING

Boone, Louis E. and Kurtz, David L. 1992. *Contemporary Marketing*, 7th ed. Ft. Worth, Texas: Dryden Press, Chapter 8.

Day, George S., Shocker, Allan D. and Srivastava, Rajendra K. 1979. 'Customer-oriented Approaches to Identifying Product Markets.' *Journal of Marketing* (Autumn): 8-19.

Lamb, Jr., Charles W., Hair, Jr., Joseph F. and McDaniel, Carl. 1992. *Principles of Marketing.* Cincinnati: South-Western Publishing Co., Chapter 5.

Lancaster, G. and Massingham, L. 1993. *Essentials of Marketing,* 2nd ed. McGraw Hill, Chapter 7.

Lipman, Joanne. 1989. 'From '60s Uniform to '90s Niche: Wrangler Targets the Family Man.' *Wall Street Journal* (3 Jul.): 12.

Lowry, James. 1988. ' "Kids Power" at $15.7 Billion.' *Advertising Age* (15 Aug.): 33.

Morton, John. 1990. 'How to Spot the Really Important Prospects.' *Business Marketing* (Jan.): 62.

Oberlink, Peter. 1987. 'Regional Marketing Starts Taking Hold.' *Adweek* (Apr.): 6.

Roberts, Keith J. 1986. 'How to Define Your Market Segment.' *Industrial Marketing Management* (Aug.): 53-58.

Shelton, Dwight J. 1987. 'Regional Marketing Works and Is Here to Stay.' *Marketing News* (6 Nov.): 1, 25.

Zikmund, W.G. and d'Amico, M. 1995. *Effective Marketing – Creating and Keeping Customers.* West, Chapter 7.

Yankelovich, Daniel. 1964. 'New Criteria for Market Segmentation.' *Harvard Business Review* (Mar.-Apr.): 83-90.

5 Consumer Buying Behaviour

Managers make decisions for the marketing mix based on what they know about their customers' buying behaviour. In this chapter, we will discuss basic principles with respect to consumer buying behaviour. In Chapter 6 we will discuss organisational buying behaviour.

In studying buying behaviour, we find that marketing has borrowed heavily from psychology and sociology for broad concepts as well as terminology. Nevertheless, marketing researchers and academics have contributed a great deal to current knowledge of consumer behaviour. While much is left to be discovered, marketing practitioners now have access to an understanding of customers that is far advanced from what it was 30 years ago.

The first section in this chapter covers the process that consumers go through in making their buying decisions. We focus on consumers who are deciding which of many brands of products to purchase, but this process can be equally applied to those who are considering several product categories, and even whether to buy or invest their resources elsewhere.

The second section of the chapter looks at major influences on buying behaviour, both internal and external (or environmental) influences. Marketers need to understand which of these influences are controllable and which must simply be taken into account.

Consumer Decision-Making

Figure 5.1 shows an outline of the major steps buyers go through in the purchase process. This process has been termed by some as the consumer's 'black box'. That is, it represents the invisible activity that goes on in the consumer's mind as he or she makes a buying decision. The process is a series of responses to various internal and external stimuli. Some of these stimuli are initiated by marketers, such as advertising or a call by a salesperson; some have other sources. Some marketer-dominated stimuli are successful in moving the consumer towards the marketer's product, and some may actually accomplish the opposite effect.

While a variety of titles exist for each stage in the process, a representative list would include:

1 Need recognised.
2 Information-search accomplished.
3 Alternatives compared.
4 Decision made and implemented.
5 Satisfaction/dissatisfaction realised.

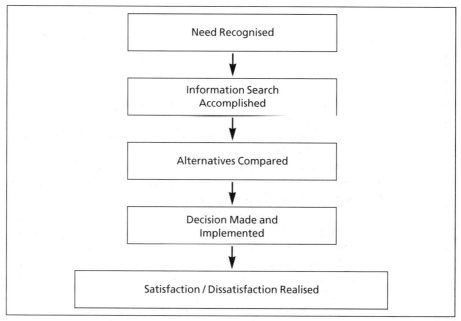

Figure 5.1 The Process for Making Buying Decisions

Need Recognised

A consumer recognises a need (or want) when something that he or she requires is found lacking. Some marketers call this 'problem recognition'. Events or conditions that stimulate need-arousal vary. You may experience hunger pangs during your noon marketing class and realise that you need to purchase some lunch. Or you may visit a fellow student and find that his computer has graphics capabilities and hard-drive capacity far superior to your 1982 model.

Alternatively, you may be influenced by marketer-dominated sources. You may read an advertisement about a shampoo and conditioner that help preserve the 'permanent' curl for which you paid a hairdresser dearly. Or perhaps your favourite sporting goods store is running a sale on ski boots.

In each of these cases, the discrepancy between what you have and what you need or want may lead you to begin the decision-making process that results in a purchase. In some cases, the need arises naturally from physiological conditions; in other cases, the influences come from sources external to you. As you can see from the above examples, sometimes a need is triggered by simply finding out that a product is available that offers 'better' features than the product you already have.

Information Search Accomplished

Information search can be internal or external. Internal search relies on the buyer's memory and prior experiences for matching problems with possible solutions. If you want lunch, you may think about various restaurants and pick one that you have enjoyed in the past. You may have also learned which ones to avoid through past experience.

Another possibility is to rely on external information by asking one of your friends to recommend a good restaurant. For a special occasion, you might even go so far as to read restaurant reviews in the local paper. External sources for different product categories include friends and family; marketer-dominated sources include advertising, brochures, packaging or salespersons; and unbiased sources include options such as consumer reports. The extent of your search will depend on such factors as the importance of the decision to you; the amount of risk involved; how familiar you already are with the product category and the alternative brands; how many different information sources are available to you; and how much time you want to spend making the decision.

Alternatives Compared

The number of brands that a consumer actually considers in making a purchase decision is called the 'evoked set'. Some brands, while known, are not deemed worthy of consideration; other brands may be unknown to the consumer. Certainly marketers' objectives include getting their brands into the consumer's evoked set.

Evaluative criteria refer to those features that the buyer uses to make a choice between brands. These include perceived quality, price, size, convenience, durability, colour and reputation (of the company or brand).

Evaluative criteria vary from one market segment to another; in fact, this variation may be the basis for segmentation. For example, one group may want cars that are moderately priced, offer good petrol consumption and retain their resale value better than other models. Another group's criteria may include leather seats, climate control, sporty design and interior leg room. Of one thing we can be certain: consumers will pay special attention to those features and benefits that satisfy their particular needs.

However, alternatives are also evaluated using criteria suggested by marketers in their advertisements. Choice of an airline might be influenced by pointing out safety record, on-time arrivals or baggage security. Thus marketers' objectives should encompass both achieving enough visibility to get into the evoked set and influencing the criteria consumers use to evaluate brands.

Decision Made and Implemented

Once consumers have identified unmet needs, searched for information and used that information to evaluate various brands, they are ready to make a purchase decision. At this point, buyers have formed intentions but have not yet carried out those intentions.

As suggested earlier, consumers' search and evaluation processes may lead them to postpone or cancel the purchase. Perhaps no satisfying brands are offered anywhere on the market; perhaps none of the local retailers carries the preferred brands. Sometimes customers decide that they have other priorities for their limited financial resources, and sometimes interpersonal influences, such as friends or family, dissuade buyers from making an intended purchase.

Often consumers will purchase a second-choice brand if their first choice is unavailable. Occasionally customers will choose an alternative brand because they do not want to shop where their preferred brand is carried. The point is that a variety of influences may thwart the ultimate purchase, even if a prospective customer has the intention of buying a given brand. It is at this stage that accessory attributes may be most important in capturing the sale: such attributes as warranties, maintenance, delivery terms and installation.

Satisfaction/Dissatisfaction Realised

After the purchase is completed, the customer's post-purchase evaluation begins. How a consumer evaluates the satisfaction (or dissatisfaction) of a particular purchase will determine whether the next buying cycle will result in the same brand choice.

A common aspect of the post-purchase stage is the *cognitive dissonance* that many buyers experience. Cognitive dissonance means that the buyer is not entirely satisfied with the purchase and discomfort results. Perhaps the chosen brand did not perform as the customer was led to believe it would. Perhaps after making the purchase the customer found the brand at a much lower price elsewhere.

These are common examples of post-purchase dissonance, but sometimes feelings are more complex. Even a buyer who would make the same decision again may regret the loss of some attributes that were associated with another brand. Cognitive dissonance results when buyers conduct an extensive search and in the end experience both positive and negative feelings towards any given choice. Once a choice is made, the rejected alternatives as well as the negative consequences of the brand selected must be rationalised.

A buyer who has to purchase a new car as a result of a car accident, for example, may regret the use of her funds even though she knew she had to replace the wrecked car. Another buyer may feel guilty for spending so much money; and another may lose satisfaction when friends fail to admire the new product as much as the buyer had anticipated.

Marketers should take these opportunities to solidify and strengthen buyer satisfaction with their brands. By providing additional information and encouragement during this phase, marketers enable buyers to work out their dissonance in positive ways.

Types of Decision

Not all buying decisions are equally critical for the consumer; not all are equally risky, nor do all buying situations demand equal investments of time and energy.

Consumer behaviour experts have identified three types of buying decisions.

Routinised Problem-Solving

This is sometimes called routine response behaviour. It refers to the purchase of inexpensive, frequently bought products for which search is minimal and several substitutions exist if the preferred brand is unavailable. Many of these products are habitual purchases; consumers do not have the time to devote to extensive information-processing every time they need a loaf of bread, a bottle of milk or a tube of toothpaste.

Limited Problem-Solving

When the product category is familiar to consumers but not all brands are familiar, customers engage in some information searching and alternative evaluation. This buying process is called limited problem-solving. These decisions are usually for products that cost more than the typical grocery item, such as a washing machine, VCR or camera. There is some risk involved in the purchase, the item is not sought routinely, only intermittently, and some features may be new to customers.

Extensive Problem-Solving

When buyers are faced with a more expensive item that is purchased infrequently and/or is in an unfamiliar product class, they face extensive problem-solving or extensive decision-making. In this situation, consumers often do extensive research and information processing, carefully weighing alternatives before they make a purchase. It is an obvious opportunity for marketers to make an impact because these buyers are in a frame of mind that is receptive to marketer-dominated sources.

In each case, customers do go through some type of decision-making process. The steps illustrated in Figure 5.1 are most apparent for extensive problem-solving. Yet these steps can be applied even to routine purchases; the difference is in the amount of time and energy invested in each stage.

Influences on Consumer Buying Behaviour

Many factors influence a person's decision to buy a given product. These factors can be broadly categorised as internal and external. Figure 5.2 summarises these factors; it also suggests some basic relationships between the individual and these factors. Notice that external influences have an impact on consumers' internal influences. That is, one's family, for example, may greatly influence one's attitude towards a particular brand of car. Another consumer's social class may determine his motives for selecting a particular college or university.

Both environmental and internal influences then interact with the decision-making process to render a purchasing decision. While marketers have very little control over these factors of influence, it is important that they take them into account.

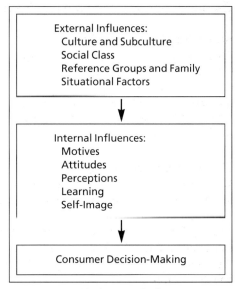

Figure 5.2 Simplified Model of Influence on Consumer Buying Behaviour

Internal Influences

In this section we will discuss some concepts that have an important bearing on the design of the marketing mix. These include motives, perceptions, learning, attitude and self-concept. Much of what we have discovered concerning these influences is drawn from psychology, but in many cases knowledge has been further expanded by research in the consumer behaviour arena.

Motives

As we have already seen in our decision-making model, the first step in the purchase decision is recognition of a need. That is, the consumer is in a state of tension because something that he or she needs is lacking. When the tension becomes strong enough, the individual will feel the drive to resolve the tension. Drive is another word for motive; it implies a strong impetus to resolve the tension.

Motives or drives are goal-directed: they seek a solution to a felt need. For example, if you are hungry, you seek food. If you are being interviewed for a job, you need a good suit.

Although psychologists have proposed lists of varying numbers of needs, no one has had more impact on the categorisation of needs than A. H. Maslow. Maslow developed a theory based on the hierarchical concept of needs. He believed that higher-level needs did not become relevant until lower-level needs were at least partially satisfied. From lowest order to highest order, Maslow's needs include:

1 Physiological needs (food, water, clothing and shelter).

2 Safety needs (concern for physical survival and preservation).
3 Affiliation and belongingness needs (love and acceptance).
4 Self-esteem (a sense of accomplishment, status, achievement and respect).
5 Self-actualisation (fulfillment, reaching one's potential and using one's talents).

To some extent, consumers are only motivated by unsatisfied needs. Once a need is met, a consumer's direction changes toward satisfying other unmet needs. In a modern society where most people's basic needs (physiological and safety) are met, the greatest interest often lies in satisfying the higher-order needs (affiliation, self-esteem, and self-actualisation). However, the physiological and safety needs are recurring needs, so that even though they are temporarily satisfied, they will periodically become important again.

Marketers use their knowledge of these motives to appeal to buyers. For example, a restaurant may advertise on the radio during the evening rush hour. People are hungry and tired; good food that they do not have to prepare themselves may have high appeal. At the other end of the spectrum, the US Army campaign slogan 'Be All That You Can Be' reflects an appeal to self-actualisation. This early 1980s promotion proved very successful.

Perception

Perception involves accumulating sensory inputs and then organising and interpreting those inputs. Different people, of course, perceive the same stimuli in different ways. For example, a car accident may be reported very differently depending on whether you are the driver, a pedestrian observer, or a passenger in the car.

The inputs that we receive are transmitted through our five senses: sight, hearing, taste, smell and touch. Once these sensations are received, the individual organises the inputs and tries to make sense of them. Perception thus becomes one's individual interpretation of reality.

Selective Perception. Selective perception means that the way people organise and interpret inputs depends on their ability to process information, their personalities, the context in which they encounter the inputs, their mood at the time and the attitudes they bring with them to the encounter. For example, the interpretation of a political debate will often depend on the prior beliefs and political orientation of the person who is watching the debate. If the viewer is a dedicated member of Political Party X, he or she will probably find much that is favourable to that party; members of another political party may observe much that is negative.

Selective Exposure. Selective exposure means that we choose the inputs to which we allow ourselves to be exposed. For example, no one sees every advertisement; there is too much clutter in the advertising environment for anyone to observe all of it. When driving down any main road, some drivers and passengers may see restaurant advertising (particularly if they are hungry), while others may see entertainment advertising (particularly if they are looking for entertainment).

Sometimes people do not want to receive certain messages. Smokers routinely ignore warnings about the harmful effects of cigarettes; overeaters routinely ignore warnings about heart disease. The easiest way to avoid these messages is simply to choose not to be exposed to the messages.

Selective Retention. Selective retention means that while we may be exposed to a variety of inputs, we choose to place some in long-term memory while others we disregard. If a marketer's message appears to have potential relevance for a consumer, he or she may file that information away for the future. For example, a local advertisement for hairdressing may be important to a consumer who has previously been driving 30 miles to have her hair done. She may not need the information immediately but will file it away for future reference.

Messages that we do not deem either immediately relevant or potentially relevant will be discarded. Marketers should be careful to give consumers a strong rationale for attending to their messages and for choosing to retain them.

Learning

Learning is a change in behaviour (including one's thinking) caused by prior experience. The first time you tasted Swiss chocolate, learning occurred. (You probably wanted to have more of that experience!) When you initiate a new experience, you are exposed to multiple stimuli. These stimuli affect various senses and result in pleasure, pain, or some combination thereof. Marketer-dominated stimuli include signs, products, advertisements and sales personnel.

Repetition of certain stimuli with the same outcomes reinforces prior experience, and thus learning is reinforced. For example, if you visit a local ice cream shop for the first time and you have an enjoyable experience, you have learned that you will obtain satisfaction from this establishment. If the same satisfaction results from subsequent visits to the shop, you will be reinforced in that behaviour and more likely to continue to patronise this ice cream shop.

Sometimes marketers try to sensitise customers to certain cues or images that will call the marketer's company/product to mind. For example, a slogan such as that used by Volkswagen, 'If only everything in life was as reliable as a Volkswagen' is intended to call to mind not only the Volkswagen brand, but also the various product attributes and benefits associated with Volkswagen.

Similarly, marketers attempt to design packages that are easily associated with their brand. Distinctive packages give brands an edge in being noticed and selected in a cluttered supermarket environment, where many brands compete in the same product category. Additionally, these packages are often designed to link positive images that have been learned in other contexts with the brand. For example, the colour blue frequently appears on laundry-detergent packaging because 'blueing' is associated with cleanliness and whiteness. Another example is the lemon scent that is often added to products, such as dishwashing liquid or furniture wax, because many people associate lemon with freshness and cleanliness.

Attitudes

Attitudes reflect a person's consistent evaluation of other people, products and ideas. Attitudes are generally thought to be comprised of several elements:

beliefs, feelings, and tendency to behave. For example, customers may believe that Hitachi television sets are the most expensive on the market. That belief, however, does not tell us how customers *feel* about Hitachi nor how they will behave towards the brand.

Perhaps customers feel that the price is too high; therefore they will not purchase Hitachi television sets. Perhaps they feel that Hitachi quality warrants a higher price, so they will purchase it. Or perhaps they feel that although Hitachi quality warrants a higher price, unfortunately they cannot afford that higher price, so they have no intention of purchasing Hitachi.

This illustration indicates why all three elements of attitude are important in understanding customer behaviour. Asking customers whether they like a product is not a determinant of whether they will purchase, as we have just illustrated. The behavioural implications of what customers believe can only be interpreted in the light of how they feel about what they believe.

Attitudes are not simply casual opinion. They are defined as deeply held behaviour; thus it is difficult for marketers to change attitudes. Certainly marketers want to do everything they can to influence attitudes and to build positive attitudes about their companies, products and brands. However, it usually takes a considerable investment of marketing resources over a period of time to develop or modify customer attitudes.

Self-Concept

Self-concept refers to the physical and mental characteristics that make up a person's total being. This self-concept has an influence on how people behave in a variey of situations, including their buying behaviour. Actually self-concept has four components:

1 Real self (an objective assessment of the person).
2 Self-image (the way people see themselves).
3 Looking glass self (the way people think others see them).
4 Ideal self (the way people would like to see themselves).

For example, people tend to buy products that they believe will enhance their ideal self. Those who want to be intellectual may join a book club or attend a prestigious university. Those who want to be glamorous may buy large quantities of cosmetics or select brands advertised by their favourite models and film stars. Those who want to be seen as physically fit may join health clubs or purchase exercise equipment for their homes.

Marketers appeal to the ideal self in many ways. The Marlboro Man has long been cited as an example of advertising that appeals to those who would like to appear as rugged individualists.

External Influences

Many factors influence a consumer's decision to make a purchase. The external factors that we will discuss in this section include culture and subculture, social class and reference groups.

Culture and Subculture

Culture is all the ideas and artifacts in a person's environment. Since human behaviour is largely learned, we conclude that much buying behaviour is heavily influenced by the culture and subculture in which we grow up. For example, in the Western World we learn to value independence, attractiveness, education and good communication skills. We learn to interpret a person's background from the cues that he or she gives, such as accent, clothing, manner of speaking and social skills.

Marketers try to keep current with changing cultural ideas. For example, the health and fitness trend of the past few years brought with it opportunities for producing and selling health clubs, fitness equipment, diet aids, and shoes and clothing for sports activities. The recent changes in women's roles have ushered in increased use of maid services and nannies, more in-home shopping, and increased sales of pre-packaged dinners.

Subcultures are groups of people within a larger culture who share values and ideas. Subcultures may be based on a variety of factors, such as race, religion, geographic location or vocation. Most of us belong to several subcultures, which may or may not overlap in our day-to-day experience.

Social Class

As discussed in Chapter 4, social class is another indicator of buying behaviour. Social classes in the United States are fairly open; that is, people can move from one social class to another on the basis of education, income and changing values. However, not all countries have social classes that are so open. Even in Western Europe, citizens have less social mobility than in the US.

To some degree, people within the same social class exhibit similar buying patterns. For example, people in the middle and upper classes place a high value on education. Upper-class people tend to send their children to private as opposed to state-run schools. Tastes in food also differ, with more fresh fruit and vegetables being consumed by the upper classes. Another pertinent example is in the choice of car driven, with many middle and upper classes seeing their car as a status symbol, therefore choosing such makes as Mercedes Benz or BMW. Lower classes tend to buy the more reliable low-cost type of car (e.g., a Ford Fiesta) and the variety of their daily diet would differ considerably from the upper classes, with cheaper types of meat being consumed.

Reference Groups

A reference group is a group with which an individual identifies in terms of values, attitudes and behaviours. Some examples of reference groups include family, peer groups, church groups, civic clubs and professional organisations.

A group can be a negative reference group if an individual wishes to avoid expressing values and behaviours that would identify him or her with that group. For example, an ex-convict might wish to distance himself as far as possible from other ex-convicts to avoid again becoming entangled in an anti-social lifestyle. A less extreme example might be someone who avoids wearing a particular type of clothing because that clothing is tyically worn by members of a negative reference group.

More often, however, people buy products so that they will be identified with a particular group. Graduates buy college ties so that they can display identification with their alma mater. Couples purchase a home in a respectable neighbourhood so that they too can be viewed as affluent and respectable.

Reference groups often have an impact on our choice of products and brands. We may use the laundry detergent that our mother always used. We may change our brand of toothpaste because our college peers recommended another brand. We may purchase a particular brand of car stereo system because that is the brand that our friends recommend.

Marketers try to use reference-group influence in advertisements by suggesting that if you buy Brand X you will be like superstar Joe Jones or Jane Jones. Advertisers are hoping that the audience will identify with the suggested reference group and want to buy products that are associated with the group to enhance the buyer's sense of belongingness.

SUMMARY

Consumers move through a decision-making process in deciding whether they will make a purchase and then evaluating the satisfaction or dissatisfaction derived from that purchase. At each step in the process, marketers try to influence customers to consider the marketer's brand. These steps include need recognition, information search, comparing alternative product offerings, making and implementing the decision, and evaluating the outcomes in terms of satisfaction/dissatisfaction.

There are a number of influences on consumer decision-making. Some of these are internal influences and others are external influences that we receive from our environment. Again, marketers try to appeal to consumers through the mechanisms of these various influences.

Internal influences include motives, attitudes, perceptions, learning and self-concept. Motives are unmet needs that drive us to make purchases to satisfy those needs. Perceptions represent the filter through which consumers receive and interpret inputs from their surroundings. Marketers try to manipulate these inputs to present their product offerings in the most favourable light. Attitudes include knowledge about our environment and the way we feel about what we know, and in many cases also include a predisposition to behave in a certain manner. Learning is a change in behaviour as a result of experience, and self-concept is the way we see ourselves as well as the way we would like to see ourselves.

External influences include culture and subculture, social class and reference groups. Each of these social groups represents values, behaviours and attitudes that we have learned over time and with which we feel comfortable. Marketers try to use these influences to enhance our comfort with their products and our desire for those products.

FURTHER READING

Assael, Henry. 1985. *Marketing Management*. Boston: Kent Publishing Co., Chapter 5.

Bennett, Peter D. and Harrell, Gilbert. 1975. 'The Role of Confidence in Understanding and Predicting Buyers' Attitudes and Purchase Intentions.' *Journal of Consumer Research* (Sept.): 11–117.

Cardozo, R. 1965. 'An Experimental Study of Consumer Effort, Expectations, and Satisfaction.' *Journal of Marketing Research* (Aug.): 244-249.

Hoyer, Wayne. 1984. 'An Examination of Consumer Decision-Making for a Common Repeat Purchase Product.' *Journal of Consumer Research* (Dec.): 822-829.

Kerr, Kevin. 1990. 'Confusion Reigns Supreme Down on Aisle 3.' *Adweek's Marketing Week* (8 Oct.): 24-25.

Kotler, Philip. 1991. *Marketing Management,* 7th ed. Englewood Cliffs, New Jersey: Prentice Hall, Chapter 6.

Lamb, Jr., Charles W., Hair, Jr., Joseph F. and McDaniel, Carl. 1992. *Principles of Marketing*. Cincinnati: South-Western Publishing Co., Chapter 5.

Pride, W.M., Ferrell, O.C., Dibb, S. and Simkin, L. 1994. *Marketing – European Edition,* 2nd ed. Houghton Mifflin Co., Chapter 4.

Schiffman, L.G. and Kanuk, L.L. 1991. *Consumer Behaviour*, 4th ed. Prentice Hall.

6 Organisational Buying Behaviour

Examples of business-to-business marketing are wide and varied. Many organisations assume the role of support services. One such example is in the catering industry. A small company based in Scotland by the name of Creative Cakes initially started off by supplying dinner parties and functions organised by friends. This network soon widened as news of the high quality product spread. Personal contact with local theatre groups introduced the company to the idea of creating food for scenes in plays, primarily of a banqueting nature. This area of the business soon took over as the main focus, with the company supplying produce for use as a prop in theatre productions.

This example demonstrates the often invisible and sometimes under-rated role played by many small companies, operating as support services to larger organisations. In the last decade much of UK industry has become much more service than production oriented, so the area of business-to-business marketing is an important element of marketing in today's society.

Most of us think of the final consumer when we hear the word customer. However, more purchases are made by industrial and other organisational buyers than by final consumers. In this chapter we will look at the three types of organisational markets and examine the nature of each of these markets. We will also discuss market structure and demand in the industrial sector as well as the decision-making and buying processes.

Organisational Markets

The three major types of organisational markets include the industrial market, the reseller market and the governmental market. Each has its own specific set of needs and procedures as well as attributes. Although they share some operational factors, each must be analysed on its own if you have a desire to do business in that market.

Industrial Market

The industrial market encompasses everyone who must buy goods or services in order to manufacture other products and services, which are then sold or rented to others. This is a very large marketplace. In Europe the industrial market consists of millions of organisations, both large and small, contributing billions in revenue to the local and national economies. Most of the discussion in this chapter will centre on the industrial marketplace, although the reseller and government markets have some similarities to the industrial market.

Reseller Market

The reseller market consists of firms that acquire products for the purpose of reselling them to others. This market includes thousands of wholesalers and retailers, who combined similarly account for billions of transactions on a national and international level.

The role of resellers is to act as purchasing agents for their customers. They are responsible for accumulating want-satisfying assortments and for setting prices for these goods and services. The assortments must reflect the demand generated at the retail and, ultimately, the final consumer levels. As we will see in Chapters 11 and 12, which deal with wholesaling and retailing, resellers may carry products from only one supplier, from several related suppliers, or even a broad assortment of unrelated products from many suppliers.

Government Market

National and local governments purchase a multitude of goods and services to carry out their functions. The UK government is a large purchaser of goods that will aid in the provision of public services. These purchases vary from hospital beds to component parts for military aircraft.

Governments throughout Europe differ in their structure and the way in which they purchase services. In the UK for example, government is divided into different departments, e.g., the Department for Trade and Industry (DTI), the Department of Transport, etc. Each of these departments is responsible for purchases in its particular area, and the purchasing decision is often being complex, involving many group decisions.

State and local agencies include such entities as school districts, road departments, and city water and sewer services.

Characteristics of Organisational Markets

Although organisational markets are like consumer markets in that customers with unmet needs are looking for solutions to those needs, there are also some differences. In this section we will cover the four areas in which those differences are most pronounced: market structure and demand; the nature of the buying unit; the types of buying situations; and how the purchase is completed.

Market Structure and Demand

Organisational markets are generally comprised of fewer and much larger buyers than are consumer markets. Yet the same company may be both a supplier to consumer markets and a supplier to a much smaller number of organisational buyers. For example, Sony television sets are marketed to millions of consumers through department stores, appliance stores, discount houses and other consumer retailers. But Sony also depends on getting orders from a few rather large hotel chains in the industrial sector.

Geographic Concentration

Organisational markets by their nature are smaller than consumer markets. Consumer markets can be spread throughout Europe, but in the case of industry, these tend to be concentrated around the areas of traditional heavy industry, for example the Rhine valley where many manufacturing plants are concentrated. Silicon Glen as the Central Belt of Scotland is known, has a concentration of computer software companies and the Southern countries of Europe have traditionally provided fresh produce.

SIC Codes

The Standard Industrial Classification System (SIC) is a detailed numbering system that the US government uses to identify American business and government organisations according to their primary economic activity. As shown in Table 6.1, each of the 11 major categories is assigned a unique two-digit number. The US Census Bureau compiles and publishes data on total industry sales and employment for each two-digit category.

TABLE 6.1 Two-Digit Standard Industrial Classification.

01-09	Agriculture, Forestry, Fishing
10-14	Mining
15-19	Contract Construction
20-39	Manufacturing
40-49	Transportation and Other Public Utilities
50-51	Wholesale Trade
52-59	Retail Trade
60-67	Finance, Insurance and Real Estate
70-89	Services
91-97	Government Federal, State, Local and International
99	Other

The two-digit numbers are further subdivided into three-digit and four-digit sub-units that represent finer distinctions within a broad category. For example, 34 is the two-digit SIC code for companies in the fabricated metal industry. Number 342 is assigned to cutlery and hand tools, and number 3425 refers to handsaws and saw blades.

These Standard Industrial Classification codes have been adopted worldwide to achieve a standard unit of understanding as to the type of organisation in question.

Marketers use SIC code data much as they do consumer demographic information. For example, marketers can use SIC codes to determine the number of firms in a particular category, what their sales volumes are, and the number of employees in each firm. If your company analyses its sales and finds that a large proportion of your business comes from producers of fabricated metals, you will want to identify and target similar companies in that industry. This is an excellent way for marketers to uncover prospects with high potential for becoming new customers.

Demand

Organisational markets are characterised by demand that is derived, joint and generally inelastic.

Derived Demand. Organisational demand is unlike consumer demand in that it is derived. This means that organisational demand ultimately flows from consumers' demand for goods and services. For example, car and truck manufacturers account for the major share of rubber sales in the United States. General Motors alone spends more than $600 million on tyres. If the consumer demand for cars drops, so do sales of rubber.

Joint Demand. Joint demand means that multiple products are purchased at the same time because they are used in combination. For example, molybdenum is used to harden certain alloys of steel. When steel is not being demanded by carmakers, the demand for molybdenum virtually disappears.

Inelastic Demand. The demand for products by the organisational market tends to be fairly inelastic. This means that an increase or a decrease in the price of the product will not significantly affect demand for the product. Generally, fluctuations in a small component of a product has little or no effect on the final price of the product and, therefore, little effect on consumer demand. For example, if the price of car paint increased 200 per cent, do you think that the price of cars would rise significantly?

Nature of the Buying Unit

Organisational buying is more complex than most consumer purchases. Consequently, company sales representatives must be well-trained to handle sophisticated purchasing agents and demanding buying committees.

Purchasing Agents

Organisational buying is often in the hands of professional purchasing agents. These employees spend their working lives learning how to bargain, how to find the best buys for their companies, which suppliers are reliable, and which suppliers offer the best prices, quality products and on-time service. Some purchasing agents earn the designation of certified purchasing manager (CPM) after successfully completing a rigorous certification programme. Sellers must approach these business buyers in an acceptably formal manner, having done their homework with respect to the prospect's needs, the nature of the business the prospect is in, and the requirements for doing business with this company.

Buying Committees

Frequently, however, a business-to-business purchase will involve sufficient capital investment or affect so many units within the buying firm that several people will participate in the decision-making process. Buying committees (also known as buying centres) are not uncommon. These are made up of technical experts and managers who have a stake in the final outcome.

However, not all company buying committees have the same make-up. In marketing-oriented firms, such as Toyota or IBM, marketing and engineering have almost equal authority. In consumer packaged goods firms, such as Procter & Gamble, product managers and other marketing decision-makers may dominate the buying process. In small manufacturing companies, the buying committee may include all plant supervisors.

Roles in the Buying Committee

Following are a list of roles that individuals may adopt while functioning as members of the buying committee:

Initiator. The person who first suggests making a purchase.

Influencers. Those who help define the attributes sought and provide information used in evaluating alternative product offerings.

Gatekeepers. Group members who have control over the flow of information concerning the purchase. Purchasing agents often assume this role. Salespeople have to convince gatekeepers that they have something desirable to offer; otherwise no one else on the buying committee can be approached.

Decider(s). The person or persons who have the authority to make the final purchasing decision.

Purchaser. The individual who carries out the mechanics of actually placing the order and setting the purchasing process in motion.

User(s). The person or persons who will actually use the product once it is purchased.

Types of Buying Situation

Industrial buyers face a variety of decisions when making purchases. The nature of these decisions varies according to the type of buying situation they face. There are three major types of buying situation: the straight rebuy, the modified rebuy and new-task buying.

Straight Rebuy

Straight rebuys require no changes from previous purchase specifications and procedures. These are essentially re-orders of products that have been satisfactory in the past, and these orders are handled on a routine basis. Sellers often like to have these situations set up so that re-orders are automatic once the stock has dropped to a given level. Thus continued sales are assured.

Straight rebuys are usually low-cost, standardised items, such as notepads or personal computer disks. However, even expensive items that have been custom-designed for a particular operation may be routinely purchased as the need arises.

Modified Rebuy

Modified rebuys occur in situations where purchasing agents are ready to re-evaluate their available options and consider new alternatives. This can happen if sellers become complacent about their customers and allow product quality and/or service to deteriorate. Buyers may want to renegotiate prices, terms, specifications or suppliers. When buyers are dissatisfied, marketers other than the present supplier have a real opportunity to gain new business.

New-Task Buying

New-task buying involves a situation where the company is purchasing a good or service for the first time. The greater the cost and the more important this purchase is to the welfare of the company, the more likely it is that several people will participate in the purchasing decision.

In this type of buying situation, buyers will seek information on payment terms, order quantities, delivery terms and schedules, alternative products and suppliers, various price levels, and many other considerations. Although new-task buying is not the usual buying mode, it does give suppliers the best opportunity to secure business with a new client.

How the Purchase is Completed

Although each company has its own methods and procedures for making purchases, there is a general process that is common to most. It includes the following steps (similar to those in the consumer purchasing process): need recognition, information search, supplier identification, sales call or proposal, and supplier selection.

Need Recognition

Machinery failure, or simply being out-of-stock of a particular item, could be the triggering event that sets in motion the purchase process. Or it could be the growing awareness of a new type of process or equipment in the firm's industry.

Information Search

Once the need for a new purchase is recognised, purchasing agents or buying committee members begin collecting the information they will need to make intelligent buying decisions. This may include reading pamphlets and other technical information, talking with salespeople or looking at products.

Supplier Identification

A pool of potential suppliers is identified. These must have product offerings that conform to the specifications of what is needed, and they must also price in a range that is acceptable to the buying firm.

Sales Call or Proposal

At this stage, buyers will invite qualified suppliers to submit proposals and/or make presentations to the buying committee. Some suppliers merely respond by sending a catalogue of their products and a price list. When the desired product is complex and expensive, however, vendors are expected to submit detailed proposals that conform to the specifications the buyer wants.

Supplier Selection

After all presentations have been made and all proposals read and analysed, members of the buying committee will meet to select a supplier. Consideration will undoubtedly be given to how well the proposed products meet the buyer's needs, what prices are being offered, what kinds of warranties and maintenance agreements go along with the product, and a supplier's ability to provide good overall service on time. Honest communication, as well as a reputation for ethical behaviour, will often be considered.

Another consideration in selecting a supplier is called *reciprocity:* the practice of extending preferential status to suppliers who are also customers. Reciprocal arrangements usually occur in industries with homogeneous products that have similar prices, such as chemicals, paints, petroleum, rubber and steel. It is important to enter into these arrangements carefully, since the authorities may view reciprocal agreements as attempts to reduce competition.

SUMMARY

Organisational markets are made up of three broad areas: industrial buyers, resellers and government markets. Each of these has some distinctive characteristics, but they also have much in common. These markets all have potential customers who are looking to fulfil unmet needs and must find suppliers who can provide solutions to those needs.

Organisational markets have fewer buyers but these usually purchase in much larger quantities than do consumers. Organisational markets are also more geographically concentrated than are consumer markets, with the largest volume of industrial sales being between the more Northern member countries of the EC. SIC codes identify the different types of businesses that are represented, and marketers can use these codes to identify prospective customers.

Organisational markets deal with a slightly different demand structure than do consumer markets, including derived demand, joint demand and inelastic demand. Purchasing agents are professional buyers employed by organisations to help these companies find the best suppliers to meet their needs. Sometimes companies will also use buying committees (or buying centres) made up of individuals who have the needed expertise and/or special interest in the purchase decision. The three types of buying situations include the straight rebuy, the modified rebuy and new-task buying.

Making the purchase involves a series of decision-making steps similar to the ones consumers employ. These steps are need recognition, information search, supplier identification, sales call or proposal submission and supplier selection.

FURTHER READING

Baker, M.J. 1991. *Marketing – An Introductory Text,* 5th ed. MacMillan, Chapter 7.

Hutt, Michael D. and Speh, Thomas W. 1985. *Industrial Marketing Readings Management*, 2nd ed. Hinsdale, Ilinois: Dryden Press.

Kotler, Philip. 1991. *Marketing Management,* 7th ed. Englewood Cliffs, New Jersey: Prentice Hall, Chapter 7.

Meeks, Fleming and Sullivan, R. Lee. 1992. 'If at First You Don't Succeed . . .' *Forbes* (9 Nov.): 172-180.

Pride, W.M., Ferrell, O.C. Dibb,S. and Simkin, L. 1994. *Marketing – European Edition,* 2nd ed. Houghton Mifflin Co., Chapter 4.

'Survey of Industrial & Commercial Buying Power.' 1987. *Sales and Marketing Management* (27 Apr.): 26.

Suss, Warren H. 1984. 'How to Sell to Uncle Sam.' *Harvard Business Review* (Nov./Dec.): 136-144.

Webster, Jr., Frederick E. and Wind, Yoram. 1972. *Organizational Buying Behavior*. Englewood Cliffs, New Jersey: Prentice Hall.

7 Marketing Research and Information Systems

Marketing research and marketing information systems are the tools marketing managers use to help them make good marketing decisions. We have discussed the highly competitive nature of today's marketplace in earlier chapters. Because marketers are now operating in such a sophisticated marketplace, they can no longer afford to make 'seat of the pants' management decisions.

In this chapter, we will look at the definitions of marketing information systems and marketing research. We will examine the sources for marketing information and then look at the process for gathering that information ourselves. Finally, we will discuss data analysis, reporting, and decision-making from an informed perspective.

Marketing Research and Information Systems Defined

A marketing information system (MIS) is a standardised, ongoing procedure for accumulating, analysing, storing and retrieving data. The keyword here is 'ongoing'. An MIS is designed to prevent managers from having to make decisions based solely on intuition. While much information is available given sufficient time and money to discover it, most managers need information that is accessible in the short term, with little expense incurred.

The information for an MIS is collected from inside and outside the organisation. Data is compiled from internal records, from secondary sources, and from marketing research projects. This central databank provides a continuous flow of information about sales, advertising expenses, competitors' activities, pricing and distribution figures.

Figure 7.1 shows an overview of a typical MIS, including both internal and external sources of information, the databank where information processing occurs, and then the final stage, output, where reports are issued to managers.

Marketing research is the design, collection, analysis, interpretation and reporting of information geared to solving a particular problem. That is, marketing research projects are conducted on an 'as needed' basis. An example of a marketing research project might be surveying customers to assess satisfaction

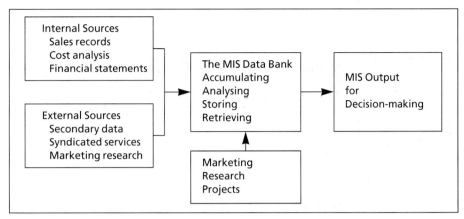

Figure 7.1 A Marketing Information System

with the company and its products; or testing two different advertising themes in two separate markets; or doing a location analysis for the establishment of a new retail store.

Information Systems and Decision-Making

Sometimes the difficulty of an MIS is that there is too much information rather than too little. Some marketing managers are inundated with massive reports that are nearly impossible to assimilate. There is a vast difference between 'data' and 'information'. When an MIS is designed, several questions should be asked to ensure that much effort and money is not wasted.

First, does the marketing information system have the full support of top management? No major improvements in the marketing area or any other can really be successful unless they are supported from the top down in the organisation. Next, managers should be consulted as to what decisions they wish to make from the output. Then knowledgeable individuals must decide what data will be necessary to make those decisions and in what form those data must be presented to be meaningful. Unfortunately, far too often computer technicians – with little or no knowledge of management's questions or the kind of data that will address these questions – are allowed to design information systems without input from decision-makers. Thus huge piles of useless data are accumulated, and a lot of time and money is wasted.

Another aspect to consider is the difference between 'nice to know' and 'essential for decision making'. The company must decide whether the benefits of a certain type of information outweigh the costs in obtaining that information. The critical factor here is how the information will be used. For example, if the results of a particular study will allow the firm to make £50,000, but the study costs £60,000 to do, that research is not an economically feasible investment.

The Marketing Research Process

Marketing research often begins with an assessment of available information concerning a problem or opportunity. Before a company can decide whether to embark on a research study, it should first determine what kinds of information already exist. This information is called secondary data.

Secondary Data

Secondary data are already available from some source. They are distinguished from primary data, which will be discussed later, because they are not generated by the researcher but rather by some other individual or, perhaps, by the organisation itself.

Secondary data can be either internal to the firm or external. Internal data are those normally compiled by the organisation, such as salesforce call reports and marketing expenditures. If the company has an MIS, much or even most of those internal data may be found already in the marketing databank. Sometimes the identification of a problem and the subsequent search for pertinent information within the firm points out additional modifications that can improve the effectiveness of the MIS.

External data can be obtained from many sources. Commercial databases contain a considerable amount of published information. These consist of reference databases, which refer the researcher to more information on a specific topic; full databases which offer entire articles on a topic; and source databases which provide detailed information listings. Some of the best-known commercial databases include CompuServe, Dow Jones News/Retrieval and Data Resources Inc.

In the UK, Keynote and Mintel produce industry-specific reports, showing trends, industry sales and development. Due to increased accessibility via CD-ROM systems, many world-wide databases can now be accessed using, for example, the Internet Worldwide Web system.

Syndicated data services routinely collect valuable marketing information, which they then sell to clients. Arbitron, for example, documents viewership/listenership and media behaviour for television and radio stations. This kind of information is used by media departments at ad agencies and by anyone who is interested in purchasing radio or television time.

Selling Areas Marketing, Inc. (SAMI) disseminates market share data on a monthly basis. A. C. Nielsen Company produces a retail index that documents brand/product movement in food and other shops. Some other services include Information Resources, Inc., Market Research Corporation of America (MRCA) and Mediamark Research, Inc. Each of these companies offers somewhat different types of information.

Secondary data can provide important information that is too costly for marketers to collect for themselves. They can often be obtained more quickly and with lower cost than can primary data. However, secondary data have their drawbacks.

The needed information may not exist or may not be in a usable form. Even when available, secondary data must be carefully evaluated. Are they relevant? Accurate? Impartial? How good a job did the researcher do in collecting the data? Secondary data collection is a good starting point for a research project, but it often is only a beginning.

Managers often must make decisions that require information not customarily available on a routine basis. For example, Coors Brewing Company tested a new beer, Keystone Dry, in eight markets before national distribution. The cable TV channel Sky carries out multiple research projects each year. These are designed to more accurately ascertain the programme requirements of what, at a European level, can be a very diverse audience.

A marketing information system, with its routinised data-gathering, is not designed to address these special cases. These cases call for formal studies in which primary data are gathered through the research process to address a particular situation.

Primary Data

Primary data collection (that is, data collected by the researcher) is sometimes conducted by untrained employees rather than trained professionals. Marketers should realise that research is a technical skill that requires some years of education and experience before the researcher becomes proficient. We will see in the following sections that knowledge of the entire research process, including sampling procedures as well as the vehicles for data collection, is critical if the research is to be accurate and useful to its intended audience.

A marketing research study follows a fairly standardised procedure. As indicated in Figure 7.2, there are broadly five steps in the research process.

Figure 7.2 The Marketing Research Process

Problem Definition

Sometimes it is easy to identify the problem. One company found that sales of its technical product were dropping because the product required so much maintenance. Another company found that its target market of baby boomers were no longer interested in its products as they aged; the firm needed a new definition of its target market. An academic journal targeted at the Chinese market found that it was priced far in excess of what Chinese educators were accustomed to and could afford.

In many cases, however, defining the problem is a difficult task. Sometimes marketers confuse root causes with symptoms. Sometimes the problem seems to be advertising when, in reality, the salesforce is not motivated to sell the product. In other cases, a company may be spending large amounts on advertising, but the product is faulty. Or maybe the problem stems from the external environment: competitors, regulations, or changing trends in consumer preferences.

The departure from normal standards or functions often signals a problem. Dropping sales, increased costs, and failure to achieve reasonable marketing objectives are all indicators of a problem. Researchers should work on problem definition until it is clear what should be derived from the research and how the data will be used. Otherwise the results of the study may not answer the real questions or address the real problems.

Hypotheses

Hypotheses are thoughtful guesses about the problem at hand. If sales of Product X have dropped by ten per cent during the past year, one hypothesis is that we are not advertising enough. Other hypotheses might be that our product does not perform satisfactorily or that our packaging is out-dated and needs a facelift. An example of a formally-stated hypothesis in this latter situation might be: Sales of Product X will increase by ten per cent if we introduce new, modern packaging for the product.

Research studies are undertaken to provide support for, or to get evidence against, a hypothesis. As a result of the study, marketing managers will know which of their guesses is most accurate, and they will then be able to make informed decisions.

Data Collection

Data collection is the step in which researchers actually obtain information to analyse and evaluate. However, the type of hypothesis that is being tested dictates the general approach to data gathering that will be used.

There are three broad types of study: exploratory, descriptive and causal (or experimental).

Exploratory research is conducted when problem definition is still unclear. If sales of a product are declining but you cannot work out why, you need to conduct an exploratory study to uncover the true issues.

Descriptive studies are the most frequently used types of research in marketing. Descriptive studies are a snapshot in time of certain conditions. For example, if you want to know how many people are interested in opening a new museum in town, you would conduct descriptive research. Your results would show what percentage of respondents reacted favourably to the proposal and would provide estimates of how much revenue would be brought in by their patronage. Descriptive research could be used to estimate how many people were planning to vote for a particular political candidate or how much tourism revenues have increased in France in the past ten years.

Causal research is more complex than either of the other types. It is conducted to determine the effect one variable, X (or group of variables: X1, X2 and X3) has on another variable, Y. For example, what effect does varying the amount we spend on advertising (X) have on sales (Y)? Or what effect does better service (X) have on customer satisfaction (Y)?

If a researcher is to achieve accurate results from these kinds of studies, he or she must exercise a great deal of control over the study. If you want to find out how advertising affects sales, you must hold every other variable constant or you will not know which one caused the variation in sales.

Sampling. Time and resources are limited, so it is virtually impossible in most cases to do a census: that is, to obtain responses from every member of the population of interest. Rather, by systematically choosing a representative group from the population, the researcher can generalise the results from the sample to the entire population. Samples can be classified as probability and non-probability samples.

A probability sample is one in which every member of the population has a known chance of being selected to participate. One type of probability sample is a simple random sample; every participant has an equal chance of being selected. Random assignment to a group means that sample units are chosen on a strictly random, objective basis. When sample units are selected in this manner, they are considered to be equivalent before one starts the study. This procedure ensures that results are not attributed to influences extraneous to the testing context but to actual difference among groups based on the experimental treatment.

A stratified sample is composed of subgroups such that a probability sample is selected from each subgroup. The intent is that each stratum of a population is represented. For example, subgroups could be male/female, different age groups, or various levels of income. Area sampling is a variation of stratified sampling and consists of two stages: a probability sample is selected of geographic areas, for example, by postal code; units or individuals within the selected areas are selected for the sample.

Non-probability sampling uses methods of obtaining respondents that do not lend themselves to statistical testing because these methods do not conform to the principles of randomisation underlying the statistical tests. For example, a convenience sample is a non-probability sample of respondents who are readily available. Man-on-the-street interviews are one type of convenience sample.

A quota sample is a non-probability sample selected so that some prescribed minimum number of respondents from specific groups are included in the sample. If you wanted to sample college students, you might specify that at least half the sample be undergraduates and postgraduates. Such an approach would represent quota sampling.

Because non-probability sampling error cannot be measured, this type of sampling is often reserved for exploratory research. These samples can be very useful in helping to pinpoint a problem, but they are not appropriate for making generalisations about an entire population.

Survey Methods. There are three main types of survey: mail, telephone and personal interview. Each of these methods has its advantages and disadvantages. Because respondents have a low tolerance for most methods of data collection, it is imperative that the survey be as brief as possible while still covering the topic. Researchers must keep to the subject, eliminating questions that unnecessarily prolong the interview.

Other problems concern the difficulty in hiring qualified interviewers and the problems of uniformity among interviewer approaches with respondents. The use of market research as a cover to hide sales tactics has made many respondents reluctant to co-operate with legitimate research efforts. Other individuals are concerned about privacy issues and the amount of time required for participation. Finally, some researchers are concerned about the problem of 'professional' respondents, people who take part in research projects on a regular basis. If these people differ systematically from the general population, then the results obtained from using them in a study will be similarly biased.

Mail surveys are printed questionnaires sent to respondents, who then fill them out and return them by post or to a central drop-off point. The advantages are that postal surveys are the most inexpensive method of data collection, and that much larger numbers of respondents can be handled at one time. The disadvantages include the possibility of a low response rate, as well as the inability to probe more deeply in the event of superficial responses.

Response rates have been increased by using multiple mailings, by personalising requests for assistance, by offering an incentive for responses, and by giving respondents advance notification of the project and asking for their willingness to participate.

Telephone interviews are also relatively inexpensive. They can be very efficient for obtaining small quantities of information. However, subjects are generally reluctant to provide personal information over the telephone.

Disadvantages include the possibility of bias as a result of overlooking unlisted numbers and households that have no telephone. Random-digit dialling is a technique designed to eliminate the problem of unlisted phone numbers.

Personal interviews can be classified into several types. The first is the in-depth interview, in which the respondent is questioned fact-to-face by the researcher or a trained interviewer. Another type is the mall intercept, which, as its name suggests, means that the interviewer stops shoppers and asks them to co-operate in a research project.

The last type is the focus group interview, consisting of eight to ten qualified individuals. The procedure with focus groups is to recruit certain types of individuals to participate in a group discussion on the topic of interest to the researcher. A moderator will guide the discussion so that researchers will obtain the needed information. For example, in a study conducted for the Cadillac Division of General Motors, two focus groups were used to get ideas for a new advertising campaign. One group was made up of Cadillac owners, and the other of owners of foreign competitors' cars.

Personal interviews have several disadvantages. They take much longer to carry out than other types of surveys. They are also the most expensive form of data collection because the sponsor must pay interviewers for their work. But interviews also have some important advantages. They allow the interviewer to establish some rapport and trust with the respondent, so that the respondent is more willing to answer sensitive questions and often to answer more questions. Face-to-face interviewing also allows the interviewer to obtain feedback, thus adjusting his or her approach to individual respondents. Finally, there is the opportunity for probing beneath the surface to get more in-depth, thoughtful information from respondents.

Observation research relies on methods other than direct contact with subjects.

There are a number of observations methods. Some are administered by people; others by machines.

'Mystery shoppers' have become quite popular. Companies hire an organisation to send people, unidentified, to their own company for a business transaction. These 'shoppers' then report on the level of customer service that they received and how satisfied they were as consumers with the client's marketing effort.

Mechanical devices, such as cameras and recorders, can be used to observe customers. Other devices count traffic, and some measure physiological changes as a result of the subject's having been exposed to some type of marketing stimulus, such as a television commercial. Electric scanners in supermarkets record the purchase of products and brands. While the technology to make full use of this information is still very expensive, marketers hope that one day they will be able to assess the relationships between product purchase and such variables as the advertising that was shown on television the night before.

Observation has the advantage of usually being unobtrusive, so that people behave in their customary fashion instead of fabricating answers to satisfy the researcher. However, it is difficult to probe beneath the surface to uncover motivations or opinions. Observation must sometimes be interpreted in which case the results may reflect the biases of the researcher. Still the elimination of interviewer bias remains one of the strengths of observation.

Questionnaire Design. Regardless of the method chosen for data collection, the design of the instrument that will be used is of critical importance. One of the first rules of thumb is to always pre-test your questionnaire. No matter how good you think it is, you will inevitably find that some changes must be made. Your questions may be unclear to your subjects; or you may have failed to include important options in your list of possible responses. Sometimes respondents find certain formats confusing or overwhelming. It is even a good idea to check the length to see if respondent-fatigue is causing low-quality answers to the later questions in the interview.

Be sure that all your questions pertain to the objectives of your research study. Most information is of some interest, but you should be ruthless in rejecting questions that will not provide the specific information you need to make your decision. This is why you need clearly-stated objectives for the research project and a clear understanding of the information you will need to solve your problem.

There are two broad types of question that you can use in your surveys. First are the open-ended questions, e.g., 'What are the most important considerations for you in choosing a new car?' These have the advantage of allowing the respondent to speak his or her mind and to choose the information that seems most relevant to him or her.

The disadvantage of open-ended questions is that responses are difficult to classify and tabulate. Also, if you give respondents too much discretion in how they can respond, you may not get the information you are seeking.

The second type of question is the closed question, where responses are restricted to the selections prescribed by the researcher. One type of closed question is the dichotomous question, a question offering only two alternatives, e.g., 'Are you presently a full-time college student?' Here, the only possible answers are 'yes' and 'no'. Dichotomous questions are easy to code and classify, though they usually do not provide marketers with much meaningful information. However, they are often used to select respondents who should be interviewed further, or to determine which set of questions would be most relevant for different individuals.

The other type of closed question has a multiple-choice format. This type of question has the advantage of specifying alternatives in which the researcher is interested and makes the data much easier to code and classify. It is important in designing the questionnaire to be certain that all critical alternatives are included.

Analysis and Conclusions

Once the data have been collected, they must be analysed to determine their meaning. Some research is qualitative, that is, it is basically exploratory in nature. It usually consists of interviews conducted in an unstructured manner with small samples of people. This type of research is often intended to generate ideas and hypotheses that can then be further developed. Focus groups are a type of qualitative research, and it is not possible to apply statistical measurement to these types of studies.

Quantitative research involves data that can be measured and subjected to statistical analysis. This type of study uses larger samples and collects responses that can be counted. An understanding of the appropriate statistical techniques and the assumptions behind the use of those techniques is essential for skilful and complete data-analysis.

The first step is to edit and code the data. Editing eliminates such problems as inconsistencies, ineligible responses, and improperly answered questions. Coding simply involves deciding how the responses will be recorded.

The next step is to analyse each question by itself. A frequency distribution provides a tabulation of how many subjects chose a given response. Next, researchers should compare sample means for different groups. For example, which markets in the region have the highest average incomes?

Cross-tabulation is a simple statistical technique that can yield much insight. It compares frequency distributions for different subgroups. An example might be to compare the answers of males versus females on the question of a recent car purchase. Additional techniques, such as regression analysis or analysis of variance, are beyond the scope of this book. These can offer a wealth of information if properly applied to the data, but they should be administered by someone who is experienced in their proper use.

One of the most critical and often overlooked aspects of doing a research project is how its results will be interpreted. That is, what conclusions will be drawn. The most carefully-done research in the world can be useless unless it is properly interpreted. Interpretation often requires a benchmark to indicate how something has changed. For example, suppose we find that twice as many women as men bought cars last year. Is that unusual? Does that represent a deviation from the norm, or is it standard consumer behaviour?

Interpretation requires that the researcher be able to distinguish between relevant and irrelevant information and to then take that information and organise it into coherent patterns. Although many marketing researchers are technically competent, the ability to understand the meaning of the data that have been collected is a much rarer commodity.

Reporting

The final stage of the marketing research process is the preparation of a formal report for management. It is at this stage that the value of the study may be inadvertently undermined by the researcher. Most managers are reluctant and simply do not have the time to wade through a detailed, technical report. Researchers should be aware of the make-up of their audience – that is, how much technical detail decision-makers are likely to demand. The report should be prepared with readers' preferences in mind.

In any case it is a good practice to include an executive summary of the findings at the very beginning of each report. This enables the reader to glean the basic findings at a glance, with the option of going over the details of the study at his or her leisure.

SUMMARY

Marketing information systems are set up to receive, organise, store and retrieve valuable data for marketing managers. The design of an MIS should be implemented with the support of top management, keeping in mind the information needs of the company.

Marketing research is conducted on an 'as needed' basis when important projects are pending. Research can be exploratory, descriptive or experimental, depending on the characteristics of the situation. Secondary data are data from sources that have already gathered them. Primary data are new knowledge gleaned from various research methods.

Primary research is conducted through survey methods and observation. It is important in the research process to take into account proper sampling procedures, as well as the careful design and testing of the questionnaires that will be used in the study. Finally, the analysis is carried out and the conclusions are formulated. These steps may require the assistance of a trained statistician in order to achieve the most reliable results.

FURTHER READING

Alsop, Ronald. 1986. ' "People Watchers" Seek Clues to Consumers' True Behavior'. *The Wall Street Journal* (4 Sept.): 29.

Baumann, Trish. 1989. 'How Quaker Oats Transforms Information into Market Leadership.' *Sales and Marketing Management* (Jun.): 79

Boone, Louis E. and Kurtz, David L. 1992. *Contemporary Marketing*, 7th ed. Ft. Worth, Texas: Dryden Press, Chapter 5.

Chisnall, P.M. 1991. *The Essence of Marketing Research*. Prentice Hall.

Fahey, Alison. 1992. 'Pepsi Bridges "Generation" Gap in Ads.' *Advertising Age* (20 Jan.): 1, 60.

Feinstein, Selwyn. *1986.* Computers Replacing Interviewers for Personnel and Marketing Tasks. *The Wall Street Journal* (9 Oct.): 37.

Lamb, Jr., Charles W., Hair, Jr., Joseph F. and McDaniel, Carl. 1992. *Principles of Marketing*. Cincinnati: South-Western Publishing Co., Chapter 6.

'Let a Data Base Get You the Facts.' 1981. *Changing Times* (Oct.): 47–49.

Luck, D.J. and Rubin, R.S. 1987. *Marketing Research*, 7th ed. Prentice Hall International.

'Marketers Increasing Their Use of Decision Support Systems.' 1989. *Marketing News* (22 May): 29.

McDaniel, Stephen, Verille, Perry and Madden, Charles. 1985. 'The Threats to Marketing Research: An Empirical Appraisal.' *Journal of Marketing Research* (May): 74-80.

O'Brien, Terrence. 1990. 'Decision Support Systems.' *Marketing Research* (Dec.): 51-55.

Pyle, Diane. 1990. 'How to Interview Your Customers.' *American Demographics* (Dec.): 41–45.

Teinowitz, Ira. 1992. 'Coors Rolls Out Keystone Dry.' *Advertising Age* (20 Jan.): 3.

Winski, Joseph M. 1992. '"Addicted" to Research, Nick Shows Strong Kids' Lure.' *Advertising Age* (10 Feb.): S-2, S-22.

Zikmund, William G. 1986. *Exploring Marketing Research*, 2nd ed. Hinsdale, Illinois: Dryden Press.

8 Product Management

What do the following have in common: a shampoo and set, a new Mazda Miata, a tooth filling, and an air-conditioning system for your home? Answer: they are all products. Some are tangible and others are intangible, but they all represent the first element of the marketing mix that companies must develop and market.

In this chapter, we will look first at the definition of a product. Then we will look at product classifications to understand differences among products. Next, information on product relationships and life cycles will offer pointers on managing products within the marketing mix. Finally, there are sections on branding, packaging and labelling, including tips on how to refine the details of the product offering to better accomplish a firm's marketing objectives.

Definition of a Product

The product, the focus of a firm's marketing programme, is the sum of everything the buyer receives as a result of the exchange. Note that what is received may be favourable or unfavourable, depending on the buyer's perspective.

Products are usually thought of as goods, that is, tangible items. A box of Corn Flakes is a good; so is the Mazda Miata and the air-conditioning system. However, services, such as the shampoo and set, are also products. These are largely intangible, and thus more difficult to evaluate. Services account for more than 60 per cent of the US gross national product; about 70 per cent of the US workforce is employed in service industries. These range from the food and beverage industries to professional medical, dental and legal services.

The service sector in Europe is just as important, with 59 per cent of the workforce being employed in the services industry. In the UK this percentage is even higher, standing at 67 per cent of the workforce.

Some organisations market ideas. If you cast your vote for a political candidate, you are in some sense buying his or her ideas. The currency of the exchange is your vote rather than cash, but the essential process is the same as any transaction. Other ideas that are being successfully marketed today include recycling, the fall of communism, and the European Economic Community.

When people spend their resources on a product, they are buying benefits that they hope to obtain from the product. Petrol, for example, is a nasty smelling liquid. It has no intrinsic worth to most of us; its value lies in the fact that our transportation system (car) will not function without it. So when we pull in to a petrol station, we are not really buying the petrol per se, we are buying the convenience of being able to drive our car.

This distinction is not merely semantic. To market a product successfully, marketers must clearly understand what benefits and satisfactions the buyer expects, not just the functional form of the product. Charles Revlon, the founder of Revlon cosmetics, illustrated this point clearly when he said, 'In the factory we manufacture cosmetics, but in the store we sell hope.' Think about it.

There are two broad classifications for products: consumer products and industrial products. Consumer products are bought for personal and/or family use. Industrial products are used to make products for resale or in the firm's operations. The same product, such as a light bulb or pencil, could be classified as either consumer or industrial, depending on its usage. The importance for marketers in these classifications is that the nature of the product dictates, to a large extent, how it should be marketed. We will look at each of these classifications in the next sections.

Consumer Product Classification

There are several ways to classify consumer products, but the most widely recognised and useful scheme uses four categories:

1 Convenience products.
2 Shopping products.
3 Specialty products.
4 Unsought products.

The basis for this classification is the degree to which consumers are willing to expend their resources in searching for the product. Table 8.1 summarises the differences between these four categories.

TABLE 8.1 Characteristics of Consumer Products

	Shopping Effort	Purchase Frequency	Price	Channel Length	Number of Outlets	Store Image
Convenience	Very little	Frequent	Low	Long	Many	No Importance
Shopping	Some	Occasional	Moderate	Fairly short	Few	Important
Specialty	Extensive	Rare	High	Very short	Very few	Very Important

Convenience Products

Convenience products are those that are brought frequently, e.g., bread, milk and petrol. Consumers expect to find these products in easily accessible locations, and they are not willing to expend time and energy making a lot of price and quality comparisons. For this reason, there are many substitutes for these products. That is, if one brand is unavailable, consumers will substitute another brand.

Since consumers are willing to accept substitutes, it behoves marketers of convenience products to distribute them intensively in every available outlet so that sales are not missed. Because these products have high inventory turnover, they also carry low gross margins. Little promotion is carried out at the retail level, so the manufacturer must engage in fairly high levels of advertising and promotion for the brand. Packaging is also important. Since most convenience items are purchased on a self-service basis, the package may have to sell the product.

Shopping Products

Shopping goods differ from convenience goods in several ways. The prices are higher, and shopping products are found in fewer stores. Customers are willing to expend much more effort in the search process to compare prices, styles, colours, warranties and other features. Often the reputation of the store that carries the product is as important as the brand of the product. Because consumers engage in shopping trips to make these comparisons, the location of a store is important. It should be convenient for the customer to include it in his or her shopping expedition.

Because shopping products are purchased less frequently, the inventory turnover is much lower. Thus gross margins must be higher so that middle-men can make a profit. Consequently, fewer middlemen are involved in distribution than with convenience products.

Some shopping goods, such as washing machines and refrigerators, are considered homogeneous; that is, the consumer views them as essentially the same. Other products, such as furniture and clothing, are heterogeneous or have significant differences. Consumers tend to compare homogeneous shopping goods on the basis of price and heterogeneous shopping goods on the basis of features.

Specialty Products

Specialty products have unique characteristics for which buyers are unwilling to accept substitutes. These products are distributed in very few outlets, but consumers will expend the effort to seek them out. The products are usually high in price and purchased very infrequently. Gross margins must be high because inventory turnover is quite low. Some of these brands are famous: Cartier watches, Porsche cars and Steinway pianos.

Unsought Products

Unsought products are those that consumers may need but are reluctant to seek out, or they are newer products that consumers are still unaware of. Usually these items require considerable selling effort to convince prospects to buy. Typical examples are encyclopedias, cemetery plots and arrangements, and insurance.

Industrial Product Classification

Industrial products, unlike consumer products, are classified according to how they will be used rather than by customer buying patterns. The job of the industrial buyer is to get the best deal for his or her company. Consequently, psychological satisfactions are likely to be much less important in an industrial transaction than in consumer purchasing. Industrial products can be divided into the following five categories: major equipment, accessory equipment, component parts and materials, raw materials and industrial supplies.

Major Equipment

Major equipment is purchased infrequently and is expected to last a long time. Heavy machinery, computer systems, and even buildings are included in this category. Since these decisions involve a high capital outlay, negotiations may take place over a period of months and involve numerous high-level decision-makers in the organisation.

Price is not usually the deciding factor. Industrial buyers are concerned with efficiency, performance, maintenance costs and technical assistance from the seller. For these reasons, the seller's salesforce is a critical factor in making the sale. These salespeople often have technical backgrounds and will be responsible for maintaining customer satisfaction long after the actual sale takes place.

Accessory Equipment

Though essential to the smooth functioning of the buyer's operation, these items cost less and require less technical assistance than do products classified as major equipment. Consequently, fewer decision-makers are involved in the purchase, and industrial purchasing agents rather than top-management executives make the final decision. Buyers are also likely to be more price-conscious, although quality is still an important factor.

Accessory equipment calls for continuous representation and widespread distribution. Thus an industrial distributor, a type of wholesaler, is often used, and manufacturers of accessory equipment use advertising more than do producers of major equipment.

Accessory equipment is used in the manufacturing process or in running the office. Examples include copying machines, word processors, portable drills and filing cabinets.

Component Parts and Materials

Component parts and materials are the finished industrial goods produced by one manufacturer that actually become part of the final product of another manufacturer. Tubing, wiring, electronic chips, and batteries are examples. General Mills purchases flour to be used in its Betty Crocker Cake Mixes.

Buyers need a continuous and reliable flow of these goods in order to stay in business. Therefore parts and materials are often supplied on a contract basis to ensure constant availability. Direct sale of these items is common, although wholesalers are sometimes also used.

Raw Materials

Raw materials consist of two types. Farm products are things like eggs, milk, cotton, pigs and soybeans. Natural materials include coal, copper, wood, oil and fish. These are similar to component parts and materials in that they too become part of the finished product.

Since nature's produce is not uniform, these products are usually graded. Top-grade fruits, for example, find their way to produce departments in grocery stores where consumers buy Sunkist oranges and Dole bananas. Lower-grade fruits end up as juices or in ready-made meals.

As with component parts, raw materials are generally required on a regular basis and in the right grades. Thus customers often sign long-term contracts, sometimes at guaranteed prices, for a supplier's output.

Supplies

If major equipment represents the 'speciality' goods of the industrial sector, then supplies represent the 'convenience' goods. Supplies are purchased frequently and in large quantities but are not part of the final product. You will sometimes see supplies referred to as MRO items: maintenance, repair and operations. These items include cleaning supplies, light bulbs, nuts and bolts for repairing machinery, heating fuel and office stationery.

Most of these purchases are made by the firm's buying agent and are considered fairly routine. Low prices with small margins suggest that the products must be widely available. Thus the use of wholesalers is common.

Product Relationships

To develop co-ordinated marketing mixes, managers must understand the relationships among products offered by their firm. A product item is a single product offering, an entity distinct from the other products offered by a company. Tide is a product item for Procter & Gamble, and Kellogg's Corn Flakes is a product item for the Kellogg Company.

A product line is a group of products that are closely related because of marketing, technical or end-use characteristics. All of Kellogg's cereals constitute a product line, and Campbell's Chunky Soups in various flavours make up another product line.

A company's product mix is the total group of products, including all product lines, that are marketed by one organisation. For example, all the detergents, soaps, toothpastes, deodorants and other products that Procter & Gamble produce and market make up its product mix.

The depth of a product line is the number of product items in it. Campbell's Chunky Soups have several different versions, such as Sirloin Beef, Vegetable and Chicken Corn Chowder. The width of a product mix refers to the number of product lines that an organisation offers. Gillette, for example, offers a fairly narrow width: four product lines, including blades and razors, toiletries, writing instruments and lighters.

The Product Life-Cycle

Just as human beings are born, move from infancy to childhood, to adulthood, and to old age, so products also have a pattern to their lives. Products typically move through four stages in their life-cycle, as depicted in Figure 8.1. These stages are introductory, growth, maturity and decline. Note that in discussing the product life-cycle, we are referring to product categories rather than individual brands.

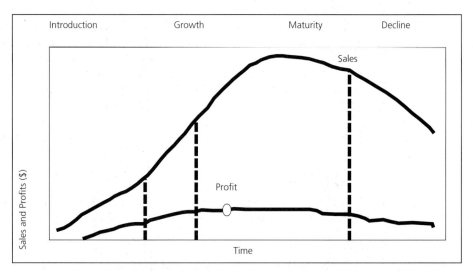

Figure 8.1 The Four Stages of the Product Life Cycle

Introductory stage

In the introductory stage of the product life-cycle, the objective is to get the product launched and to stimulate initial sales of it. Profits are negative in this stage because of extensive research and development and heavy promotion costs. Other characteristics of the introductory stage include high product-failure rate, little competition, limited acceptance by both consumers and middle-men, and some product changes to eliminate any unforeseen problems.

The length of the introductory stage varies according to how quickly the product is accepted by the target market. The more radical a departure it is from products that are already available, the longer it will take to gain acceptance and usage. Promotional costs are also high during this period, since consumers must be informed as to the product's benefits.

Shopping and specialty products require personal selling effort, and convenience products need a lot of advertising support. The focus is on stimulating primary demand rather than demand for individual brands.

Growth

During the growth stage, sales rise rapidly and profits peak then start to decline. The firm has also recouped its research and development costs, and prices begin to fall. These price reductions result from economies of scale and increased competition. The focus now is on increasing or, at a minimum, maintaining market share, since the product's success is apt to attract competitors to the category. Distribution is an important key to success, and companies strive to build strong relationships with middle-men.

Maturity

Industry sales peak and start to decline in the maturity stage, while profits continue to decline. By this stage many competitors have entered the industry, and the weakest will be weeded out or absorbed by more profitable companies. Marketers have also discovered the product benefits that are most appealing to consumers, so most versions have similar features and are often promoted similarly. Since one of the easiest forms of differentiation is price, many firms will cut their prices. Unfortunately, since this is also one of the easiest tactics to mimic, price-cutting may escalate into a price war, with all firms losing money.

Decline

In the decline stage of the product life-cycle, the product is losing market appeal. Many companies have already stopped carrying the product, and fewer and fewer consumers are purchasing it. Consequently, sales fall rapidly and marketers begin to consider what to do with the product.

A product can be phased out gradually, especially if the company has new product offerings to take its place. In such a case promotional support would be withdrawn, and the product allowed to fall into disuse as a natural course of events.

Another option, of course, is to take the product off the market abruptly. One advantage of this approach is that the company eliminates any further costs and losses that this product may incur. A disadvantage is that it might alienate loyal customers who still depend on the product's availability.

In contrast, it is sometimes possible to infuse new life into a product by finding new markets and/or new uses for it. The soft drink Lucozade is an example of a product which was successfully repositioned from being a drink to be taken along to a sick relative to one which is now seen as an energy booster for sports enthusiasts.

Branding

Brands are associated with products and are an important element in the overall bundle of attributes and satisfactions that consumers derive from products they buy. A brand is a name, term, design, symbol, or any other feature that identifies one seller's good or service as distinct from those of other sellers. A brand may identify one item, a family of items, or all items of that seller.

There are other terms that relate to branding. A brand name is the spoken part of a brand, including the words, letters or numbers that are associated with the brand.

A brand mark is a visual symbol or sign associated with a brand. The Coca Cola logo falls into this category; so does the Shell sign and the Legal & General Umbrella. When these elements are registered with the Patent Office they are called trademarks, a legal term that indicates that the owner has exclusive right to the brand, brand name, and/or brand mark. Finally, a trade name is the legal name of a company or organisation.

Benefits of Branding

Branding was first practised in the Middle Ages in Europe when craft guilds used marks to identify their products. The intent was to help buyers determine who consistently produced good quality (or poor quality) merchandise.

Branding in the United States seems to have had its beginnings with patented medicines. However, other manufacturers soon began branding their products also. Some of these are still being marketed today, including Ivory Soap and Quaker Oats.

Branding has some advantages for both buyers and sellers. Customers can feel reasonably confident when they buy the same brand over and over again that they will be getting consistent quality. If products were not branded, customers would be unable to judge differences in quality or preference until they got the product home and used it after each purchase. So branding speeds up the shopping process, as well as giving consumers the ability to support their favourites and avoid brands they dislike. For marketers, branding helps them build a loyal base of customers that stabilises market share. Judicious investment of resources into building a well-known and liked brand name enables marketers to charge a premium price for their product. And introduction of new products into the market under a common brand makes acceptance of these new products much easier for consumers.

Types of Brands

If a company produces more than one product, it must decide whether to use a different brand for each product or to choose a family brand that covers a variety of related products. For example, Coca Cola brand covers several different products: Coca Cola Classic, Diet Coke, Caffeine-Free Coca Cola, and Caffeine-Free Diet Coke. Procter & Gamble, however, decided to differentiate each of their laundry detergents with a different brand name altogether: Tide, Bold, etc.

By using the same brand with several products, a company can take advantage of the goodwill built up for the original brand. All the resources that have already been invested will work in some measure for the new item. This situation then cuts promotional costs for each individual product.

Individual branding makes sense if products are of a varying quality or type. Procter & Gamble's brand differentiation is based partly on the theory that if any brand cannibalises a P&G brand, it should be another P&G brand. Careful positioning is thus required to provide distinctive identities for each laundry detergent.

Generic brands are essentially unbranded products. The only identification on these products is the type of product and the manufacturer. Because resources have not been poured into establishing a strong brand identity, generic brands are usually much less expensive than well-known brands.

Private brands (also known as private label brands, private distributor brands, store brands or dealer brands) are indicative of the reseller who carries that brand rather than the manufacturer who makes it. Black and Decker makes and markets tools under the Black and Decker brand name; Black and Decker also makes tools for Sears under the Craftsman name.

Brand Selection and Maintenance

When selecting a brand name, marketers should be careful to observe some guidelines and answer some questions that will give the brand a better chance of success. Are our objectives for the brand name clear? What product attributes, if any, do we want the brand name to evoke? How can we make the brand memorable? Is it unique or would it be easily confused with existing brands? Is it positive, or is there something about the brand that could be interpreted as negative by the customer? Is it easy to remember and associate with the correct product? Is this a legal brand mark and brand name, or is someone already using it?

Marketers should also choose brand names and design brand marks that can be easily protected. If these special identities can be confused with someone else or if they are likely to fall into general usage as a generic term for the product category, the company will lose exclusive rights to the brand. Given the tremendous resources that a company typically invests, such an occurrence is judged a major disaster.

For example, not all cola-flavoured soft drinks are Coca Cola, and the company spends a lot of money to protect that distinction. Some words that used to be protected brands have fallen into generic usage – escalator, aspirin, shredded wheat, cellophane, nylon and kerosene.

Packaging

As far as its role in the marketing mix is concerned, packaging is generally considered part of the product, although the case can be made that it also serves a promotional function. Nevertheless, the traditional function of packaging has been to protect the product and to hold the product during distribution.

Package design can make a great contribution to the success of a product. Certainly packages make products easier to identify and more attractive at the point of purchase. In fact, a new package can even be the focus of an updated marketing strategy, one in which the package helps create a 'new' product or generates appeal for a new market.

For example, many years ago Avon found out that innovative packaging for their products was as attractive to customers as the products themselves. Since then, Avon bottles have become collectable items. More recently, single-serving containers have opened up new opportunities for food marketers among single-person households.

Packaging is sometimes used to make the use of a product easier or safer. Tamper-proof packages have become common in the wake of some very unpleasant tampering incidents. The Pringles potato crisps resealable box keeps the product fresh for longer and is much easier to close than traditional potato crisp bags.

At a basic level, packaging helps protect products and can reduce distribution costs by reducing the rate of damaged goods. Good packaging will also give a firm some advantages with promotion. After all, the package is a firm's last opportunity to win the customer's attention and elicit a purchase.

As affluence has increased, consumers have demanded more sophisticated and attractive packaging. Gone are the days when a plain brown paper wrapper held much appeal. Packaging upgrades add to the overall cost of the product, but with effective planning, the attractive package can affect sales to the extent that the increased revenue more than offsets the increased costs.

Labelling

Labels come in various forms, and marketers have various objectives for their labels to accomplish. For some, simply identifying the product is sufficient; for others, the label is a source of information for customers. For some marketers, the label is an integral part of their total promotion mix.

Consumer Protection Acts throughout Europe have made some labelling information mandatory. For example, many food items must now display nutritional information, such as the percentage of saturated fats, in addition to the standard volume and weight details. 'Best Before' and 'Use By' dates are now expected by many consumers on foodstuffs.

SUMMARY

Product decisions are among the most important that a marketer can make. In this chapter we saw the need to correctly classify products because of the impact that different classes of goods have on marketing-mix decisions. Convenience products are intensively distributed, have low margins, and have many substitutes. Shopping goods require more search effort and have some qualities that induce consumers to engage in comparison shopping. Specialty items have unique attributes that cause consumers to make a special effort to obtain them and to be unwilling to accept substitutes. Industrial product categories parallel consumer product categories in some respects; however, there are fewer emotional attachments associated with industrial purchases.

The relationships between product items, product lines and product mixes, as well as product depth and width, were discussed. Marketers must make decisions concerning how best to position their product offerings.

Sometimes a common brand name for a group of related products helps tie them together and produces economies of scale in terms of promotion and distribution. In other cases, marketers want to establish a carefully differentiated position for each individual product item.

Choosing and protecting brands is an important aspect of product management. Brands should be easily recognisable, not confused with other brands, and suggestive of some of the positive qualities of the product. Protecting a brand means that marketers must discourage its usage as a generic term for the entire product category, lest the owner lose the exclusive rights to the brand.

FURTHER READING

Assael, Henry. 1985. *Marketing Management*. Boston: Kent Publishing Co., Chapter 10.

Baker, Michael J. and Hart, Susan J. 1995. *Product Strategy and Management.* Prentice Hall (Simon Schuster).

Bennett, Peter D. 1988. *Dictionary of Marketing Terms*. Chicago: American Marketing Association: 18.

Bennett, Robert C. and Cooper, Robert G. 1984. 'The Product Life Cycle Trap.' *Business Horizons* (Sept./Oct.): 7-16.

Howsam, Peter S. and Hughes, G. David. 1981. 'Product Management System Suffers from Insufficient Experience, Poor Communication.' *Marketing News* (26 Jun.): S-2, 8.

Lamb, Jr., Charles W., Hair, Jr., Joseph F. and McDaniel, Carl. 1992. *Principles of Marketing*. Cincinnati: South-Western Publishing Co., Chapter 7.

Lazer, William, Lugmani, Mushtaq and Quareshi, Zahir. 1984. 'Product Rejuvenation Strategies.' *Business Horizons* (Nov./Dec.): 21-28.

Pride, W. M., Ferrell, O. C., Dibb, S., and Simkin, L. 1994. *Marketing – European Edition,* 2nd ed. Houghton Mifflin Co., Chapter 7.

9 New Product Development

The marketplace is dynamic; that is, it is constantly changing. Marketing mixes that have been successful in the past must be constantly modified to adjust to the changes and remain successful in the future. Existing products must be adapted and new products developed to meet changing needs.

In this chapter, we will examine the organisational structure for managing products. We will discuss changing the product mix by deleting or adding products. The main thrust of this chapter, however, will be the new product development process. We will look at the various stages of new product development and how marketers can best manage these stages for ultimate success when the product is introduced.

Organising Around Products

Marketing managers are confronted with a complex set of products, markets, customer needs, and environmental influences. In many cases, the traditional organisational structure does not enhance a marketing manager's ability to handle these demands. Consequently, some managerial alternatives have been developed that enable marketers to bring to bear a specialised focus on some of these areas.

For example, a product manager takes complete responsibility for a single product item, a product line, or, in some cases, several related product lines. A brand manager, similarly, takes charge of a single brand and all the product items that fall under that brand.

These managers co-ordinate the activities involved in marketing the products/brands under their responsibility. They set up distribution channels, plan advertising and promotional campaigns, set pricing policies, and instigate marketing research projects. Product brand managers must also agree on package design, and they work closely with engineering as well as research and development.

A market manager takes a slightly different approach. Rather than focusing on the products, he or she takes responsibility for a particular group of customers. Customers may be divided according to industry, by geographic region, or by some other designation.

A venture team is a group whose members have been drawn from various operating departments. They are brought together to provide impetus and the expertise for developing and marketing a new product or venture. These products may be line extensions (products that appeal to new market segments but are closely tied to existing product lines), or they may be entirely new products.

One consideration in introducing new products is to avoid negatively impacting existing products. A product that sells at the expense of another product in the same product line is cannibalising that line. Although in the case of line extension some cannibalisation is likely, market research should help managers keep these occurrences to a minimum. Clearly differentiated product offerings that appeal to new market segments is the best way to minimise cannibalisation.

Stages in New Product Development

As mentioned in Chapter 8, the failure rate of new products is extraordinarily high, somewhere between 60 and 90 per cent. This fact alone makes the development of new products risky, apart from the additional fact that the development process itself is also expensive.

There are many causes of new product failure. Inadequate market research is certainly one factor. Other causes include technical or design problem with the product itself, errors in timing the introduction, failure to offer a unique benefit, and competitive counter-attacks.

All products advertised as 'New' must be able to prove their claim, either by being a different size from previous versions of the product or by being functionally different from previous options. The Code of Advertising Practice is intended to ensure that all products are what they profess to be. Additional acts which support the above are the Trade Descriptions Act, 1968 and the Fair Trading Act, 1973.

Realistically, there are relatively few truly new products; most are just variations on products that are already on the market. However, some new products introduced in the past 30 years come easily to mind: VCRs, compact disc players, personal computers, cellular telephones and quartz watches.

Variations on existing products qualify as 'new' if they are:

1 New to the company that is marketing them.
2 Represent a significant change from what has previously been available.
3 Enter a new market with a totally new use. For example, when Dr. Pepper introduced Diet Dr. Pepper it was considered a new product, since a diet version of the drink had never before been available.

Sometimes companies move too quickly when introducing a product. Actions that are not well-thought-out can lead to disaster. However, if a company is too slow to respond to market opportunities, competitors may have already taken advantage of those opportunities. To be able to move quickly and still avoid many of the pitfalls of introducing a new product, good marketers follow a logical sequence of stages. These steps are portrayed in Figure 9. 1.

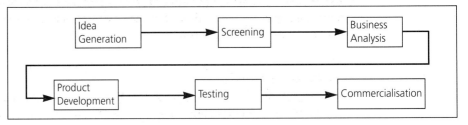

Figure 9.1 The Six-Stage Process of New Product Development

Throughout the stages of new product development, marketers should be evaluating the idea with respect to profitability and return on investment. The burden of proof should be to show that the concept can be successful rather than that it cannot. Such an approach will tend to lead marketers to discard marginal ideas and retain only those that make a good case for themselves.

Idea Generation

Successful new products begin with just one good idea. But most companies have to generate a lot of ideas just to come up with one that is really profitable. That idea can come from sources inside the firm, such as the salesforce, engineering, research and development, and marketing managers. Many companies have implemented reward and incentive plans, which encourage employees to submit their product ideas.

Other ideas come from sources external to the company. These include customers, advertising agencies, management consultants, and research organisations. Sometimes even competitors provide the stimulus for new products either to compete directly or to keep ahead of competitors technologically.

Customers are a particularly good source of new product ideas. Customers themselves are often the most in tune with unmet needs and can give the company sound direction in coming up with a new product.

Screening

At the screening stage, those ideas with the greatest potential are identified; others are eliminated from further consideration. For this reason, relatively few ideas survive the screening stage.

Many companies have a formalised procedure for submitting ideas to the new product screening committee. Write-ups of new ideas may include such aspects as the proposed target market, market size, proposed sales volume, revenues, margins, development costs and time period involved, equipment needs and manufacturing costs. Another critical question that must be addressed is whether the new product meshes well with the firm's overall objectives and its current resources.

Some companies also have a rating system whereby each proposed project can be rated on a variety of dimensions and only the most promising projects pursued. One advantage of a rating system is that it tends to encourage objectivity among managers. It also enables them to prioritise new product ideas when there are many from which to choose.

Business Analysis

The evaluation that takes place in the business analysis stage covers aspects similar to those of the screening stage. The difference is that in the screening stage many of the factors evaluated are somewhat subjective. However, for ideas that survive screening, the figures and projections that will be made during business analysis require much more in-depth research. In fact, you might say that business analysis is an attempt to provide substantiation (or to disprove the claims, as the case may be) of those assumptions made in the screening process.

For example, managers will again examine potential costs and profits, return on investment, and sales projections. Market growth and the future of the product category will be examined. Anticipated environmental changes and competitors' reactions will also be examined.

Much of this information will come from secondary data sources, but it is not unusual at this stage of new product development to conduct a customer survey to provide concrete evidence for the product's potential sales. These surveys can also contribute to understanding customers' needs and wants with respect to the proposed product.

Product Development

In the product development stage the product idea in some respects becomes a reality. Although extensive work has already been done on the idea, it is now time to get feedback on the actual product itself. At this point a prototype is made; a company may even go into limited production of the item to see whether it is technically feasible to produce and can be made at a reasonable cost.

Bear in mind that by the product development stage most ideas have already been discarded. Only a very few warrant the investment necessary to convert the idea into a physical product. This stage is very expensive for a company, and it is important that only the best ideas come this far.

Development can also be a lengthy process. It is here that intangible product attributes can be evaluated, and product characteristics can be linked to the wants and needs of the target market. Here too is where flaws in the design and/or functioning of the product should be found. Safety features must also be evaluated, since companies can be found liable by the courts if product-use results in injury to a customer. The fact is that sometimes a product looks better on paper than it performs in reality; companies must uncover cases where this is so.

Testing

While limited testing can occur in the product development phase, among employees for example, the test market is the crucial phase in deciding whether to add the product to the firm's marketing mix. During testing, a product itself is test-marketed, along with its complete marketing mix: the promotion, distribution, pricing, branding and packaging.

The company will learn how customers respond, whether middle-men will pick up the product, and competitors' counter tactics. As a result, marketers will know whether they want to complete the product roll-out: the process of offering it on a national or international basis. If the product needs some improvements before it can be successfully marketed, limited testing prevents the entire customer base from having had negative experiences with the initial version of the product.

There are some pitfalls in doing a test. For example, the costs of running a test market are very high. This stage should therefore be reserved for only the most promising new products.

Testing may also tip your hand to your competitors. That is, while you are testing, your competitor may do a national roll-out of its own version of the product. Since being first in the marketplace often represents a considerable competitive advantage, this fact alone can make the difference between success and failure. An additional pitfall is that if the testing is a failure, the company may lose credibility with customers and distributors.

Testing is usually done when the costs of developing and introducing the product are high. In such a case, the test market can help a company avoid even more expensive mistakes, either in the decision to market the product or in some aspect of product design or the marketing mix.

Testing is less likely to be done when management has overwhelming confidence in the new product or when it is merely a revised version of a successful product that is already on the market.

Commercialisation

Products that reach the commercialisation stage are those that have completed the new product development process and are deemed suitable for introduction. At this point the marketing mix should be refined based on findings from the test market(s), and sufficient production capability must be assured to meet anticipated market demand once the product is available.

The commercialisation stage is usually the most expensive step in the process, but marketers should not proceed with this stage unless the preceding steps have given them clear go-ahead signals. Even so, it is generally customary to roll-out the product step by step, still weighing its impact in the marketplace. The product will often be introduced either regionally or in select major markets. This is viewed as a risk-reduction strategy. Based on its continued success, the new product will then be introduced nationally or even sometimes internationally.

Industries and companies vary with respect to the speed with which they attempt to launch new products. In mature industries, firms usually take their time and proceed carefully. In industries where technology is rapidly changing and is a key factor in offering a competitive edge, it is extremely important that a company does not waste much time. Otherwise it may be pre-empted by its competitors.

Product Positioning

Positioning refers to what marketers do to influence the minds of customers and to set certain products apart, thus giving these products a distinctive identity. For example, what company do you think of when you think of computers? Photocopy machines? Rental cars? These examples represent companies that have successfully forged a unique niche; in a sense, they 'own' that place in the consumer's mind.

Being first is one way to garner a unique position. However, as with 7-UP being positioned as the 'uncola', other products have found ways to position themselves and create an advantage. Avis is positioned as the company that practises 'we try harder!' Crest is the toothpaste that fights cavities, and Gillette 'owns' the razor market.

Sometimes brands position themselves to fight head-to-head with market leaders. However, the market leader has a tremendous advantage, and most companies do not have the resources to dislodge a company or brand from a firmly embedded position. A better strategy, and one that works even better, is to find an unclaimed position and take it. This has come to be called niche marketing, a relatively new term for a concept that has been around quite a long time. An example would be Volvo claiming the 'safety car' niche in the car market.

SUMMARY

To manage products most effectively, marketers have devised several alternative management structures to handle products. These include the product or brand manager, the market manager and the venture team. The approach that is chosen depends on the characteristics of the organisation, the product and the markets that are being served.

New product development is a very important and risky venture for a firm. To counteract some of the risks, a formalised procedure is usually implemented to evaluate new product possibilities. The six-stage process includes idea generation, screening, business analysis, product development, testing and commercialisation.

In idea generation, the objective is to come up with a large number of ideas. Screening then eliminates most ideas from consideration. The ones that survive are analysed to determine market potential, costs and profitability. New product ideas that have good business potential are then developed and tested in limited markets to further refine the products and the marketing mix. Commercialisation is the final stage, in which the product is eventually introduced to its entire market.

FURTHER READING

Boone, Louis E. and Kurtz, David L. 1992. *Contemporary Marketing*, 7th ed. Ft. Worth, Texas: Drysden Press, Chapter 10.

Deveny, Kathleen. 1987. 'Maytag's New Girth Will Test Its Marketing Muscle.' *Business Week* (16 Feb.): 68.

Giges, Nancy. 1987. 'Colgate Sets 2nd New Product Unit.' *Advertising Age* (9 Feb.): 12.

Guiltiman, Joseph P. and Gordon W. Paul. 1988. *Marketing Management,* 3rd ed. New York: McGraw Hill Book Co., Chapter 7.

Hart, Susan J. 1995. *New Product Development: A Reader.* Dryden Press.

Hisrich, R.D. and Peters, M.P. 1991. *Marketing Decisions for New and Mature Products,* 2nd ed. Maxwell MacMillan International Editions.

Kotler, Philip. 1991. *Marketing Management*, 7th ed. Englewood Cliffs, New Jersey: Prentice Hall, Chapter 12.

Ries, Al and Trout, Jack. 1981. *Positioning. The Battle for Your Mind*. New York: McGraw Hill Book Company.

Statman, Meir and Tyzoon T. Tyebjee. 1986. 'Trademarks, Patents, and Innovation in the Ethical Drug Industry.' *Journal of Marketing* (Summer): 71-81.

Wall, John. 1987. 'State of the Mart Product Packages.' *Insight* (19 Jan.): 62.

Yonovich, B.G. 1981. 'Competition Jumps the Gun.' *Advertising Age* (9 Feb.): S-18.

10 Marketing Channels

Marketing channels (also called channels of distribution) are the pipelines through which goods and services pass from the producer to the ultimate customer. Some of these channels are for industrial products; some are for consumer products. A variety of possible intermediaries may be involved in moving the product along its way. Some of these take title to the product; they are called merchants. Others are responsible for physically moving the product from one place to another; these are agents or brokers. And still others simply facilitate the product's passage along the pipeline such as financing companies or advertising agencies.

Regardless of who is involved in the final structure of a distribution channel, the decision about how to distribute products is among the most important facing management. Pricing depends on whether the product is sold by mass merchandisers or in exclusive specialty stores. Whether to use a salesforce and how to advertise the product are decisions that depend on how the product will be distributed.

In this chapter we will examine the structure and functions of distribution channels. We will look at some considerations for choosing various types of channels, and we will examine the need for skilfully managing channel members.

Structuring Marketing Channels

Channels vary in the number of intermediaries involved in the product flow from the producer to the customer, as can be seen in Figure 10.1.

However, each middle-man in the channel performs some work that moves the product closer to the final customer. For example, Channels A and E are direct marketing channels, which means that there are no intermediary levels between the producer and the customer. Companies like Avon and World Book Encyclopedia send their salespeople to the final consumer, instead of funnelling their products through a wholesaler or retailer.

Other channels use at least one intermediary to facilitate the exchange process. IBM, for example, uses a Channel B format to market its micro-computers to home-users. Singer sells its sewing machines through its own stores.

Channel C is used by many food, drug and hardware producers. Because a typical retailer will stock many brands, that retailer will rely on a wholesaler to

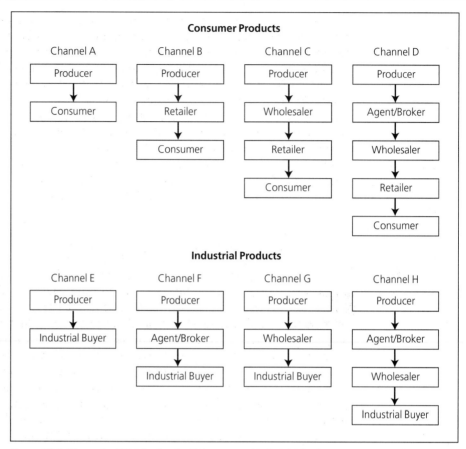

Figure 10.1 Channels of Distribution for Consumer and Industrial Products

provide an assortment of needed products and brands. Most consumer products are sold through channels similar to B and C.

Channel D is often the choice of mass-distributed products, such as confectionery or some foods. A confectionery manufacturer may hire an agent or broker to represent its products with wholesalers, who in turn provide a variety of products for supermarkets and convenience stores.

Channel E, the direct-marketing channel in the industrial sector, is often used by producers who make expensive products, such as aircraft and earth-moving equipment. Salespeople call directly on corporate buyers and make the sale to them without going through intermediaries. Channel E is more often used in industrial sales than in consumer sales and is frequently the choice for raw materials, major equipment, processed materials and supplies.

Channel F would be used when the producer is too small to maintain its own salesforce or when it is entering new markets with which it has little experience. Agents/brokers who represent producers in Channel F would undoubtedly carry several non-competing product lines and would offer a cost-effective way for numerous small producers to reach their customers.

Channel G would be used under similar conditions, except that a wholesaler would be particularly effective if the products are to be marketed to a large number of buyers and do not require intensive personal selling effort. Many construction products, for example, are sold through Channel G.

Finally, Channel H can be used for specialised cases in which a small manufacturer without a salesforce markets products that must be re-ordered on a regular basis or purchased in small quantities by a large number of users. Overseas producers of electronic components, for example, may use export agents to sell to industrial wholesalers in the countries where the producer has customers.

In each case, you should note that the characteristics of the producer, the product itself, and the market being served all enter into the decision as to which distribution channel will be most effective and efficient.

Performing Channel Functions

Most producers lack the resources to use direct-marketing channels and in many cases direct marketing is impractical. For example, Coca-Cola's distribution system flows through the bottlers to the retailers and then to final consumers. Suppose Coca-Cola decided to market its product direct. Should they set up small stores in a multitude of locations to make Coke available to everyone who wants it? Or would it be feasible to sell Coca-Cola door-to-door? Or by post?

Economies of scale would only be realised if Coca-Cola also began to sell other products as well, so that customers found it convenient to make several purchases in one stop. Now Coke is operating its own convenience store or supermarket, and we are essentially right back where we started. The point is that distribution channels are set up to perform needed functions.

One of the most important axioms in marketing is that you can eliminate the channel intermediary, but you cannot eliminate the functions he or she performs. The purpose of this section is to describe the functions channel members carry out and to convince you that eliminating them will not necessarily save the customer money.

Facilitating Exchange

In some countries today, women still spend a very large proportion of their time shopping. They buy their bread from one vendor, their meat from another, and their produce from yet another vendor. This process is time-consuming at best; in Western society, for many people it would simply be impossible to find enough time.

Figure 10.2 shows how the addition of a middle-man can eliminate duplicated effort and minimise the number of transactions required to complete a shopping expedition for five shoppers. Notice how the insertion of a retailer in the distribution channel brought the number of transactions down from 25 to ten. In similar fashion, middle-men in many different distribution channels reduce the amount of work that must be done to get products to customers at the right place, at the right time, in the right form, and in the right quantities.

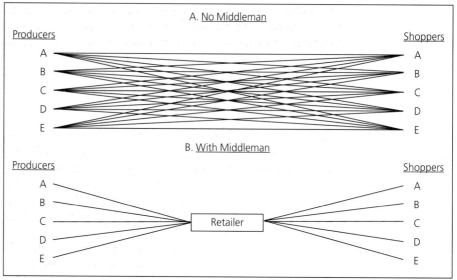

Figure 10.2 How a Middleman Increases Shopping Efficiency

To accomplish these goals, distribution channels are set up to perform many key functions. Some members carry out research to gather valuable information on marketing the product to other channel members and to customers. Others develop effective promotions that help to gain acceptance for the product among buyers. Many channel members engage in negotiations, selling, storing, inventorying, and physically moving products from one place to another. Some facilitating agencies provide financing and assume some of the risk involved in moving the product through the channel.

Resolving Discrepancies

Let's look again at our Coca-Cola example. Assume a Coca-Cola plant can produce 5,000 gallons of syrup each day. What shall be done with this production? First, there is a form discrepancy: syrup is not what Coke drinkers want. They want the syrup combined with carbonated water and packaged in small amounts that can be easily consumed. Second, there is a place discrepancy: consumers do not want to drive to the plant in Atlanta to pick up their Coke. Third, there is a quantity discrepancy: no one wants that much syrup at once, particularly along with the form discrepancy. And finally, there is a time discrepancy: customers cannot get a drink of Coke when they want it in its present form.

Channels of distribution are designed to resolve these discrepancies for customers. This is accomplished through several processes. *Sorting out* consists of breaking down a heterogeneous bulk into relatively homogeneous groups. Grading agricultural products, such as eggs, meat or fruit, is a typical example. *Accumulation* involves combining groups of similar products. For example, Red Delicious apples from many orchards may be combined to provide a stock from which smaller units will be then taken in individual boxes, called *breaking bulk* or *allocation*. *Assorting* combines groups of products into collections that buyers want to have available at the same time and place. A tennis player would expect to find an assortment of tennis products, racquets, shoes, balls, shorts and shirts, at his or her favourite sporting goods store.

Integrating Channels

The traditional marketing channel is a network of entities that are loosely aligned, at best. In some cases there is poor co-ordination and co-operation among members of the channel. Because each member is autonomous, members may have different goals, procedures and philosophies of operation, which can eventually result in customer dissatisfaction. For this reason, traditional channels are often more expensive and less efficient than other types of channels that we will now examine.

When two or more members of the distribution channel are combined under one management, such an arrangement is called 'vertical channel integration' or 'vertical marketing integration'. This can be accomplished by one member purchasing the operations of other members or by taking on the functions that they perform – in effect, eliminating the need for them. Total vertical integration can be seen in the oil industry, for example, where oil fields, wells, pipelines, refineries, terminals, transportation fleets and service stations are owned by one company.

Generally in vertical integration, one member of the channel takes the lead in co-ordinating the activities of the other members. Such a member is called a *channel leader* or *channel captain*.

Types of Vertical Marketing System

There are three types of vertical marketing system (VMS): corporate, contractual and administered.

Corporate VMS

The corporate VMS is formed when one of the intermediaries in the channel acquires the other channel members. For example, a supermarket chain that also owns food-processing plants and food wholesalers would be an example of a corporate VMS.

Contractual VMS

A contractual VMS, as the name implies, is a group of independent channel members bound together by a contractual agreement that specifies each member's rights and obligations to other members. Franchise operations, such as The Body Shop, Holiday Inn, and car dealerships, are all contractual vertical marketing systems.

Administered VMS

An administered VMS means that the size and power of one of the channel members gives that organisation control over the successive stages in the distribution system. Technically, channel members are independent; in reality, one channel member dominates the administered VMS. Marks & Spencer and Safeway are retailers that have been able in numerous instances to exercise a strong influence over other members of their distribution channels. Sometimes manufacturers are the dominant members of a channel. What supermarket can afford to alienate the Kellogg Company or Campbell's?

Horizontal Marketing Systems

Horizontal integration occurs when members at the same level in the distribution channel pool their resources to achieve economies of scale in research, purchasing, advertising or negotiating. Some of these organised groups are called co-operatives, such as American Hardware, which has more than 3,700 members. Others are wholesale horizontal marketing systems. And some occur at the retail level when other stores are bought out, as was the case when the Argyll Group purchased all the Presto stores in the UK in 1989.

Selecting Distribution Channels

A new producer may start with just a few channel members. As the company grows and sales increase, new channel members may be added. In some cases, entirely new distribution channels may be set up. For example, the company may sell directly to retailers in small markets but require the assistance of wholesalers to reach the top 100 mass markets in Europe.

But a distribution system should not just 'grow'. It is a critical element in the company's marketing mix and, as such, it should be carefully designed. Choices with respect to distribution should reflect the company's resources and objectives, customer needs and wants, and product constraints. It is important that decision-makers set channel objectives and carefully evaluate channel alternatives before making commitments that will have far-reaching repercussions for the firm's future.

Intensity of Market Coverage

One of the basic issues is the degree of market coverage necessary to successfully market various products. As we have seen in Chapter 8, there are three types of product: convenience, shopping and specialty. The intensity of market coverage is directly linked to the consumer behaviour patterns associated with these three types of product.

Intensive distribution means stocking the product in as many outlets as possible. Intensive distribution is appropriate for convenience items because consumers purchase these products frequently, the products have a high replacement rate, and consumers are likely to substitute other brands when their favourite is not available. Toothpaste, sweets, bread and milk are good examples of products that can be purchased not only in supermarkets but in convenience stores and even in petrol stations.

With *selective distribution* – only a few outlets in a given geographical area are chosen to carry a product. This type of distribution generally applies to shopping goods and, occasionally, to some specialty items. Selective distribution is effective when customers are willing to spend some time looking for their preferred brand or when products require special service at the point of sale. By using more than one but less than all outlets that are available in a given area, a producer can develop strong relationships with the best outlets. Such arrangements conserve resources and allow the producer to maintain more control over the selling effort.

When only one outlet is used in a given geographical area, we call this *exclusive distribution*. This form of distribution works best for specialty products: those that are purchased infrequently, consumed slowly, and/or require special tailoring for the buyer. Customers are willing to engage in considerable search activity for these products.

The advantage to the producer is the control that he or she has over the reseller. For example, exclusive dealing may be in effect, wherein the manufacturer requires that the retailer does not carry competing products. An advantage to the reseller is that there is virtually no competition for that product within his or her selling area.

Exclusive distribution is often found with prestigious cars, such as Porsche, Bentley and Rolls Royce, and with prestige women's apparel brands. Steinway piano outlets enjoy exclusive distribution, as do many types of industrial equipment.

Markets and Buyers

The first obvious distinction a producer must make is that between consumer and industrial channels. Industrial buyers are more likely to purchase direct from the manufacturer than are consumer buyers, but even industrial producers face a wide selection of options in terms of designing their channels.

The geographical location of the market is one factor to consider. Direct sales are possible when a company has a few customers concentrated in one location. As a firm's customer base spreads out geographically, the need for additional intermediaries in the distribution channel tends to increase accordingly, and the intensity of customer distribution becomes an issue. At this stage, manufacturers' representatives, salespeople, who represent several non-competing clients at the same time, might be the best solution. However, if the majority of the company's customers were concentrated in, say, two geographical areas, a salesforce of two representatives might be feasible.

It is also important to consider buyer behaviour when selecting a channel. Market research can provide information concerning what quantities customers want, when they buy, and where they buy. Producers can use shorter channels when customers buy in large quantities; however, most consumer products are purchased in small quantities at a time and thus call for wholesalers to be part of the channel. On the other hand, some large retailers, such as Marks & Spencer and Debenhams, order in large quantities and provide their own warehousing so that it makes sense for a manufacturer to deal with their sales offices directly.

Shifts in buying behaviour sometimes alter the channel decision. For example, the growth of self-service, the greater use of mail-ordering, and the demand for convenience have changed many distribution channels in recent years. Consumers now order clothing from catalogues through the post, buy cosmetics from their Avon representative where they work, and do their banking and pay their bills where they shop for groceries.

Product Attributes

In general, the lower the unit cost of an item, the longer the distribution channel. Usually such items must be part of a larger assortment to justify handling on a cost basis. Also, the more perishable the product, such as some food items and fashion products, the shorter its shelf life and the shorter the distribution channel. Finally, more customised products, both consumer and industrial, tend to have shorter channels. A computer system, for example, must be tailored to the needs of specific users. Thus the producer must supply additional services as well as custom-designing the product. When consumers want services such as delivery, credit, repairs, maintenance, installation and replacement parts, marketers must provide a higher level of channel service.

Environmental Factors

The company that is designing its distribution channels must find middle-men who are willing and able to perform the necessary tasks. Companies that have adequate financial and marketing resources are more likely to supply their own support; however, many successful companies have had to forge relationships with intermediaries to be able to do business.

New technology has changed distribution practices for some companies. Electronic scanners, automated inventory systems, and telemarketing make it easier for firms to perform some of their own distribution functions. These developments also make it more difficult for undercapitalised and unsophisticated companies to survive, much less compete successfully.

Even changes in the social fabric have forced some firms to change their distribution patterns. Avon used to concentrate entirely on door-to-door sales to housewives. Now a large part of its revenue is generated through sales in the workplace.

There are also some legal factors that companies must take into account. For example, horizontal arrangements – say, among competing retailers or wholesalers – have been ruled illegal by the US Supreme Court if the intent is to limit sales by customer or territory. This is called collusion and its result is to limit competition.

Correspondingly, some vertical relationships may be found illegal if they serve to limit competition. Sylvania won an important case in 1977 when the US Supreme Court ruled that it could limit distribution of its television sets through stores that specialised in TVs and that provided additional services for customers, such as TV repair. Sylvania argued that it could not compete if customers could gather information at these stores and then go to a self-service discount store to actually make the purchase on a price basis.

Some vertical relationships are not very formalised, but nonetheless the companies work together. This is most evident in the retailing industry, with the large retailers being in a position to exercise a great deal of control over their suppliers, without actually buying them out. One example is that of the retailer Marks & Spencer, with stores throughout Europe. This retailer establishes very close relationships with suppliers. One supplier, namely Marshalls, provider of ready-made meals for M & S, has a special division dedicated solely to this customer. Companies must ensure that with or without a formal agreement, their arrangement does not endanger competition.

Managing Distribution Channels

There are many good reasons for channel members to get together and co-operate in building a unified distribution system that will be mutually profitable and satisfying for all the members involved. Sometimes the channel works this way; often it does not. Channel conflict is so common as to be written up in nearly all principles of marketing texts. We will look briefly at the bases for co-operation, the reasons for conflict, and the role of leadership in channel management.

Co operation

If members of a channel do not co-operate, then none of the members realises its goals. Channel members must view themselves as a unified team, and policies must be developed that enable each channel member to benefit from the relationship.

Different producers will experience different responses from prospective channel members. For example, Phileas Fogg has no trouble recruiting retailers to carry its tortilla chip range; the snack food assortment would be incomplete without this brand. However, some producers have to promise selective or exclusive distribution before retailers and wholesalers are willing to handle their product lines.

On the other hand, producers should carefully examine the credentials of other members of the channel to determine those with the characteristics of effective middle-men. Years of experience, other lines carried, profit potential, levels of service, and reputation with customers can be important clues to selecting middle-men with whom a producer can have a good relationship.

Power

Channel power means the ability of one channel member to influence, even control, the behaviour of other channel members. The leadership role in the channel is typically assumed by the member with the most power; as we have already seen, this can be a producer, a wholesaler or a retailer. Several bases of power exist, and leadership may be assumed on the basis of one or several of these.

Reward power means that channel members believe that another member can help them achieve their goals. If a retailer gets exclusive distribution rights from a producer, that arrangement may place the retailer in a highly advantageous position competitively.

Coercive power means that one member of the channel has the ability to threaten another member. An example might be if IBM threatened to withdraw the option of selling its products from a retailer.

Legitimate power simply means that the channel leader has a right to make decisions. Legitimate power usually derives from a company's widespread and respected reputation. Examples include Procter & Gamble, Campbell's and Xerox.

Referent power develops when one member has accrued a great deal of prestige, and other members want to identify with that prestige. For example, some manufacturers list prestigous department stores, such as Harrods, Debenhams and John Lewis in their advertising.

Expert power is based on the belief that one channel member's experience and marketing ability can provide benefits to all other members of the channel. Retailers often allow important suppliers to put up special displays or to advise them on how to most effectively merchandise the producer's products.

Conflict

While there are many good reasons for co-operation among channel members, there are also reasons for conflict. Decisions can be made by one channel member that adversely affect other members. Horizontal conflicts occur when one middle-man infringes another's territory, or when different types of retailers carry the same products. Vertical conflicts can occur when, for example, the producer lowers the suggested retail price, which in turn lowers the retailer's profit. Another example could be when a retailer carries private brands in addition to a supplier's nationally advertised brands. Vertical conflict occurs more often than does horizontal conflict.

SUMMARY

There are two broad types of distribution channel: consumer and industrial. Within each of these two types, there are also several options as to how to set up the channel. Some channels are direct from the producer to the customer; others have more intermediaries, such as the typical producer-wholesaler-retailer-consumer channel.

Channel decisions are very important for a company, since place is a critical element in the marketing mix. Channel decisions should be made with a strategic plan in mind. Executives should set objectives that are compatible with the company's overall goals and that take into account the firm's resources and expertise. Most important to remember is that a certain number of channel functions must be performed. Either some intermediary in the channel or the customer will have to perform these functions.

Wise channel decisions also depend upon characteristics of the market, customers, and the general competitive situation, as well as the characteristics of the product itself. For example, is the product a convenience, shopping or specialty good?

Sometimes it is effective to integrate the channel either horizontally or vertically, depending on the objectives of the producer and the needs of customers. Types of vertical marketing systems include corporate, contractual and administered. Some horizontal marketing systems are called co-operatives. In any channel there is likely to be a certain amount of conflict. While co-operation is the ideal, conflict may still arise. Firms should therefore be sensitive to how their decisions will affect other members of the channel and what repercussions they can expect.

FURTHER READING

Agins, Teri. 1989. 'Clothing Makers Don Retailers' Garb.' *Wall Street Journal* (13 July): B1.

Boone, Louis E. and Kurtz, David L. 1992. *Contemporary Marketing*, 7th ed. Ft. Worth, Texas: Dryden Press, Chapter 12.

Christopher, M. 1992. *Logistics and Supply Chain Managment*. Pitman Publishing..

Kiley, David. 1987. 'Lever in a Lather over Shelf Space.' *Adweek's Marketing Week* (2 Nov.): 1, 6.

Kotler, Philip. 1991. *Marketing Management*, 7th ed. Englewood Cliffs, New Jersey: Prentice Hall, Chapter 19.

Lamb, Jr., Charles W., Hair, Jr., Joseph F. and McDaniel, Carl. 1992. *Principles of Marketing*. Cincinnati: South-Western Publishing Co., Chapter 9.

Payne, A. 1993. *Relationship Marketing*. Wiley.

Rosenbloom, Bert. 1987. *Marketing Channels*, 3rd ed. Hinsdale, Illinois: Dryden Press.

Stern, Louis W., El-Ansary, Adel I. and Brown, James R. 1989. *Management in Marketing Channels*. Englewood Cliffs, New Jersey: Prentice Hall.

11 Retailing

The Currie Family with one child of three and a baby of five months live in Glasgow. They have varying shopping needs. Alastair, the husband, enjoys French-cured sausage; another family favourite are Mexican Tortilla Chips. With a young baby in the household, they are often required to make extra purchases at the last minute. Since the whole family enjoys experimenting with cooking, they expect their local supermarket to stock fresh herbs from various countries of origin.

Retailers create the convenience for this family to have their needs satisfied, without having to travel to various locations. The time utility offered by retailers also helps the family to make last-minute purchases and gives them a wide range of products to choose from.

Retailers buy and stock merchandise for the purpose of reselling it to the final consumer. Consequently, retailers are both customers and marketers in the channel of distribution. They provide products and services for consumers, but they are also customers for manufacturers and, wholesalers.

Retailers create place utility by having products in a location that is convenient for consumers. Time utility involves having the products or services available when the customer wants them, and possession utility means that the retailer makes it easy for consumers to buy.

Retailers are the most visible of all marketers and are probably who consumers think of, when they think of marketing. However, not all retailing is done by supermarkets and department stores. Some non-traditional retailers include mail-order marketing, automatic vending machines, and in-home retailing. These other forms of retailing will also be examined in this chapter.

Types of Retail Outlet

There are several ways to classify retailers: amount and extent of service, product lines sold, relative prices and control of the outlets.

Self-service retailers are represented by supermarkets, superstores and many discount chains. They usually carry convenience goods and nationally-branded, fast-moving shopping goods.

Limited-service retailers provide some sales assistance, along with credit and some delivery services. Additional services increase operating costs and, thus, prices.

Full-service retailers are found in specialty stores and more sophisticated department stores. These establishments are able to charge higher prices than other retailers because of the added value in additional services that they offer. These services may include liberal return policies, credit plans, free delivery, home servicing and alterations.

Product Lines

Product lines can be measured by their depth and breadth. Depth refers to the number of versions available in a given product category, such as men's shirts; short-sleeved and long-sleeved sport shirts, athletic shirts and dress shirts in varieties of colours, styles and fabrics reflect a fairly deep product assortment. Breadth means that a variety of product categories are featured in a given store. For example, in addition to men's shirts, a men's clothing store might offer trousers, suits, ties, belts, shoes, socks, handkerchiefs and accessories.

Pricing

Stores can also be classified according to pricing policy. Discount stores offer low prices; full service department stores offer relatively high prices. These higher prices are easy to understand when you recognise the numerous 'free' services that the store provides to its patrons; the cost of those services must be recovered.

Control of Outlets

Some stores are part of a chain, a series of similar stores under a common ownership. Others are independently owned and operated. And still others are franchised operations, a popular and growing form of store ownership. The franchisor is paid for the use of a store name, co-operative advertising, training and guidelines for running a successful operation. The franchisee has certain responsibilities to adhere to the franchisor's standards for doing business. Often the products and even the advertising are standardised among individual operators.

Department Stores

Department stores are large stores that are organised into many separate departments, with each specialising in a particular product line or group of related product lines. In some ways the department store is like a series of specialty or limited-line shops, with such groupings as women's clothes, accessories, shoes, children's wear, men's wear, housewares, home furnishings and textiles. Some well-known department stores are Harrods, Frasers, Debenhams and John Lewis. It should be noted that specialty department stores can also be found, notably

Next and Principles, which carry only clothing, shoes, gift items, cosmetics, accessories or luggage. General merchandise department stores are those that have expanded their product lines to attract more customers. Some additional departments might include automotive, electronics, sports equipment and computer supplies. Some added services are provided by specialists who lease the space and pay 'rent' to the department stores, such as travel agents, beauticians and optometrists.

Department stores specialise in offering many services to their customers, such as charge accounts, gift-wrapping, free delivery and liberal return privileges. As a result, they have high operating costs, averaging between 45 and 60 per cent of sales. Chain stores, such as Sears, average somewhat lower operating costs – about 35 per cent of sales – because of successful marketing integration with suppliers.

At first, department stores were located in the central shopping district of towns. After World War II, however, middle- and upper-income groups began a mass exodus to the suburbs. In response to changing customer demands, department stores began opening branch stores in the suburbs, usually in shopping centres.

Another serious source of concern for department stores has been the rise of two other distinct forms of retailing. The discount store has posed a threat to the department store in the form of lower prices; the specialty retail store competes on the basis of more variety and product depth within a specified product line. Department stores' responses have been varied. Some have added 'bargain basements' and expanded parking facilities. Others have increased their services to provide added value for more affluent shoppers.

Mass Merchandisers

Traditional retailers have a philosophy of 'buy low and sell high'.

Mass merchandisers have challenged them with a new philosophy of 'low prices, faster turnover, and higher volume'. By appealing to large markets with a low-price, high-volume strategy, mass merchandisers have virtually changed the face of retailing since the 1930s.

Supermarkets

In the US supermarkets made their appearance in the 1930s, but were not established in the UK until the 1960s. They offered a wide assortment of merchandise, lower prices than the corner shop and the introduction of the self-service concept. Their success was due to several factors. Consumers were very cost-conscious at this time. The widespread use of the car enabled customers to move beyond the neighbourhood grocery shop, so supermarkets were able to generate the higher volumes they needed to make lower prices profitable. Also, improved packaging and refrigeration techniques gave products longer shelf life, so customers were able to do their shopping periodically rather than every day.

A typical Asda superstore in the UK is approximately 40,000 sq.ft., with many supermarkets being of around 25,000 sq.ft. In the UK the majority of larger supermarkets are part of a national chain, some of the most important being the Argyll Group, Tesco, Asda and Sainsbury's.

In the UK during the 1970s the number of supermarkets grew dramatically, at the expense of the small corner shop. The reduction in small shops per year was over 3,000, but between 1986 and 1987 this reduction slowed to only 530 per year. Although there are thousands of supermarkets operating throughout the UK and Europe, they are rapidly reaching saturation point and many stores have adopted the concept of recreating the small store within the large supermarket: for example, the delicatessen counter and fish sections, where service is personal and not on a self-service basis.

Supermarkets in the US are also reaching a saturation point because of increased competition from other forms of food retailing, such as convenience stores, discount food stores, superstores, and more eating out in restaurants.

Supermarkets have rather thin margins: net profits of one per cent or less of total sales. Consequently, they are focusing on some strategies to improve their competitive position. One approach is to convert to discount or warehouse retailing, thus scaling back services and reverting to a 'bare bones' operation. These operations carry more non-perishable items than supermarkets, packaged goods and canned items with fast turnover.

The other approach has been to add services and expand the types of shopping activities that customers can perform while in the store. This has led to the rise of the superstores and hypermarkets.

Superstores and Hypermarkets

Superstores, originally from Europe, not only carry food but many non-food items as well: housewares, small appliances, lawn and garden products, clothing and hardware. They may also offer such services as ATM (automatic teller machines) machines, film developing, dry cleaning, travel reservations, bill paying and banking. These stores try to meet all the customer's routine needs with one-stop shopping.

Superstores typically carry about 50,000 items and may offer large 'sales' to customers to entice them to travel a little farther for the cost savings and the convenience of everything under one roof.

Store size is the major difference between superstores and hypermarkets. Hypermarkets typically have more than 200,000 sq.ft. of selling space and combine discount store and supermarket shopping in one location. They offer an average of 45,000 to 60,000 different types of products at low prices. With only 40-50 per cent of selling space allocated to grocery products, these hypermarkets have been referred to as 'malls without walls'. The remainder of the space includes such varied products and services as hardware, soft goods, building materials, auto supplies, appliances and prescription drugs, as well as a restaurant, beauty salon, barber shop, branch bank, specialty food shop, florist and bakery.

Discount Houses

Discount houses offer low prices and fewer services than traditional department stores by accepting lower margins and by selling in higher volume. First appearing after World War II, discount houses rapidly grew in favour with consumers. The conventional retailer, Kresge, opened its version of the discount house, Kmart, and received widespread response from consumers.

Elimination of many of the 'free' services has enabled discount houses to keep their markups 10 to 25 per cent below their competitors'. Originally discount houses sold mostly appliances, but it was not long before they branched into clothing, furniture, lawn and garden, automotive, housewares and textiles. Over time many discounters added services, such as credit, and also nationally advertised brands to their product assortments.

Wholesale Clubs

Wholesale clubs, sometimes called warehouse clubs, sell a limited selection of brand name items: food, appliances, electronics, clothes and other categories. Members pay an annual fee, usually £25 to £50, for shopping privileges. Often small, local retailers will shop at a wholesale club, since they may be unable to obtain wholesaling services elsewhere; they average about 60 per cent of the wholesale club's sales. Consumers generally pay a premium of five per cent above the marked price.

Wholesale clubs are the newest form of mass merchandising, and they operate the most spartan of any retail operation. They are housed in large warehouse buildings with concrete floors and aisles wide enough to accommodate fork lift trucks. Products are stored on pallets or pipe racks, and customers are required to manoeuvre their own trollies to their cars.

Product ranges are very limited – usually only four to five thousand different products – and it is often necessary to buy in large quantities to get the typical 20 to 40 per cent reduction off supermarket and discount store prices.

The earliest wholesale club was founded by Price company in the late 1970s. Price has been joined by Costco Wholesale Clubs and BJ's Warehouse Club (owned by Zayre Corporation), as well as Sam's Wholesale Clubs in the US Wholesale clubs do not constitute a large number of retailers in the UK, Costco being the largest. This may be due to cultural differences in shopping behaviour, but has surely also been affected by the recession in the 1980s.

Catalogue Showrooms

Catalogue showrooms send catalogues to customers and display samples of items on the showroom floor. The main draw of catalogue showrooms is, like other mass merchandisers, cost savings that accrue through high volume and low overheads. Low prices are made possible by few services and warehouse storage of inventory, which reduces shoplifting losses and the number of personnel needed.

Merchandise is primarily brand name, quality merchandise and includes such items as jewellery, power tools, camping equipment and sporting goods, toys, cameras and other electronic products, luggage and small appliances. Well-known catalogue showrooms in the UK are Argos and Index, which is part of Littlewoods group.

Catalogue showrooms were introduced during the 1960s and quickly became popular. Their popularity, however, waned during the 1980s, when department stores and discount retailers were able to run regular sales that beat warehouse showroom prices. Additionally, off-price retailers, a form of specialty retailers, have consistently been able to offer better prices on the lines that showrooms carry. Many showroom chains are in the process of upgrading services and product lines to be able to compete.

Specialty Retailing

Specialty stores only offer deep assortments of one product line or of select products within a product line. However, within the product lines they carry, they do offer in-depth assortments. These types of products include tobacco, kitchen equipment, books, sporting goods, electronics, cards and gifts, and toys.

The growth of specialty retailing in recent years can be traced to several factors. First, an affluent society becomes more discriminating in its taste and desires greater variety with respect to styles, models, price ranges and product features. Two-income households have contributed to greater discretionary income; but busier lifestyles have contributed to less time for shopping. Thus consumers want to find high-quality products at close locations with convenient shopping hours and lots of services.

Off-price retailers could be classified in many cases as mass merchandisers. However, we have chosen to classify them as specialty retailers because they tend to specialise in terms of the product lines offered. These retailers buy well-known brands and labels, usually at negotiated prices that are less than the regular wholesale price because these purchases may be overruns, seconds or end-of-season inventory. The savings are then passed on to the consumer.

As with most mass-merchandisers, off-price retailers rely on turning their inventory over rapidly, perhaps as much as twelve times a year (three times the rate of most specialty retailers). Consequently, their merchandise assortments change frequently and the composition of assortments is sometimes unusual. Some examples include PriceSavers and What Everyone Wants.

Off-price retailing is expected to continue to grow. In the US, Marshall's and T.J. Maxx, two of the fastest growing, are opening an average of 20 to 40 stores per year. These stores have introduced a powerful means of attracting large traffic volume: the outlet mall. These malls, made up entirely of off-price retailers, are growing rapidly in number and popularity.

Retailing Strategies

A number of years ago a noted retailing expert was asked what were the three most important factors of retail success. He replied, 'Location, location, location'. And certainly experience has repeatedly demonstrated the importance of retail location. As previously mentioned, retailers have historically located in the central business district, but changing demographics and consumer habits have forced retailers to relocate in the suburbs.

While some retailers occupy a free standing (that is, physically unattached to other outlets) location, many of them choose shopping centres because of the high traffic that a cluster of shops will draw.

Regional shopping centres are the largest cluster of shops and have the largest department stores (anchors) of any of the shopping centres. Generally, these large structures with 40 to 100 stores require a minimum of 150,000 to 200,000 consumers in the area to support their sales volume. Newer ones are enclosed malls to make shopping comfortable all year round.

Community shopping centres are larger than neighbourhood shopping centres. Community centres serve 40,000 to 150,000 people and usually provide a small department store along with a number of specialty stores. *Neighbourhood shopping centres* are quite small, with several convenience stores, such as a supermarket, dry cleaners, beauty shop and petrol station. These neighbourhood centres serve 7,500 to 40,000 people who live within their shopping areas.

A few other characteristics must be noted with respect to traditional retail stores today. First is the notion of 'scrambled merchandise'. As you may have already observed, the classification of retailers has been complicated by the practice of carrying dissimilar lines. For example, a chemist not only fills prescriptions and carries over-the-counter medications, but it may also carry greeting cards, picnic supplies, magazines and even small appliances.

Atmospherics is a term that relates to the physical layout and characteristics of a shop. Every shop imparts a 'feeling' to its patrons. One may be quiet and formal; another noisy and chaotic. It is important to plan a store's atmosphere to coincide with the store image that management wishes to convey to customers. Features that impact on store atmospherics include such things as carpeting (or lack thereof) colours, merchandise layout, space (for example, wide or narrow aisles), music and odours.

The product assortment makes an important statement about the image that the shop conveys and about the type of shopping experience that it provides to the customer. The most important consideration is to match customer expectations, so that they will be encouraged to shop there again.

Retailers make decisions about the assortment width and depth. A wide assortment means many product lines; a deep assortment means many choices within a given product line. For example, a wide assortment of women's clothing might include dresses, suits, sports separates, lingerie, shoes, coats, accessories, belts, purses, jewellery, scarves, etc. A deep assortment means that the dresses come in many styles, colours, sizes, fabrics and labels.

The Wheel of Retailing

The wheel of retailing is a theory suggesting that firms come into the market as low-price, low-margin, few-services operations and then, when successful, evolve slowly into the opposite. That is, as they grow, retailers tend to add services and improve the atmosphere, thus raising their overheads, which, in turn, causes them to raise their prices.

The result is that a new vacuum is created at the lower end of the retailing spectrum and a need re-appears for low-price, low-margin, few-services competitors to emerge. Supermarkets and mass-merchandisers are examples of the wheel of retailing in action.

Non-Store Retailing

Non-store retailing includes direct selling, direct marketing and automatic vending. Each of these broad areas can be further broken down into more specific types of customer approaches.

Direct Selling

Direct selling includes a variety of direct-to-consumer marketing channels, such as door-to-door, home party plans and demonstrations, and telemarketing. Each of these has some strengths and weaknesses.

Door-to-door selling has been losing popularity for many years. In the past, successful door-to-door companies included Fuller Brush and Avon. But without a pre-arranged appointment, sellers are likely to find no one at home in these days of single heads-of-household and dual-income families. Rising crime rates have also made householders reluctant to admit strangers, and busy customers resent the time taken by unsolicited salespeople.

Home-party-plan selling has been very successful in the past. Customers like the opportunity of viewing products at their leisure and the convenience of home delivery. They also enjoy individualised attention and the social atmosphere of buying among friends. Some well-known party-plan/demonstration companies include Tupperware, Mary Kay Cosmetics and Home Interiors. Other companies, such as Encyclopaedia Britannica and Kirby Vacuum Cleaners, contact prospects in shopping malls, at trade fairs, or by referral before calling on them at home.

However, with more people working, even fewer consumers are willing to spend their leisure time attending home demonstrations and parties. It has also become much more difficult to recruit and retain well-qualified sales personnel.

Telemarketing and teleshopping have become important contact tools for many companies, even those with other well-established marketing strategies. Telemarketing can be used to set up appointments with customers or sell directly over the phone – many companies specialising in home improvements use this method. New technology has also introduced us to the possibility of buying through TV channels, where companies display their merchandise and customers can view, without having to visit the shop. This is still in its infancy in the UK, but may grow in importance. An early example of using technology in retailing is that of a computer-linked selection and ordering system, installed in a local community centre for the benefit of less mobile shoppers. The Gateshead Shopping and Information Service, launched in 1980 through the collaboration of Tesco and the local authority, established the service; subsequently the Bradford Centrepoint was launched with the co-operation of Morrison superstores.

Direct Marketing

Direct marketing uses a variety of media to make contact with the customer and solicit a direct response. These media include direct mail and catalogues, television, and magazine and newspaper advertisements. A number of years ago it was felt that only inexpensive items could be sold through direct marketing. Now it is customary to sell everything from records, tapes and compact discs to expensive jewellery, home furnishings and electronic equipment.

Catalogue marketing in the past was dominated by Kays, Littlewoods and Janet Freeman. The scenario is changing, with specialty catalogues appearing, offering a more dedicated product range, e.g., Next and Racing Green. Some of these catalogue retailers also have retail outlets; others do not.

Some companies are experimenting with videotape catalogues and have even suggested selling them in video shops.

Magazine and newspaper advertisements may solicit direct response, either through a convenient telephone number or by post. Television shopping is also on the rise. At first commercials were generally 60–120 seconds long and focused on getting the viewer to call an 0800 number. Now home-shopping channels that are devoted simply to selling goods and services on television have begun to appear.

With more and more of the population entering the workforce during the 1990s, it is certain that the time-savings and convenience of direct marketing will continue to have appeal for busy consumers.

Automatic Vending

Today, automatic vending machines can be found everywhere: schools, factories, office buildings, recreational facilities, even in churches. They offer a variety of products, including soft drinks, coffee, snacks, cigarettes, newspapers, hosiery and stamps. Vending machines are expensive to operate relative to their volume, so margins must be higher than in other forms of retailing. Consequently, their prices are often 15–20 per cent higher than other retailers. However, vending machines provide a great deal of place utility in that they are located in high-traffic areas where these products would otherwise be unavailable.

Franchising

When we think of franchises, we often think of the fast-food operations, such as McDonald's or Wendy's. But the largest franchise operations in the United States by sales are car and truck dealers, petrol service stations and restaurants.

Franchises work in one of three ways:

1 Manufacturers authorise retailers to sell their brand names.
2 Manufacturers authorise distributors to sell to other resellers.
3 The franchisor supplies virtually an entire marketing strategy – names, advertising, processes, and standard operating procedures – for a retailer.

Your local Rover dealership is an example of the first case, Coca-Cola an example of the second, and McDonald's an example of the third.

Franchisors benefit from fees paid up-front and ongoing royalties throughout the life of a successful franchisee's operation. Franchisees benefit from a proven marketing strategy. In fact, only five to eight per cent of franchises fail during their first two years, compared with an average of 54 per cent among independents, a dramatic reduction in the risk of opening a new business.

There are some disadvantages, however. Many businesspeople become disenchanted with conforming to franchisors' dictates with respect to product offerings, store layout or advertising. Franchisors may find that franchisees are not as conscientious in maintaining high standards of performance as the franchisors would like them to be. In extreme cases, poorly-operated franchises have been known to hurt the image of the entire franchise.

SUMMARY

Retailing has come a long way since the early days of the 'general store'. Retailers have added large assortments of products, have become more specialised in many respects, and have begun offering many new services to customers. As the wheel of retailing suggests, retailing is always evolving. New forms today will become obsolete tomorrow, and newer forms will take their place.

Retailers may be classified as self-service, limited-service, and full-service, according to the number of 'extras' they offer customers. The major types of retailers include department stores, mass-merchandisers and specialty retailers. Mass-merchandisers offer several variations as well: supermarkets, superstores, discount houses, wholesale clubs and catalogue showrooms.

One area of retailing that is growing tremendously is the area of non-store retailing. Direct sellers, such as Tupperware and Home Interiors, offer customers the convenience of home shopping and delivery. Other companies – World Book and Encyclopaedia Britannica, for example – locate in heavy-traffic areas, such as malls and trade fairs.

Cataloguing, too, is on the rise. Some maintain traditional retail outlets; others operate strictly out of a warehouse facility. Automatic vending machines can be found in nearly every conceivable public location. Finally, franchising operations, such as petrol service stations and restaurants, have become very popular. Many people who could otherwise not afford to open their own businesses see franchises as a viable business opportunity.

FURTHER READING

Assael, Henry. 1985. *Marketing Management*. Boston: Kent Publishing Co. Chapter 17.

Brown, Stephen. 1990. 'The Wheel of Retailing: Past and Future.' *Journal of Retailing* (Summer): 143-149.

Davies, R. L. 1985. 'The Gateshead Shopping and Information Service.' *Environment and Planning*, 12, pp.209-220.

Dawson, J.A. 'Independent Retailing in Great Britain: Dinosaur or chameleon?' *Retail & Distribution Management,* 11(3):29-32.

Hollander, Stanley C. 1960. 'The Wheel of Retailing.' *Journal of Marketing* (Jul.): 37-42.

Kaikati, Jack G. 1986. 'Don't Discount Off-Price Retailers.' *Harvard Business Review* (May/Jun.): 85-92.

Kotler, Philip. 1991. *Marketing Management*, 7th ed. Englewood Cliffs, New Jersey: Prentice Hall, Chapter 20.

Lusch, Robert F. 1982. *Management of Retail Enterprises.* Boston: Kent.

McGoldrick, Peter, J. 1990. *Retail Marketing*. McGraw Hill.

Milliman, Ronald. 1982. 'Using Background Music to Affect the Behavior of Supermarket Shoppers.' *Journal of Marketing* (Summer): 86–91.

Pride, William M. and Ferrell, O.C. 1991. *Marketing*, 7th ed. Boston: Houghton Mifflin Co., Chapter 12.

Saporito, Bill. 1991. 'Is Wal Mart Unstoppable?' *Fortune* (6 May): 50–59.

Strand, Patricia. 1987. 'Kmart Dangles Lure for Affluent Shopper.' *Advertising Age* (24 Aug.): 12.

Trachtenberg, Jeffrey A. 1990. 'Largest of All Malls in the U.S. Is a Gamble in Bloomington, Minn.' *Wall Street Journal* (30 Oct.): A1, A8.

12 Wholesaling

While some retailers are large enough and diverse enough to bring goods from the manufacturer to the final consumer and perform a lot of functions that make the product more available and usable to consumers, another common level of distribution is wholesaling.

Wholesaling in the United States today is virtually a two-trillion-dollar business. Wholesalers perform the entire range of marketing functions involved in bringing products and services to resellers and business users. As we shall see, not all wholesalers perform all functions; nevertheless, without the services that wholesalers provide, most products would actually be more expensive and less satisfying to customers.

Wholesalers perform some or all of the following functions. They:

- Buy products from a variety of producers and build new assortments that satisfy their customers' (resellers or businesses) needs.
- Receive and store products, keep inventory records, and ship outgoing orders.
- Provide timely delivery to buyers.
- Finance retailers by allowing credit and provide cash flow to manufacturers by purchasing inventory.
- Absorb risks by taking title and possession of products.
- Provide both producers and resellers with marketing information and assistance.

The last function includes such tasks as selling, doing competitive analyses, analysing market trends and environments, training sales clerks, improving store layout, merchandising, promotion and inventory control.

As you can see from this list, some of these activities are done on behalf of manufacturer-suppliers and some on behalf of customers, resellers and business operators.

The activities done by wholesalers make it possible for manufacturers and resellers to lower their costs and operate more efficiently. When wholesalers regroup products and provide desirable assortments, resellers can obtain stock at lower cost. By stocking inventory, wholesalers absorb carrying costs. By granting credit, wholesalers reduce the need for resellers to borrow working capital and also enable them to operate more efficiently.

Types of Wholesaler

For this discussion we will cite 'classic' definitions of various types of whole-sales. Students should realise that in practice it may be difficult to actually find many wholesalers that precisely characterise the following textbook definitions. That is, most wholesalers are a mix of several types of classic wholesaler. To further complicate the situation, the names commonly used in a given industry may be confusing. Some so-called 'agents' may occasionally be brokers; some 'manufacturers' agents' may perform the role of a full-service wholesaler. Through the years, the customs and practices of what certain parties in the distribution channel were called have made the issue somewhat imprecise and confusing. The following discussion should help in the analysis of existing wholesalers and in understanding various characteristics when they are encountered in real-channel units.

Merchant Wholesalers

Merchant wholesalers take title to and possession of the products they handle. In the US, they account for the majority of wholesaling transactions, some 58 per cent, which represents more than $1 trillion in sales. Similarly in Europe, whereby merchant wholesalers make up about two-thirds of all wholesaling activities. Merchant wholesalers often specialise by type of product or customer, and they tend to service fairly small geographical areas. Competition is fierce among merchant wholesalers; even the largest firms hold only a small percentage of the market within a given industry. There are two kinds of merchant wholesalers: full-service wholesalers and limited-service wholesalers. Full-service wholesalers provide a wide range of wholesaling functions, while limited-service wholesalers provide only some marketing services and specialise in relatively few functions. Producers, or sometimes retailers, perform any remaining functions that are not performed by limited-service wholesalers.

The two most common types of full-service wholesalers are the wholesale merchant and the industrial distributor. Wholesale merchants offer a complete assortment of services for retailers and may store merchandise convenient to retailers, maintain salesforces that call on retailers, make deliveries to those retailers, and extend credit to retailers. Industrial distributors operate much like a wholesale merchant, servicing retailers; however, they supply goods such as equipment, accessories for equipment, and supplies to industrial users.

Limited-service wholesalers might include the following types: cash and carry wholesalers, truck wholesalers, drop shippers, rack jobbers, producers' co-operatives and mail-order wholesalers.

Cash-and-Carry Wholesalers

The cash-and-carry wholesaler performs almost all wholesaling functions, with the exception of financing and delivery. These wholesalers evolved out of the needs of the Great Depression in the 1930s when retailers, in an attempt to reduce their costs, began picking up and paying cash for their own deliveries. Although this option is still available, relatively few stores – and small stores at that – still use this type of wholesaler.

Truck Wholesalers
Truck wholesalers, sometimes also called truck jobbers, sell food items that are perishable. They make regular deliveries to their retail customers and depend on their drivers to perform the sales and collection activities.

Drop Shippers
Drop shippers usually own the products that they sell but do not handle, stock or deliver those products. When they receive an order from a customer, they ship directly to that customer. They keep operating costs relatively low because they perform no storage or handling functions. Drop shippers tend to be popular in sectors where products are bought in large, bulky lots.

Rack Jobbers
Rack jobbers sell non-food products through grocery stores and supermarkets. They provide their own storage units, usually racks. Health and beauty aids, reading material, hardware, housewares and toys make up rack jobber merchandise. Many operate on consignment and take back products that have not been sold by the time periodic inventories are taken.

Producers' Co-operatives
Producers' co-operatives perform many of the functions of a full-service wholesaler but are owned by the co-operatives' customers, who are also members. These co-operatives have arisen in agricultural markets where individual small producers have relatively little market power apart from through co-operating with one another.

Mail-Order Wholesalers
Mail-order wholesalers are limited-function merchant wholesalers who use catalogues and other direct-mail vehicles rather than a salesforce to contact customers. Choices are made from that material and orders are placed by mail or telephone.

Brokers
Brokers have the function of bringing potential buyers and sellers together. They exist primarily to provide information in initiating and helping to complete the transaction. They can represent either a buyer or a seller in a given transaction but typically not both. Brokers exist in a wide variety of product lines as diverse as real estate services, capital equipment and perishable foods. If the channel members are likely to be interacting frequently, a broker will often retire from the relationship equation. Once a buyer and seller are brought together and made aware of one another, the broker's function ends.

Agents

Agents do not take title to goods but represent a manufacturer or many manufacturers in the marketplace. There are several types of agents, including manufacturers' agents, selling agents and commission agents.

Manufacturers' Agents

Manufacturers' agents, sometimes also called manufacturers' reps, may work for a number of manufacturers of related but non-competing products and receive commissions based on a specific percentage of sales. Many of these call on institutional markets that might have an interest in their full line of products from a variety of manufacturers.

Selling Agents

Selling agents have full authority over marketing decisions, such as pricing and promotion, as well as providing financial assistance for their manufacturer client. Selling agents operate in many commodities markets, such as coal and lumber, and seem to serve small, poorly financed manufacturers by assuming control of the entire marketing decision-making process.

Commission Agents

Commission agents, also called commission merchants, handle products shipped by sellers and perform the functions necessary to complete the sale minus the commission, which is then returned to the seller. They are most common in agricultural markets where someone in a central market is needed to take care of the sale of a load of agricultural commodities.

Manufacturers' Sales Branches and Offices

Manufacturers' sales branches and offices appear to perform many of the functions of merchant wholesalers. They differ in that sales branches are owned by a manufacturer who has set them up to sell products and provide support services to that manufacturer's salesforce. They are usually located where large customers are concentrated and where demand for their products is high. They perform such functions as delivering goods, offering credit and helping the promotional programme.

A sales office is also a manufacturer-owned operation but is normally associated with agents. Unlike a sales branch, it carries no inventory, although it is also located in a strategic place.

Facilitating Agencies

A variety of organisations are not wholesalers as such, but they do provide services that are similar to those provided by full-service wholesalers. These facilitators tend to specialise in single functions, however.

Public Warehouses

Public warehouses can be of a variety of types, but their primary function is to provide storage for a fee. In many cases these warehouse facilities relieve wholesalers from maintaining a much larger seasonal capacity warehouse or specialised types of storage facility. Some public warehouses, called bonded warehouses, will store goods and at the same time enable the owner of the goods to borrow money using the stored goods as collateral. The bonded warehouse must assure a financial institution that it has control of the goods.

A second type of specialised public warehouse is the field warehouse. Many bulky goods are not actually taken to a warehouse but are, in fact, stored on the owner's site under the control of the field warehouse. Again, money can be borrowed against these goods, since they are not under the actual control of the owner but under the control of the field warehouser.

Finance Companies

Several types of financial institutions have grown up to service the special needs of wholesale distribution. They enable wholesalers and retailers to carry larger amounts of inventory than they would otherwise or, in some cases, help free working capital for other purposes. Sales finance companies sometimes 'floor-plan' inventory for a retailer. Floor-planning is the process by which inventory is financed and must be paid off if the goods are actually sold. Car and major appliance dealers, for example, are able to afford a much larger inventory than they would without this assistance.

Another type of specialised finance company is called a factor. Factors buy accounts receivable from a retailer or wholesaler to free up working capital for other purposes. Factors frequently have some control over what accounts are sold and for how much if they have agreed to buy all of the accounts. They specialise in an industry and offer more services than do commercial banks.

Transportation Companies

Public carriers such as rail, truck and air facilitate wholesaling by bringing goods to the appropriate place at the right time. A recent example of the creative use of a transportation company is the many wholesalers and retailers who are now using overnight delivery service companies to both store and quickly deliver small products, as well as technical or higher-priced items that they handle. One consumer travel video company has used Federal Express, with a free telephone number, to store all of its videos sold through catalogues. When an order is placed, Federal Express is contacted about the order and delivery destination. Within 24 hours of receiving the order, the goods are delivered.

Trade Shows and Trade Fairs

Trade shows are a service provider in that they help companies periodically identify prospects and occasionally eliminate the need for other intermediaries in the channel. Trade shows enable sellers to show their goods and, at the same time, develop prospects and probable future sales. Trade marts are similar to trade shows, except that they go on all the year round and are housed in permanent facilities. They tend to be set up to sell a particular class of goods, such as furniture or apparel.

Wholesaler Strategic Market Decisions

Wholesalers are also marketers and must use marketing-mix decisions to build their businesses and serve their customers. This section discusses one area with which wholesalers must be concerned.

Target Market Decisions

Intermediaries choose their markets by customer size, types of services needed, product line, or sometimes promotional strategies used by those customers. A typical wholesaler might specify the size of customer, either large or small, that it would seek to serve. Further, it would target customers with particular types of needs for which services are then provided.

In the UK, Booker Cash and Carry has established itself well as a food wholesaler. They have a national network of warehouses, stocking fresh and frozen foods, wines and spirits, cigarettes and fresh meat. They sell solely to the trade and in bulk to hotels, restaurants and the catering industry.

Product Assortment and Services

The actual product of a wholesaler is defined by the width and depth of assortment of products and services it offers. The services offered by wholesalers tend to differentiate them and bind their customers to them based on services needed. Successful wholesalers find a mix of services needed by many of their customers and change that mix only when those needs for services change. Some wholesalers, agents for example, carry no inventory, while others are full-line wholesalers and provide every service and virtually every product that a retailer could request.

For example, Super Valu is a full-service wholesaler that provides a wide selection of services to a carefully-defined target market: food retailers. Super Valu offers complete store planning and layout services, including architectural and engineering consultation. It also offers a wide and deep selection of quality products at competitive prices, assistance with merchandise and advertising concepts, electronic services for managing payroll, inventory, and labour management, and insurance coverage specifically tailored to the food-retailing industry.

Pricing Decisions

Pricing by wholesalers is directly related to the services that are provided and the economies that a given wholesaler can create for its customers. Pricing may vary when a wholesaler is trying to penetrate a new market or going to a new geographical area with other services. Over time, however, a wholesaler's pricing is dependent on both the quality and the number of services provided.

Place Decisions

Where a wholesaler will operate geographically varies by the scope of the market it serves, the number of service functions that are provided, and its role in the market. Some wholesalers provide very carefully placed warehouses to facilitate rapid delivery, while other special-function wholesalers, such as drop shippers, may operate out of a post-office box. Because of the geographic or spatial problems that are solved by wholesalers, the place decision is quite important.

Promotion Decisions

While wholesalers have historically relied more on personal selling than any other form of promotion, some of the more progressive wholesalers of late have done a good job of trade advertising as well as very carefully building relationships with customers. Once these relationships are established, many use their salesforces to keep the relationship sound.

Trends in Wholesaling

Recent years have seen wholesaling change as much as in the three previous decades. First, there is a tendency among wholesalers now to consolidate power into larger and fewer wholesaling companies. This does not always change the operational size of a wholesaler unit but might enable it to have more power when buying. Second, there are many variations on the classical forms of wholesalers. As different services have been demanded by innovative retailers, wholesalers have evolved to meet those needs. Third, there is a trend toward US wholesalers crossing international borders. One of the largest wholesalers in North America recently opened an operating division with a local partner in Mexico and, within a year, also did the same thing in the UK. While all wholesalers have not moved in this direction, many observers believe that wholesaling will become more of an international activity in the future.

SUMMARY

In this chapter we have defined the various broad classes of wholesalers: merchant wholesalers, brokers and agents, and manufacturers' sales branches and offices. Merchant wholesalers, a very important category, take title to and possession of products. Essentially, they assume the risk of inventorying and transporting the product to the customer. There are two categories of merchant wholesalers: full-service wholesalers, who can be further subdivided into wholesale merchants and industrial distributors; and limited-service wholesalers, who can be divided into cash-and-carry, truck wholesalers, drop shippers, rack jobbers, producers' co-operatives and mail-order wholesalers.

A broker's function is to bring buyers and sellers together. This intermediary is usually only involved in the transaction on a temporary basis. Merchants, on the other hand, tend to have an ongoing relationship as a representative for a single manufacturer or a group of non-competing suppliers.

Manufacturers' sales branches and offices are set up to provide services on the part of a manufacturer in a convenient location. Facilitating agencies perform a variety of services to enhance the functioning of the marketing channel.

Wholesaling is growing and changing rapidly. Computerisation, consolidation and internationalisation are all trends that are changing the way wholesaling operates.

FURTHER READING

Boone, Louis E. and Kurtz, David L. 1992. *Contemporary Marketing*, 7th ed. Ft. Worth, Texas: Dryden Press, Chapter 13.

'Four Strategies Key to Success in Wholesale Distribution Industry.' 1989. *Marketing News* (March 13): 22.

Hlavacek, James and McCuistion, Tommy. 1984. 'Industrial Distributors – When, Who and How?' *Harvard Business Review* (Mar./Apr.): 96-101.

Lamb, Jr., Charles W., Hair, Jnr., Joseph F. and McDaniel, Carl. 1992. *Principles of Marketing*. Cincinnati: South-Western Publishing Co., Chapter 10.

Lusch, Robert, Coykendall, Deborah and Kenderdine, James. 1990. *Wholesaling in Transition*. Norman: University of Oklahoma.

Pride, William M. and Ferrell, O. C.. 1991. *Marketing,* 7th ed. Boston: Houghton Mifflin Co., Chapter 11.

Reinhart, Thomas C. and Coleman, Donald R. 1978. 'Heyday for the Independent Rep.' *Sales and Marketing Management* (Nov.): 51-54.

'Wholesalers as Retailers.' 1987. *Supermarket News* (30 Nov.): 8.

13 Physical Distribution

This chapter examines how companies provide place utility for customers. That is, how companies inventory, handle and transport goods so that customers will have them at the right time, in the right place and in the right quantities.

We will look at how physical distribution (PD) systems are set up, at the advantages and disadvantages of various modes of transportation, and at warehousing practices. We will also examine some aspects of managing inventory.

The Importance of Physical Distribution

Nearly half the cost of marketing a good is spent on physical distribution activities. The range of activities includes those that relate to planning, implementing and controlling the flow of goods and services from the point of origination to the final consumer. More specifically, customers want on-time delivery, merchandise that is undamaged and in a usable form, prompt installation and maintenance, a generous return policy, and generally high-quality service.

As with any of the elements in the marketing mix, distribution involves trade-offs between what customers want and what channel members can reasonably provide. If service is inadequate, for example, late deliveries or damaged goods, customers will seek alternative distributors. On the other hand, providing higher service levels will inevitably increase PD costs, thus resulting in higher prices to customers.

Setting up the System

Physical distribution systems are a complexity of interrelationships among channel members and facilitators who are responsible for getting products to customers. For marketers' organisational and marketing goals to be met, the system must function effectively; all these interrelated parts must act harmoniously. Yet marketers must also deal with a system's interdependencies.

For example, transportation costs could be cut by using a slower method of transporting goods, say water rather than air. But that would mean that inventories would have to be higher to make up for a longer wait between deliveries. And if inventories are higher, more capital is tied up at any given point, and the carrying charges are higher.

This example illustrates how difficult it can be to determine the structure of an optimal distribution system. Several elements must be included in a PD system. First, the level of customer service that a company can afford and is willing to provide must be considered. The question of what customers expect and what competitors have to offer in contrast must also be asked.

Second, mode(s) of transportation must be selected. Marketers must keep in mind the relevant costs, the speed at which deliveries should take place, any special handling requirements of the product, and the trade-offs that are incurred with respect to inventory levels.

Third, an inventory control system must be planned. Marketers must decide how much inventory should be carried at various locations. They must also put in place re-order mechanisms and establish buffers (or safety stock), so that members of the channel do not run out of inventory prematurely.

Fourth, marketers must determine the type of packaging and materials-handling to use. Packages must protect the product, but they must also identify the product, provide information about the product, and often promote the product at the point of purchase.

Fifth, an order-processing procedure must be developed. Marketers want to be efficient, but must also ensure that customers' needs are met.

Finally, marketers must decide on warehousing issues. How many warehouses to have, where they will be located, and how large they should be are some important questions. Again, decision-makers must remember that the essential trade-offs in each of these cases involves costs versus customer service.

Customer Service Standard

Companies must decide what level of service they will provide to their customers. Most companies set a minimum level and strive to maintain those standards most of the time.

For example, American Airlines has a goal of keeping passenger waiting-time for tickets down to five minutes or less for at least 85 per cent of the passengers queueing to buy their airline tickets. Reservation telephones should be answered within 20 seconds, 80 per cent of flights should take off within five minutes of scheduled departure time, and 79 per cent must arrive within 15 minutes of scheduled arrival time.

By establishing and monitoring acceptable levels of customer service, a company can pinpoint problem areas and take steps to improve performance. Some of the components of customer service include order cycle time, percentage of on-time deliveries, maintenance levels for inventory, accurate order filling, minimised damages in transit, and effective communication with customers. But, as the American Airlines example illustrates, service standards must be tailored to the specific needs of a given company and its customers.

Elements of Physical Distribution

Five general areas must be addressed in setting up an effective physical distribution system:

1 Order processing.
2 Materials handling.
3 Warehousing.
4 Inventory control systems.
5 Transportation modes.

We will discuss each of these areas in the following sections.

Order Processing

Physical distribution begins with the customer's order. This may be transmitted electronically or manually, depending on the system. Generally it is felt that manual systems can respond more quickly to special cases and rush orders. However, for large volume operations, electronic order-processing has become virtually mandatory.

When an order is received, four things must happen. First, the order must be entered into the system. Next, a credit check must take place to reveal whether this customer is a good credit risk. The order is then transferred to the warehouse, where inventory is examined to determine whether the goods are in stock. If the company experiences a lack of stock, the customer will either be offered a substitute item or may be queried as to whether this request should be back-ordered (placed on hold until the inventory is replenished).

Finally, the order is filled, packed and shipped to the customer as requested. During the process, of course, invoices will be prepared so that the customer can be billed. It is also imperative that inventory records be continually updated as each order is filled and as each new shipment of inventory arrives so that the warehouse has an accurate record of its current stock.

Materials Handling

The act of physically moving the items from point to point within the company and from one channel member to another is called materials handling. Often the key determinants as to how the products will be handled are the physical characteristics of the product itself. For example, ice cream and many other food products require freezers and/or refrigeration units.

One important innovation in the area of materials handling has been the practice of *unit loading*. This means that as many packages as possible are combined into one load on a pallet or skid for easy transporting by fork-lift trucks or conveyors. Another practice is *containerisation*, the consolidation of several unitised loads into a single, large container that is easier to transport and store than individual units. The container is typically a big box, 8 ft. high, 8 ft. wide, and 10, 20, 30 or 40 ft. long.

The process of containerisation has several advantages: it reduces loading and unloading time, it protects the contents from damage, and it works well for changes between modes of transportation.

Warehousing

Companies have to store their products until they are sold and transported to customers. This need is intensified because production and consumption cycles rarely match. For example, John Deer must produce harvest equipment all the year round to have enough products available during harvest season. Many kinds of fresh produce cannot be grown all year, but consumers want to find them in their grocery stores all year round. For these reasons, companies need storage warehouses.

Companies also need distribution warehouses. A distribution warehouse assembles and redistributes products, moving them as quickly as possible, often within 24 hours. The decision about how many distribution centres to maintain and in which locations again involves that ever-present trade-off of costs versus customer service. More locations give a company the opportunity to provide faster service. However, warehousing costs obviously increase as locations multiply.

Some companies concentrate on a few centrally located distribution centres. These specialise in break-bulk functions: that is, the process of breaking down large shipments into several smaller ones for individual customers within the distribution centre's service area.

Conversely, some distribution centres are make-bulk centres. These consolidate several small shipments that are headed for a common destination.

Warehousing facilities and technological capabilities have evolved into much higher levels of efficiency in the past decade. The new automated warehouses use advanced materials-handling systems controlled by a central computer. Few employees are necessary since the computer fills orders, directs trucks, decides scheduling and issues invoices. Such an operation requires considerable initial investment, but it yields savings in the form of lower labour costs, fewer injuries, fewer delays and mistakes, and less pilferage and breakage.

Companies can also choose whether to use public warehouses or private warehouses. Private warehouses, those owned by the company itself, offer more control but tie up capital and make location changes difficult.

Public warehouses charge for the rented space, offer flexible locations, and provide additional services (such as inspecting, packaging and shipping goods) for a price.

Inventory Control Systems

One of the major functions of the physical distribution system is inventory management. The most recent estimates of annual inventory holding costs run at approximately 25 per cent of the total value of the inventory. For example, it would cost £500 to store £2,000 worth of inventory for a year. These costs include the actual storage building(s), insurance, taxes, depreciation, and even possible obsolescence.

Because inventory levels affect customer satisfaction, marketers would like to carry enough stock to fill all orders promptly. However, these carrying charges force companies to make trade-offs between the possibility of an out-of-stock occurrence and the costs of maintaining constantly high inventory levels.

The most commonly cited technique for inventory control is the economic order quantity (EOQ) shown in Figure 13.1. Here we see a trade-off between inventory-carrying costs and order-processing costs. The carrying costs increase as inventory levels rise; the order-processing costs decrease as the quantity ordered increases, thus causing marketers to prefer to maintain sufficient inventory levels to meet any order.

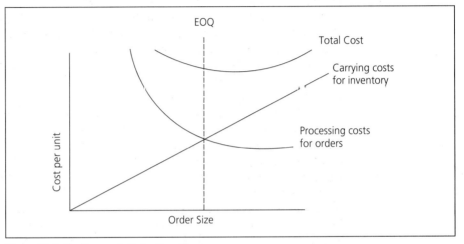

Figure 13.1 The Economic Order Quantity

The re-order point in the EOQ model is the point at which carrying costs equal order-processing costs. This is the theoretical point at which total costs are at their lowest point. This point will differ among companies depending on several factors. First, the longer the time from order placement to order fulfillment, the greater the amount of inventory that must be maintained. Second, the faster a product is used up and the need to re-order arises, the greater the amount of inventory that must be available. Finally, the more safety stock, or 'buffer' an organisation wants to maintain, the higher the level of inventory they will need.

Another approach to inventory control has more recently been borrowed from the Japanese. The just-in-time, or JIT, system is set up so that parts and materials arrive often on the same day that they will be used by production. Producers obviously like the fact that JIT greatly reduces their carrying costs. However, it is also obvious that such a system requires very careful planning, monitoring and control. It would be easy to miscalculate and end up with a stalled production line as a result of lack of stock.

JIT is heavily dependent upon co-ordination between purchasers and sellers, as well as their carriers, to ensure timely delivery. JIT also requires close relationships between suppliers and their customers, since discrepancies could prove extremely costly to both parties.

JIT works best for products that have relatively few variations and many standard features. Multiple suppliers are frequently used to hedge against price gouging, labour disputes and plant closings that might threaten shipment schedules.

Transportation Modes

Choosing transportation modes involves selecting the types of carriers and the specific companies that will transport products between channel members. Transporting provides time and place utilities, but the value added to products by moving them must exceed the costs incurred. Sometimes it is more cost-effective to produce in one location and move the products to another for distribution. In other cases, the costs of transportation more than offset these savings. Marketers must examine each situation individually before making a decision.

There are five major transportation modes: rail, road, inland waterway, pipelines and airways. We will examine each of these in more detail.

Rail

Rail is still the most frequently used transportation mode in the United States and railways are the best method for transporting bulky, heavy freight over long distances. Railways haul such commodities as chemicals, timber, coal, grain and farm products. However, it is most cost-effective to use rail for transporting full carloads rather than smaller quantities.

In the UK initiatives such as the Channel Tunnel have helped to keep the railways competitive even across water and pose a strong threat to the cross-channel ferry market.

Rail's share of the transportation market has declined in recent years due to high fixed costs, shortages of rail cars during peak shipping seasons, poor maintenance of tracks and equipment, and increased competition from alternative shipping modes.

However, railways are fighting back to regain their competitive edge. They have introduced measures to improve customer service, such as specially-designed railway cars and dual-mode vehicles that can run on the tracks and immediately convert to the road. Piggyback operations in which road vehicles ride on rail flatcars, are used increasingly. These two options combine the advantages of long-haul capacity with the flexible mobility of the truck.

Railways have also introduced unit trains and run-through trains. The unit train runs between two key points, such as a mine and a processing plant, to deliver a single product. Run-through trains are also non-stop modes but carry multiple products. Mini-trains are small but run often, ideal for JIT inventory systems.

Railways are also upgrading their computer systems and modernising their routing capabilities. Optical scanners read coded labels on the sides of cars to sort them by destination, thus speeding up the formation of outbound trains. These measures should help keep railways competitive for many years to come.

Motor Vehicles

While railways are best for large, bulky shipments of commodity products, trucks concentrate more on carrying manufactured products. Motor vehicles can offer the most flexible schedules and routes of all the transportation modes, and trucks provide fast, consistent service for both large and small shipments.

Motor carriers charge more per ton shipped than do railways. (A ton-mile refers to carrying a ton, 2000 pounds, of cargo for a distance of a mile.) But trucks offer the advantages of fast, virtually door-to-door service.

Contract carriers establish specific contracts with their customers rather than serving the general public. They generally operate for a particular industry and are not subject to as much regulation as are common carriers.

Private carriers are owned by a company and transport only that company's products. There is no rate or service regulation, but these carriers were once prohibited from soliciting business from other firms. Exempt carriers carry unregulated products, such as unprocessed agricultural goods. Brokers often bring together those who want transportation services with those who need them.

Inland Waterways

Water carriers, both inland or barge lines and ocean-going deepwater ships, offer cost advantages. They average one cent per ton-mile – clearly very economical. Certainly this is the most cost-effective way to ship heavy, low-value, non-perishable commodities, such as ore, coal, grain, sand and petroleum products.

However, water transportation is the slowest form of transportation. Sometimes it comes to a complete standstill during the winter, so that companies must ship during the summer and store their inventory during the winter. Because not all destinations have access to a waterway, this mode is often combined with other modes, such as motor vehicle or railway.

The prognosis for water transportation is very good. Because of its low costs, the shipping volume for waterways is expected to double by the year 2000 worldwide.

Pipelines

Interestingly, pipelines rank second only to railways in the number of ton-miles transported. But since pipelines are largely invisible, few people are conscious of the tremendous volume they carry. Most pipelines belong to a single company or a consortium of companies that share their services. For example, the TransAlaska Pipeline is owned by Exxon, Mobil, British Petroleum and others that transport crude oil from sites in Alaska to shipping terminals on the coast.

Because they are fixed, pipelines offer almost no flexibility, but more than 213,000 miles of pipelines serve the United States and account for about one quarter of all intercity ton-miles. Pipelines are slow, but their cost is relatively low, about 1.2 cents per ton-mile. Pipelines are also a low maintenance, dependable method of transportation.

Airways

Air freight is a relatively insignificant percentage of transportation miles (less than one per cent of ton-miles). However, this mode of transportation has been growing. For example, air ton-miles more than doubled between 1961 and 1985 world-wide.

The advantages are that airways provide a fast, safe environment for shipping valuable or highly-perishable products. However, air transport has fairly high costs and may require additional modes of transportation when the products arrive at their air destinations.

Typical shipments include computers, furs, jewels, fresh flowers, technical instruments and emergency orders. Most medium-range jets carry about 40,000 pounds of freight; some larger planes can accommodate more than 200,000 pounds.

SUMMARY

Physical distribution focuses on the process of actually moving products from the producer to the final consumer. Since nearly half the cost of marketing is tied up in PD, marketers must carefully plan their PD systems to maximise efficiency and customer service. This trade-off between costs and service is an ongoing constraint for marketers.

Most companies set minimum performance standards and then strive to meet or exceed those standards. The need for exceptional customer service extends into all areas of PD: order-processing, materials-handling, warehousing, inventory control systems and transportation modes.

One of the most important decisions that has to be made is which of the transportation modes best suits a company's marketing mix and customer needs. Of the five modes – rail, road, waterways, pipelines and airways – rail carries the most volume and airways the least. However, each of these modes has its own strengths and weaknesses. Therefore, each marketing situation must be assessed with respect to its specific characteristics before setting up the physical distribution element of the mix.

FURTHER READING

Assael, Henry. 1985. *Marketing Management.* Boston: Kent Publishing Co., Chapter 16.

Baker, M.J. 1991. *Marketing – An Introductory Text,* 5th ed. MacMillan, Chapters 9 and 14.

Galante, Steve P. 1986. 'Distributors Bow to Demands of "Just in Time" Delivery.' *The Wall Street Journal* (30 Jun.): 27.

Johnson, James C. and Wood, Donald F. 1986. *Contemporary Physical Distribution.* New York: Macmillan.

Kotler, Philip. 1991. *Marketing Management,* 7th ed. Englewood Cliffs, New Jersey: Prentice Hall, Chapter 20.

Moore, Peter D. 1989. 'New Ways to Reach Your Customers.' *Fortune* (6 Nov.): 210.

Murray, Tom. 1990. 'Just in Time Isn't Just for Show – It Sells.' *Sales & Marketing Management* (May): 62-67.

Petre, Peter. 1985. 'How to Keep Customers Happy Captives.' *Fortune* (2 Sept.): 4.

Pride, William M. and Ferrell, O. C. 1991. *Marketing,* 7th ed. Boston: Houghton Mifflin Co., Chapter 13.

Saporito, Bill. 1986. 'A Smart Cookie at Pepperidge.' *Fortune* (22 Dec.):74.

Tausz, Andrew. 1989. 'The Airfreight Payoff.' *Distribution* (Feb.): 36-42.

14 Pricing Determination

The 1980s was a prosperous decade for branded consumer packaged goods. Such well-known companies as General Foods, H.J. Heinz, RJR Nabisco, General Mills, Procter & Gamble and Kimberly Clark were big winners as their brand names became extremely valuable assets.

These companies built their brand names using heavy advertising and promotion, while also charging premium prices to cash in on the prestige of those brand names. At the same time, inflation slowed, with the result that the costs of the basic raw materials went up much more slowly than producers could raise prices. For example, prices of some soaps and cereals went up as much as five to eight per cent a year, and still consumers continued to buy.

Consequently, profits went up even faster. Heinz's earnings climbed at an average annual rate of 13 per cent. Quaker Oats' staple, oatmeal, went from 73 cents for an 18-ounce box in 1980 to $1.73 in 1991, a price three thousand per cent higher than the cost of the raw, unprocessed ingredient.

Why would consumers pay inflated prices in a low-inflation economy? Although this trend seems to be petering out, questions are still being raised about the power of the big brands to draw a loyal following who will pay premium prices.

In this chapter on pricing, we will look at the nature of a price, as well as the legal aspects of pricing. We will also look at price as a competitive tool and discuss pricing objectives that different firms may have. We will consider factors that influence how we set prices and various pricing strategies.

What is a Price?

The companies mentioned above are using the strength of their brand names to charge premium prices and, therefore, to show large profits. For these firms, as indeed for any company, pricing is a crucial element in the marketing mix. Prices that are too high result in a loss of customer confidence and patronage. Prices that are too low result in lost profits.

For the buyer, price is whatever is given up in the exchange to obtain something of value. We know 'price' by many names. It is the mortgage payment or rent on our home. It is the premium we pay for our insurance policies. We pay retainers to our lawyers, tolls to drive on the motorways in France, and fares to ride in taxis. We tip waiters, pay salespeoples' commissions, pay executives' salaries and work for wages. We make a deposit on merchandise and pay interest on loans.

In each of these cases, a financial transaction has taken place. However, in non-profit marketing and in other special cases, we may pay something other than money (or one of its forms) for that 'something of value'. For example, politicians work for our votes, the Blood Bank wants us to donate blood, and churches ask for our time to teach a Sunday school class.

Historically, barter, or negotiation between two parties, was the customary method of setting prices. The seller started high and the buyer started low; they worked together until they could reach agreement. The 'strictly one-price policy' became popular in the United States with the advent of large department stores, such as F. W. Woolworth and J. L. Hudson, because they carried so many items and had so many sales clerks that bargaining would have created chaos. Because price is the only revenue-generating element in the marketing mix (all others are cost elements), the importance of setting prices cannot be emphasised too much. Marketers must plan carefully if pricing objectives are to be met.

Legal Aspects of Pricing

Before marketers can make definitive pricing decisions, they must take into account the legalities associated with setting prices. In each of the cases that will be discussed, the intent of the legislation is to preserve competition and to protect consumers. Sometimes the intent has backfired, but generally these laws have been to the good of society.

Unfair trade practices acts put a floor on the prices that can be charged, particularly by wholesalers and retailers. That is, resellers are required to charge some minimum level above cost.

Theoretically, resellers could prove that their operating costs are lower than average so that they can charge lower prices; however, in practice this is almost never done. The intent of the law is to prevent large operations from charging such low prices that they drive competitors out of business.

Government can intervene to technically 'freeze' prices in a given industry or determine rates at which prices can be increased. Regulatory bodies can also be established to monitor pricing within the industry. For example, in the UK, OFTEL is a regulatory body established to monitor the previously public telecommunications industry.

In addition to regulatory bodies, specific acts will determine the scope of prices open to a company. The Monopolies & Mergers Commission is in place to prevent the creation of monopolistic situations. From the consumer perspective such laws as the Trade Descriptions Act, the Fair Trading Act, the Consumer Protection Act and European Community laws are all in place to protect consumers from unfair trading practices.

Pricing Objectives

Pricing objectives should be compatible with the company's overall objectives and with agreed marketing objectives. We will look at some typical pricing objectives in this section. Bear in mind that different firms will opt for different objectives; yet each may be very successful in its own right.

Profitability

The traditional pricing objective is to maximise profits. Several economic concepts govern the logic here. First,

$$\text{Profits} = \text{Revenue} - \text{Costs}$$

Since price is the sole revenue generating element in the marketing mix, you can see that pricing has a direct bearing on the profitability equation. Also,

$$\text{Total Revenue} = \text{Price} \times \text{Quantity Sold}$$

The trade-off here is that at some point, quantity sold will begin to decrease as price rises. A ten per cent price increase that leads to a five per cent decrease in units sold will add to overall revenue. However, a ten per cent price increase that leads to an 11 per cent drop in sales decreases a firm's revenue.

Economists term this approach marginal analysis, and they recommend reducing prices to the point where revenue increases just equal cost increases. In practice, few firms are able to actually identify this point; they simply make educated guesses.

Return on Investment

Companies commonly price to achieve some stated return on investment (ROI), a profit-related objective. However, here again it is difficult to identify the actual point at which returns equal investment. Some companies just aim for a 'satisfactory' ROI; that is, they just want to ensure the firm's survival and convince stockholders that management is 'doing a good job'.

While such a strategy may sound reasonable, situations arise where this would not be in the best interest of either the company or the stockholders. In highly-competitive, dynamic markets, if managers are not extremely proactive, they and their companies are likely to become casualties.

A good example might be General Motors in the era immediately before foreign cars had such an impact on the car market in the US. Many GM managers were afraid of making 'too much profit' or profits that might be interpreted by the media as 'obscene'. Consequently, they were not motivated to keep costs and prices low. Lower costs and the accompanying lower prices might result in even greater market share, which could then result in anti-trust action by the government. When low-cost competitors entered the market, GM was not in a favourable position to respond.

Market Share

It is common for companies to seek a certain market share or simply to aim for a larger market share. Market share, of course, is dependent on what competitors are doing in the marketplace. This forces marketers to be responsive to changing competitive conditions, a posture that is always in the long-term best interest of the company. Market share is a popular measurement, too, because it is easier to compare market share than to measure profitability. The company with dominant market share often has economies-of-scale advantages over weaker competitors. The strongest company may also be very difficult to dislodge from that position. Some companies choose to focus on market share in a growing or declining market, so that they can assess their overall performance in the context of changing circumstances.

Sales

Sales objectives may be geared toward some level of unit or monetary volume sales. It is important to remember that sales volume does not necessarily translate into profit. Marketers are notorious for focusing on sales and disregarding costs. In reality, sales growth may or may not lead to increased profits. This is the reason why marketing managers should co-ordinate their decisions with other functional areas within the firm, such as finance, accounting and production, to ensure moves that will be profitable in the long run.

Product Quality

Another pricing objective might be to establish your brand as the industry leader in terms of quality. Therefore, you may wish to set a price commensurate with this goal to cover the high costs of quality construction, performance, and even research and development.

Cash Flow

Cash flow recovery is often a primary pricing objective when a new product has been introduced. Such a goal does not necessarily require setting a high price; the opposite strategy might be more effective. In fact, the specific price that will result in the largest cash flow may be high or low, depending on such variables as price elasticity of demand (that is, how sensitive customer demand is to changing prices) and whether economies of scale can be realised from increased volume.

Pricing Strategies

Three broad types of pricing strategy are practised by most companies today: cost-oriented pricing, demand-based pricing and competitive pricing. Under each of these broad umbrellas are several distinct options. In this section we will discuss each of these.

Cost-Oriented Pricing

Many companies find that a good way to ensure profitability is to take their costs into consideration when they are developing a pricing strategy. The two most common forms of doing so are cost-plus pricing and markup pricing.

Cost-Plus Pricing

This is the most common approach to setting prices. Usually a fixed percentage of total cost is added to the total cost of producing and marketing a product. This method is used by construction companies, for example, when they estimate the cost of doing a building project and then add in a standard amount for profit. Many professionals, such as accountants and lawyers, follow this method of pricing.

For cost-plus pricing to work, managers must be able to identify total costs, including both fixed and variable costs. This approach results in the following formula:

$$\text{Price} = TC + X(TC)$$

where: TC = total cost of the product
X = percentage of total cost added to complete the final price

For example, jewellery with a total cost of £100 and a 200 per cent markup (not uncommon for this product category) would then be priced at £300.

This is a simple strategy that enables the company to recover its costs and make a certain profit. Unfortunately, a company's ability to assess its true costs is greatly hampered by current accounting methods. Steps are being taken to clarify this situation, but no one has yet introduced a completely satisfactory system.

Markup Pricing

Markup pricing is really cost-plus pricing when it is used by retailers and wholesalers. A standard markup is useful for firms that carry hundreds, even thousands, of products, since it is obviously prohibitive to construct demand schedules for each item. Different percentage markups, however, are likely to be used with some product categories based on management's judgement of past sales performance and the demand characteristics for the category. For example, it is common for supermarkets to mark up baby food by nine per cent, bakery products by 20 per cent and greeting cards by 50 per cent.

It should be apparent to the marketing student that there are some real flaws in this approach to pricing. Demand is largely ignored, and profits are unlikely to be optimal. Additionally, some products will probably be under-priced and some over-priced.

Demand-Based Pricing

An application of the marketing concept, discussed earlier, would suggest that prices should be set to reflect the value that customers associate with the product.

While covering costs and making a profit are essential for the firm to stay in business, it is unlikely that gross revenues or profit potential will be maximised without taking customers into account.

An example of this is the airlines' segmentation strategy and their pricing policies that reflect this strategy. Airlines recognise two important customer segments: business travellers and holiday-makers. Business travellers are more concerned with flexible scheduling and convenience, and are less price-sensitive than holiday-makers. However, holiday-makers will schedule far in advance and at the most inconvenient times to take advantage of a price break. Airline price lists reflect these differences.

Prestige Pricing

This tactic is used when customers tend to judge the quality of the product based on its price. The important element here is customer perception. The firm's costs need not be high. The fact is that with some products, such as furs, jewellery, fine liquors, etc., if the price drops too low, the product is devalued in the eyes of the consumer.

Odd-Even Pricing

Odd-even pricing is based on the theory that consumers respond more favourably to prices ending in certain numbers. That is, consumers perceive prices ending in odd numbers as substantially lower than prices ending in even numbers. For example, customers respond more favourably to £199.95 than to £200.00.

Some marketers believe that odd-even pricing suggests to customers that sellers have set the prices as low as they possibly can.

Price Lining

This technique is commonly used in retailing. Instead of using a continuous range of prices, marketers establish a limited number of price levels, and they target the merchandise at each of these pricing levels for different target audiences. Men's trousers, for example, may be offered at £75, £50 and £35 with no price points in between.

The theory is that demand between each of the price levels is inelastic. That is, marketers will sell the same number of trousers at £50 as they would at £45. Many companies produce product lines of similar items that are differentiated largely on the basis of various price points.

Loss-Leader Pricing

This is a pricing tactic that must comply with any legal restrictions, particularly unfair trade practices acts. In loss-leader pricing, a firm offers unusually low prices on a few items to attract customers who will then purchase additional products at the regular prices once they enter the store.

The best loss-leaders are products that have high demand, cannot be stored for long periods of time, are characterised by high price elasticity of demand, and are priced low enough to be extremely attractive to customers.

Competitive Pricing

One consideration in setting prices has to be the competition's pricing strategy. If your prices are seen as way out of line with your competition, you may be contributing to negative perceptions about your product among consumers. For example, if the price is too high, your products may be seen as over-priced. If they are too low, your products may be seen as being of inferior quality.

Price Leadership

Price leadership is common in industries characterised by only a few firms with large market shares. This is called oligopolistic competition. As the price leader takes the initiative in raising or lowering prices, others in the industry tend to follow suit. We have seen much of this tactic in the airline industry in recent years.

Price leaders need to be sensitive to the effects of their pricing decisions on the entire industry. For example, setting prices that are too low may force other companies out of business and bring on legal problems with restraining competition. Additionally, lowering prices sometimes results in a price war (as in the airline business in recent years) in which everyone loses.

Price leaders are typically the low-cost producers in the industry or, at a minimum, the companies that can sustain losses for the longest period of time. This does not mean that they necessarily sell at the lowest price in the industry, although they may.

Customary Pricing

Customary pricing works just as it sounds: products are priced according to custom. In the UK the customary price for a telephone call is 10p. Marketers sense that there is a perceptual barrier in the minds of consumers against raising customary prices. The standard price has remained but the length of telephone time available has been decreased. For these reasons, customary prices tend to be more stable than many other prices and are changed only when absolutely necessary.

Competitive Bid Pricing

Prices for some products are established by competitive bid. This is often used in business-to-business marketing where expensive, customised projects are involved. For example, a company may take bids from communications suppliers for a telephone system or from computer manufacturers for an area-wide network.

The auction is another well-known situation in which competitive bidding takes place. Many products are sold at auction: buildings, cars, industrial equipment and machinery, antiques and farm products.

Buyers often initiate the process in a sealed-bidding situation. Government purchases usually go to the lowest bidder who conforms to specifications, and any supplier's bid would be unknown to other bidders until the contract was awarded. (Realistically, you should be aware that specifications can be written so as to weed out all but a given preferred supplier. This is where ethics and legalities come into play.)

Firms that submit bids need to consider demand, competition and costs as well as a reasonable profit when developing a bid. It is possible to win a contract and still be unprofitable if the bid was set too low.

Penetration Pricing

Penetration pricing is often used to help a new product secure a strong hold in the market. For this reason you will most often find penetration pricing used in the introductory and growth stages of the product life-cycle.

This approach calls for setting a low price in order to capture as large a share of the market as possible.

Penetration pricing works best when buyers are fairly price sensitive and demand is flexible; that is, demand varies depending on the price. It is also helpful if the product has widespread appeal and is quickly accepted by consumers. Also, if the firm's costs are lower than competitors', penetration pricing is more likely to be an acceptable pricing approach.

One of the advantages of penetration pricing is that a low price tends to discourage new competitors from entering the market; it also tends to weed out weak competitors whose costs prohibit them from meeting the lower price. However, penetration pricing can only be used by those companies whose efficiencies allow them to have lower-than-average costs. Otherwise a penetration price will not allow them to recover their introduction costs and make a profit.

Price Skimming

In a sense, price skimming is the opposite of penetration pricing. With price skimming, a firm sets a high price initially to quickly recover costs and become profitable in the least amount of time.

This approach works best when buyers are relatively insensitive to minor price differences, and the item possesses unique benefits that make it highly desirable to customers. Price skimming is also more effective when entry into the market is restricted for competitors because of technological, production or capital requirements that are difficult to meet.

Many new products in recent years have been introduced with a price skimming policy: handheld calculators, personal computers, microwave ovens, video recorders and digital watches. (Note that a price-skimming policy is usually temporary; as the life-cycle matures, the prices of these products tend to drop dramatically.)

As with any marketing decision, a price-skimming approach carries its own pitfalls. Chief among these is the possibility that competitors will enter the market with penetration pricing and take all the business for themselves. A corollary is that the company that pioneered the product may eventually find itself with the smallest market share.

SUMMARY

Pricing is only one element of the marketing mix, but this is the element that bears directly on whether marketers will make a profit and will be able to stay in business. Regardless of the term used in lieu of price, a careful strategy must be developed for managing price. Such a strategy must be in keeping with the many regulatory aspects of pricing, with particular consideration for any anti-competitive factors.

Pricing objectives must be in line with the firm's overall objectives and the marketing objectives for the product in general. Some pricing objectives include profitability, return on investment, market share, sales, product quality and cash flow.

To satisfy these objectives, pricing strategies may include cost-oriented pricing or markup pricing. If the strategy focuses on customer demand, prestige pricing, odd-even pricing, price lining, or loss-leader pricing may be used. Finally, if the intent is to offset the effects of competition in some manner, marketers may choose price leadership, customary pricing, competitive-bid pricing, penetration pricing or price skimming. Marketers must always keep in mind that each of these strategies has its own unique advantages and disadvantages.

FURTHER READING

Assael, Henry. 1985. *Marketing Management*. Boston: Kent Publishing Co., Chapter 15.

'Can Anyone Win the Coffee War?' 1990. *Fortune* (21 May): 97-100.

Dibb, S., Simkin, L. Pride W. and Ferrell, O. C. 1994. *Marketing-European Edition*, 2nd ed. Houghton Mifflin Co., Chapter 17.

'Elasticity, It's Wonderful.' 1989. *Fortune* (13 Feb.): 123-124.

Erickson, Gary and Johannson, Johnny. 1985. 'The Role of Price in Multi-Attribute Product Evaluations.' *Journal of Consumer Research* (Sept.): 195-199.

Guiltiman, Joseph P. and Gordon W. Paul. 1988. *Marketing Management,* 3rd ed. New York: McGraw Hill Book Co., Chapter 8.

Lamb, Jr., Charles W., Hair, Jr., Joseph F. and McDaniel, Carl. 1992. *Principles of Marketing*. Cincinnati: South-Western Publishing Co., Chapter 16.

Lichtenstein, Donald and Burton, Scott. 1989. 'The Relationship Between Perceived and Objective Price Quality.' *Journal of Marketing Research* (Nov.): 429-443.

Lynn, Robert A. 1967. *Price Policies and Marketing Management*. Homewood, Ill: Irwin.

Morgenson, Gretchen. 1991. 'The Trend is Not Their Friend.' *Forbes* (16 Sept.): 114-119.

'Supermarket 1984 Sales Manual.' 1984. *Progressive Grocer* (Jul.).

Udell, Jon G. 1964. 'How Important Is Pricing in Competitive Strategy?' *Journal of Marketing* (Jan.): 44-48.

Wentz, Theodore E. 1966. 'Realism in Pricing Analysis.' *Journal of Marketing* (Apr.): 26.

15 Pricing Strategies

What economic tools are available to assist companies in setting prices? For example, a software producer knows that software prices can run from £20 or £30 all the way to £500 or £600. How can marketers decide the most profitable pricing level for their products?

Let's say you are manufacturing fine domestic chocolates. You know that you are pricing in a mature market and that the demand for your product fluctuates dramatically according to how you price the product. Again, what tools do you have at your disposal to help you make those difficult pricing decisions?

This chapter is devoted to some of the most important and useful economic analysis tools at your disposal today. While these must initially be introduced in theoretical terms to fully explain the concepts, we will also show you how these concepts can then be applied to your marketing mix.

Market Structures that Impact on Pricing

Marketers face some restrictions on the prices they can charge. There is a floor beneath which a firm cannot price or it will lose money. The costs associated with producing and marketing the product constitute this floor. At the other extreme there is a ceiling, which is determined by the size of the market and the demand for the product. Since the price/demand relationship varies for different types of markets, we will look at these various types to see how pricing is reflected in each one.

Pure Competition

Under pure competition marketers have little or no leeway in setting prices. There are many buyers and sellers dealing in a commodity product (a product that is virtually undifferentiated from others in its category, such as flour or sugar). Consequently, sellers will not raise prices, since buyers can go elsewhere and sellers have no other advantages to offer. Similarly, sellers will not lower prices, since they can sell all that they produce at the going price. Marketing strategy is very simple: produce and sell the product at the market price. Obviously, there is little need for marketing research, advertising or product development to contribute to building a competitive edge.

Monopolistic Competition

Monopolistic competition means that buyers and sellers have differentiated products and can thus charge different prices to buyers. Buyers see advantages in one product over another and are willing to pay for those advantages. Most consumer goods industries operate in conditions of monopolistic competition because the impact of other elements of the marketing mix on pricing is considerable. For example, prices for highly advertised brands that have achieved a strong brand image can generally be higher than prices for brands that are not so widely known and have a weaker brand image.

Oligopolistic Competition

Under oligopolistic competition the market consists of limited numbers of sellers who are very sensitive to one anothers' pricing and marketing strategies. If one company lowers its price, there is extreme pressure on the others to do likewise. The airline industry is a good example of oligopolistic competition. It is in such an environment that price wars often erupt. Raising prices is equally risky, since there is always the possibility that other companies will fail to follow suit, and the one who has raised its prices stands to lose a great deal of market share.

Pure Monopoly

A pure monopoly is usually regulated by the government, such as in the case of the UK Postal Service or even a private utility company. However, sometimes an innovator of technology can carve out a monopoly in the short run before competitive offerings appear. This was the case, for example, with Du Pont's nylon.

Pricing objectives under a monopoly are varied. The government may set a low price and absorb losses to provide an important product to those who could not otherwise afford it. Or a price might be set high to slow down consumption.

Non-regulated monopolies are free to price at the level the market will bear. However, they sometimes choose to price prudently so as not to attract too much attention from regulators and/or competition.

Economic Tools Used in Setting Prices

The following section deals with several economic tools that impact on pricing. We will discuss elasticity of demand, break-even analysis and marginal analysis with an emphasis on the decision-making power of these tools.

Elasticity of Demand

This key factor in pricing decisions can be defined as the ratio of the percentage change in the quantity demanded to a percentage change in price. Put more simply, this concept represents the degree to which buyer demand is sensitive to changes in price. The formula looks like this:

$$\text{Elasticity} = \frac{\text{Change in quantity demanded}}{\text{Change in price}}$$

The coefficient is often negative because price and quantity demanded are inversely related. When the price falls, quantity demanded tends to rise, and vice versa. However, the key question for marketers who are trying to determine optimum pricing is: by how much does quantity demanded change as a result of changes in price?

These concepts are illustrated in Figure 15.1. The demand curve on the left shows elastic demand. This means that as a firm raises its price from P1 to P2, the quantity demanded drops by the difference between Q1 and Q2 – a proportionate decrease in quantity demanded. Conversely, with inelastic demand (shown on the right of Figure 15.1), the quantity demanded decreases by less than a proportionate change in the price.

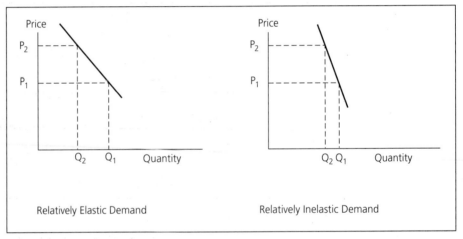

Figure 15.1 Demand Elasticities Under Varying Price Levels

The interpretation of this figure is simply that for some products, more people will continue to buy in the face of a price increase than for other products. Of course there is a range in which these relationships will hold.

For example, demand for a chocolate bar may remain relatively inelastic between 25p and 35p. However, it may be that if the price rises above 35p demand will drop faster than revenue will increase. At this point demand has become elastic: that is, relatively sensitive to the change in price.

Break-Even

Break-even analysis is another valuable tool for making strategic pricing decisions. Figure 15.2 depicts the relationships of variables in break-even analysis.

First, fixed costs must be identified. Fixed costs are those that would be present even if nothing were produced, such as rent and electricity bills. Then we identify variable costs, those that vary with the amount of goods or services produced. For example, the more airline flights produced, the more fuel that is used. Total variable costs = variable cost per unit produced X total units produced.

Finally, the fixed costs plus the total variable costs equal the total costs involved in producing a given amount of product.

The next concept we must understand is total revenue. This is found by multiplying the number of units sold by the price of each unit. Total revenue could be less than total costs, and thus the firm is operating at a loss. Conversely, total revenues could be more than total costs, and thus the firm is making a profit.

Once the total revenue equals the costs, the firm has reached its break-even point and may go on to make a profit. Another way of expressing this is that the break-even point is the point where total revenue equals total cost. As shown in Figure 15.2, if total revenue drops below the break-even point, the firm is operating at a loss. Thus pricing decisions must be made to take into account the revenue required to break even.

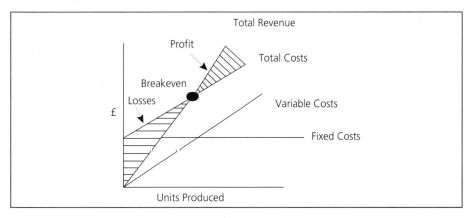

Figure 15.2 Break-Even Analysis

Let's use a simple example. Say your fixed costs are £100 and it costs you £2 per unit to produce your widgets. How many widgets must you sell to break even? That depends on the price you set. If you sell your widgets for £4 each, the break-even point (BEP) would be 100 units. This is determined by using the following formula:

$$BEP = \frac{\text{Total fixed costs}}{\text{Selling price} \quad \text{Variable cost}}{\text{per unit} \quad \text{per unit}}$$

Break-even analysis is one way to help decide what price to choose, particularly if a company has some idea of elasticity of demand and estimates of how much will sell at various pricing levels.

Marginal Analysis

Marginal analysis is another avenue to understanding cost-revenue-profit relationships. This approach uses marginal revenue (MR) and marginal cost (MC) to find the price and quantity where profit is maximised.

Marginal revenue is a simple concept; it is the change in total revenue that occurs from selling each additional unit of a product. As shown in Figure 15.3, the demand curve slopes downward. This is reasonable, as common sense suggests that if you want to sell more of a product, one way to do so is to lower the price. Thus, each additional unit sold provides less additional revenue than the previous unit sold. This is why the MR curve is also a downsloping one.

Marginal cost, similarly, is the change in total cost that results from selling each additional unit. Figure 15.3 also illustrates the average cost curve (AC) and the marginal cost curve (MC).

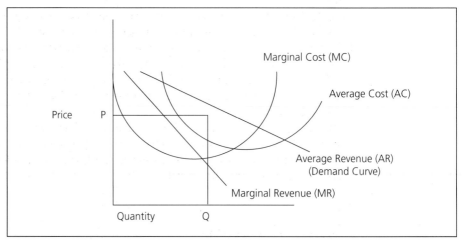

Figure 15.3 Using Marginal Analysis to Determine Profitability

To maximise profits, a company should produce at the point where marginal cost is equal to marginal revenue. The selling price at this point is determined by referring to the demand curve that shows the price consumers are willing to pay at this optimum quantity. The logic is that if a firm sells more than that optimum quantity, its costs begin to rise and eat into its profits. If the firm sells less than the optimum, it is missing out on revenues that would add to profits.

In theory, marginal analysis is very logical. In practice, costs and demand fluctuate so regularly that it is often difficult to determine them. Also, the lack of precise data on demand elasticity makes doing marginal analysis very problematic indeed.

Factors that Drive Costs

Since price, revenue and, thus, profits are so dependent on costs, it is well that we look at some of the factors that influence costs.

Economies of scale result when a firm produces higher volumes of product. The reason is that fixed costs are then spread over many more units, thus lowering the cost per unit sold.

Capacity utilisation functions similarly to economies of scale. If more is produced, then per-unit fixed costs are lowered, and a low fixed-to-variable cost ratio enables a firm to lower its prices and, theoretically, sell more products. Another method to accomplish the same end is to shift fixed costs to variable costs. For example, instead of paying a salesperson a fixed salary, establish a commission system whereby the costs are linked to the amount sold.

Firms with good supplier relationships are at an advantage. Problems such as unreliable delivery, varying product quality and inefficient order-processing can increase a producer's costs, thus adding to the price of the manufactured goods or, at a minimum, lowering the profit margins that a company can make on each item.

Sometimes firms can enter into relationships that lower their costs. For example, firms can engage in common purchasing, advertising or shipping to lower their costs. Wholesaler co-operatives are successful because they purchase in larger quantities and thus get a price discount. Another version of this is for a firm to take on some of the activities that it had previously paid others to do. For example, a firm may purchase its own fleet of trucks instead of paying another carrier company.

There are many ways in which a company can lower its costs. Often the emphasis in marketing is to sell more products as a way to become more profitable. Sometimes, however, the easiest, most efficient means for increasing profitability lies in our own backyard

Using Discounts

Management normally establishes an official price list for its products after having considered many of the factors that we have discussed in this chapter and in Chapter 14. In most retail establishments, those prices are considered fixed until such time as the management decides to hold a sale. Some retailers encourage negotiation. For example, some antique shops and art studios are willing to negotiate prices. However, you are more likely to see negotiable prices in business-to-business marketing.

Discount Structures

A trade discount (also called a functional discount) is a reduction in the price granted to a customer who performs functions that are normally the responsibility of the supplier. The discount is generally a percentage off the list price. Selling, storing and record-keeping are examples of various functions performed by some customers that entitle them to discounts from manufacturers.

A quantity discount reduces the cost of items based on the size of the order. Large orders result in lower unit costs for the supplier due to reduced selling, transportation and inventory costs. Such discounts may be cumulative or noncumulative.

A seasonal discount is a reduction given to buyers who order seasonal merchandise in advance of the normal buying period. A cash discount is offered to customers who pay their bills on time. This is often stated in a format such as 2/10, n/30. This means that if the buyer pays the invoice in full within 10 days, a two per cent discount will apply. Otherwise, the full amount (n = net) will be due in 30 days.

A rebate is a refund from the seller. Rebates are generally offered for a limited time and are not viewed as a permanent part of the seller's pricing structure. They are often used to speed up the movement of products to get rid of slow-moving inventory.

The promotional allowance is a discount given by a manufacturer to a dealer to be used for advertising expenses or for merchandise displays. The idea here is that part of the promotion function has been shifted from the manufacturer to the dealer.

Geographic Pricing

Because transportation costs vary from place to place and generally increase with distance, not all buyers will be given the same terms by a seller.

In freight-absorption pricing, sellers in effect pay part of the transportation costs to meet the price of a competitor that is located closer to the buyer. This practice amounts to price cutting by the seller.

Zone pricing sets boundaries between selling areas and ties prices to all buyers within a zone. Zone pricing somewhat simplifies pricing for managers because only a relatively few price levels must be established.

FOB or 'free on board' means that the buyer pays all transportation costs and assumes the risk of any damage or loss that may occur. Such a practice makes it difficult for sellers to compete in distant markets, but it does simplify the problem of added costs associated with serving distant customers.

A uniform delivered price means that all buyers pay the same price and some average freight charge. If shipping costs are not a major portion of the price of the product, then this policy can work very well.

SUMMARY

Firms must look at economic aspects of pricing to arrive at a pricing strategy that best meets their needs. Different types of market structure – pure competition, monopolistic competition, monopolies and oligopolies – dictate different selling environments that have an impact on price.

The three economic tools discussed in this chapter that have a bearing on price determination are elasticity of demand, break-even analysis and marginal analysis. Although each of these techniques requires some data gathering, each can be an important part of helping a firm set prices that will lead to profitability.

Companies must examine the factors that drive their costs to see whether they can take reasonable steps to lower costs. Sometimes lowering costs is the best route to increased profits.

Finally, in the business-to-business environment, a number of price-discounting methods are used. Because buyers' order sizes and geographic locations vary, firms must decide what kinds of discounts work best. It is important when applying these discounts to remember the legal aspects of setting prices that were discussed in Chapter 3.

FURTHER READING

Boone, Louis E. and Kurtz, David L. 1992. *Contemporary Marketing*, 7th ed. Ft. Worth Texas: Dryden Press, Chapter 20.

Day, George and Ryans, Adrian. 1988. 'Using Price Discounts for a Competitive Advantage.' *Industrial Marketing Management* (Feb.): I-14.

Ingene, Charles A., and Levy, Michael. 1985. 'Further Reflections on Cash Discounts.' *Journal of Marketing* (Winter): 147–148.

Kotler, Philip. 1991. *Marketing Management*, 7th ed. Englewood Cliffs, New Jersey: Prentice Hall, Chapter 18.

Nagle, Thomas T. 1987. *The Strategy and Tactics of Pricing*. Englewood Cliffs, New Jersey: Prentice Hall.

Pride, William M. and Ferrell, O. C. 1991. *Marketing,* 7th ed. Boston: Houghton Mifflin Co., Chapter 18.

'Secrets Behind the Specials.' 1983. *Fortune* (11 Jul.): 94.

Stern, Andrew A. ,1986. 'The Strategic Value of Price Structure.' *Journal of Business Strategy* (Autumn): 22-31.

Tellis, Gerard J. 1986. 'Beyond the Many Faces of Price: An Integration of Pricing Strategies.' *Journal of Marketing* (Oct.): 146–160.

Thompson, Jr., Arthur A. 1984. 'Strategies for Staying Cost Competitive.' *Harvard Business Review* (Jan./Feb.): 110-117.

Promotion Management

16

An insurance company reaped a £750,000 profit on an investment of £85,000. A retailer sold £250,000 worth of merchandise after paying £10,000 for it. A car dealership sold 25 more cars during the last quarter because management upped spending by £2,000. How did all these companies manage to spend money and yet make money? Promotion. Each of these successes was the result of a well-planned promotional programme that required a modest investment but generated remarkable returns on that investment.

Promotion is that part of the marketing mix that focuses on various types of communication with an organisation's constituencies. Usually this communication is directed at the firm's customers, who may be consumers, other businesses, or, in the case of non-profit entities, members or donors. However, marketing communication can be directed at other groups: employees, vendors, legal and regulatory groups, or the public at large.

Since all forms of promotion involve communication, it makes sense to look briefly at the communication process before moving on to specific types of promotion.

A Model of Communication

The word 'communication' comes from the Latin *communis*, which means 'a sharing of meaning'. The various elements involved in this sharing of meaning are depicted in the model of communication shown in Figure 16.1.

The model not only shows the elements that make up a communication loop but also the flows of information between the parties involved.

Sender

The originator of a message is termed the sender or source. The sender may be an individual, but marketing communication often has an entire company as its source.

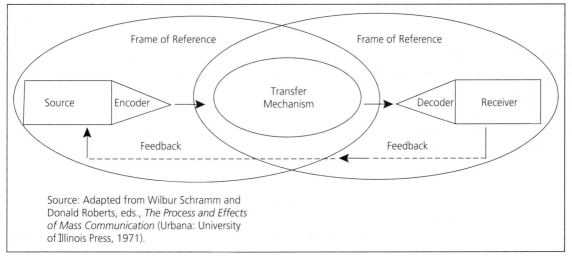

Source: Adapted from Wilbur Schramm and Donald Roberts, eds., *The Process and Effects of Mass Communication* (Urbana: University of Illinois Press, 1971).

Figure 16.1 Adaptation of Schramm's Model of Communication

Receiver

The receiver is the recipient of the communication. A receiver may be an individual, as in the case of one-on-one selling, but is often an entire audience, everyone that is exposed to the message. And if the message is conveyed through television or magazines, that audience may be composed of thousands of individuals.

Message

The message itself consists of the ideas and information that the sender wishes to share with the receiver. Messages can be long or short, complex or simple. The degree of accuracy with which meaning is transmitted depends on several factors that are identified in the communications model.

Encoding/Decoding

First is the encoding process in which the sender puts information into the appropriate words or symbols. The receiver then decodes the words and symbols. The correspondence between what the sender intends to say and what the receiver perceives that the message says depends on the accuracy of the encoding and decoding processes. For example, suppose an advertiser says, 'Our company directors have your interests at heart.' Then suppose that the receiver interprets this message as the following: 'Our bank offers higher interest rates than any other bank in town'. Obviously, what the advertiser claimed and what the customer heard were two different messages.

Frame of Reference

Another element that affects accuracy is a common frame of reference. This simply means that the receiver attaches the same meaning to a word or symbol as the sender. Suppose a salesperson says to a client, 'I'll meet you at your place on Thursday'. If, by chance, the client interprets 'your place' to mean his home, while the salesperson intended to convey the client's office, then a misunderstanding has occurred.

Medium of Transmission

The last element that affects the accuracy of meaning is the transfer mechanism or the medium of transmission. We will see that the best transfer mechanism for communicating accurately is face-to-face. Here the receiver can express confusion to the sender, ask questions, and generally provide the sender with direct feedback that enables the sender to adjust the message accordingly. The opportunity to carefully tailor the message to meet the needs of a specific customer is one of the great advantages of personal selling as opposed to advertising, sales promotion or publicity.

Two other elements in the communication process can have a significant bearing on the accuracy of the message and on how the message is received. Noise or interference in the channel can distort the message or disrupt the process entirely. An inaccuracy in a printed advertisement, radio static, or constant interruptions during a sales presentation are all examples of noise in the transmission channel. Channel capacity also has a bearing on the delivery of a message to an audience. One of the major problems in mass media advertising today is that the major media, such as television, magazines, newspaper and radio, offer a very cluttered environment with respect to advertising messages. Channels that try to carry too many messages are apt to overload the audience and thus be ignored.

Applying the Communication Model

The application of the communication model to marketing is very important. Marketers should plan their advertising and all their promotion with their target market and its characteristics in mind. The language should be language that the audience understands and uses with respect to the product being advertised. The symbols and images used in the message should be positive and relevant for the target audience.

It is also important to determine the response sought before designing the communication plan.

The audience to be reached, the medium that is chosen, the execution of the message, and the symbols that are used should all be a function of clearly defined marketing objectives. In other words, make 'how you say it' conform to why you are saying it and the response you hope to get.

The Adoption Process

A good promotion programme requires careful planning. As we have already seen, many factors can interfere with successful communication. Therefore several areas must be decided upon before we actually begin to make our promotion plan.

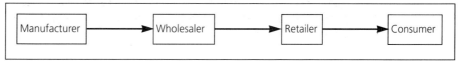

Figure 16.2 Hypothetical Distribution Channel for Brand XX

First, we must understand how the product that we are promoting moves through the distribution channel. Figure 16.2 shows a hypothetical channel for Brand XX. To increase the likelihood that our brand will move from the manufacturer to the wholesaler and on to the retailer it may be necessary to employ any or all of the following: advertising, sales promotion, publicity/public relations, or personal selling. Which of these to use depends on individual situations; however, the promotion plan must take into account the different characteristics of each channel member and what it will take to get the product into his or her hands. The type of promotion that is best varies with each step in the channel.

Push Strategies

Push strategies are used to promote products to intermediaries in the marketing channel. A manufacturer may want the wholesaler to inventory more products; the distributor may want the retailer to give her more shelf space. Push strategies involve motivating the next member of the channel to purchase the product and 'push' it to the next step in the channel. Volume discounts, special deals, sales-force contests, and various business-to-business promotions are very common.

Pull Strategies

A pull strategy means that various intermediaries in the channel are attempting to increase demand on the part of the consumer. The objective is to get the consumer to ask for the product, thus inducing the retailer to order it from the distributor, who then orders it from the wholesaler, and so on. Pull strategies assume that the product will be 'pulled' through the channel of distribution by consumer demand at the retail level.

Channel Members

Now we must look at the adoption process as it relates to each member of the channel. The adoption process consists of awareness, knowledge, trial, liking, preference, conviction and purchase. For example, a wholesaler may have become aware of Brand XX through samples brought in by a salesperson. The retailer may have noticed Brand XX being advertised in a trade magazine, and consumers may have seen Brand XX on television or perhaps cut a money-off coupon out of the Sunday newspaper. In each case, awareness was generated by a completely separate promotional medium.

Customers

Different aspects of promotion may also increase demand, depending on which stage of the adoption process most customers are in. Having generated awareness through television and newspaper advertising, a marketer may want to stimulate trial through direct-mail sampling or perhaps through supermarket demonstrations. Preference and conviction, on the other hand, may be induced through strategically-placed publicity articles that tout the superior performance of Brand XX.

Product adoption has been represented by more than one series of steps. The oldest and most common is called AIDA, for awareness, interest, desire and action, but any of these models is useful for showing how an individual moves through the adoption process.

It is also useful to observe how markets as a whole move through the adoption process. Research has shown that markets move through various stages, producing what is known as the adoption curve.

The first to adopt are *innovators*, those willing to take the risk associated with a new, untried product. Making up approximately three to five per cent of the market, innovators tend to be younger, more mobile and better educated than the average member of the market. They also tend to be information-seekers and will search for new ideas and products.

Early adopters (ten to 15 per cent) are an important group for marketers, since they are well respected by their peers and tend to be opinion leaders for this market. Like innovators, early adopters are also younger, more mobile and consumers of information. Unlike innovators, however, they have less contact with influences outside their respective groups.

The word-of-mouth activity generated by early adopters is an important influence in product adoption by other market segments, particularly the *early majority* (34 per cent). The early majority avoids risk, takes time to consider new products and ideas, and has a great deal of contact with information sources: salespeople, mass media and opinion leaders.

The *late majority* (34 per cent) tend to be older, less educated, more set in their ways, and risk-aversive. They do make use of some marketer-dominated sources of information, such as mass media and salespeople, but word-of-mouth communication tends to be confined to other late adopters.

The final segment of the market is composed of the *laggards* and, in fact, those who may never adopt, the non-adopters. Also older and less educated, laggards are not just risk-aversive but actually suspicious of anything new. Their incomes are lower than the average for their social class, and they generally avoid marketer-dominated sources of information.

An advertiser whose market consists of businesses rather than final consumers can expect segments of the business market to exhibit the adoption curve and these stages in the adoption process. Since a business organisation is made up of people, the company culture reflects the characteristics of the dominant individuals within the company.

Setting the Objectives

It should now be clear that the starting point for setting objectives is to pinpoint where the company is in terms of product life-cycle and where the market is in terms of product adoption. Strategies can then be developed to address where the company wants to go from here.

Promotion can have many possible objectives. It may be used to introduce a new product or announce a sale; obtain leads for the salesforce or address misperceptions about an organisation; sell season tickets or solicit new memberships. In fact, the various uses of promotion are nearly limitless.

One obvious objective is to provide information to an organisation's target markets. Informational promotion tells consumers and business buyers what products are available, where to find them, when they will be on sale, and sometimes what the advertising company itself is doing to contribute worthwhile products to the marketplace.

Another promotional objective might be to level fluctuating sales figures. A cabinet-maker in Germany finds that sales boom during the spring and summer but drop significantly during the winter months. What to do? Business-to-business advertising to the rescue! Advertising during these months, coupled with strong selling efforts, enable this company to avoid lay-offs and to generate revenue during those normally slow months.

Promotion can be designed to stimulate demand for a product or service. Primary demand is demand for the product or service category. Stimulating selective demand requires focusing on a specific brand, such as Yamaha, Sharp or Sony.

Some promotion plans are intended to get customers more involved with a given brand or company. A new bank's grand opening is geared towards drawing in new customers. Once inside, these guests are plied with food and drink, as well as imprinted gifts, to create goodwill for the new bank and to induce the guests to do business with the new bank. This special event is a combination of several promotional tools: public relations, advertising (to announce the event to the public), and specialty advertising or promotional products (gifts that generate goodwill and double as an advertising medium).

Choosing the Promotional Mix

Not every marketing situation calls for the use of all promotional media. In fact, budgetary constraints would prohibit unlimited expenditure. So the real test of promotional acumen depends on the wise selection of the promotional mix. What blend or combination of promotional tools will enable the marketer to get the message across to the right audience at the least expense and with the most impact?

Knowledge of each of the promotional tools is necessary for making informed decisions. The promotional mix is divided into two broad areas: personal, and non-personal or mass communication.

Personal Communication

Personal communication is usually defined as personal selling. Selling involves an individual or several individuals who meet face-to-face with a customer or a customer group. Occasionally this definition is expanded to include telephone marketing and, sometimes, direct mail.

Non-Personal Communication

Advertising can be defined as a non-personal, paid form of communication with an identified sponsor. Advertising is intended to be persuasive and elicit some positive response from the audience. Generally, it is unabashedly sales-oriented in nature. However, sometimes advertising is informative – for example, introducing a new product or educating the public concerning a company's contributions to society in the form of scholarships or new technology.

Sales promotion is a category of very specific types of promotional devices. Sales promotion to consumers includes coupons, money-off offers, in- or on-pack premiums, contests, sweepstakes, demonstrations and samples. Some sales promotion, also called trade promotion, is targeted at the middle-men in the distribution channel. These devices include volume discounts, trade shows, merchandise allowances, and even contests to stimulate sales among distributors or retailers.

All companies have public relations, whether good or bad. Public relations involves communications with all of a company's publics. When we talk about public relations in marketing, we are implying an element of the promotion mix that should be managed by the company in a professional manner and in such a way that the company reaps long-term benefits as a result. Public relations can make use of a variety of approaches, such as special events, company or product spokespersons and publicity.

Publicity is non-paid, mass communication about a company, its products or its people. Publicity is perceived as being more objective and credible than advertising, over which the sponsor has obvious control. Publicity will be read or listened to by many who would never pay attention to conventional advertising. Since publicity is not paid for, the releases must be newsworthy items or the media will refuse to run them.

The Promotional Budget

Setting the promotional budget can be a difficult undertaking for marketers. Many years ago the great retailing marketer Lord Leverhulme said, 'I know that half of my advertising is wasted, but I don't know which half.' How much is enough? How much is too much? A variety of allocation methods are used, and some are better than others.

Percentage-of-Sales Method

First is the percentage-of-sales method, which relies on past sales as the base from which current promotion will be calculated. This method is riddled with problems, not the least of which is simply that it has the cart before the horse. It assumes that sales cause promotion instead of the other way around. It is probably widely used because it sounds so scientific and also because it keeps spending down when revenues are down. Unfortunately, since we do believe that there is a cause-and-effect relationship between promotion and sales, the percentage-of-sales method may ensure that revenues continue to be down. It has been suggested that this method can lead a company into a downward sales spiral from which it will never recover. The same arguments can be applied to another version of the same approach, the percentage-of-profits method and the fixed-sum-per-unit method.

Competitive Parity

Another popular approach is competitive parity. Here one simply attempts to spend approximately what one's competitors are spending. The idea is not to let anyone get ahead of you. However, your objectives may not be those of your competitors; your resources may be better/worse/different from those of your competitors; your market positioning and/or niche may differ from those of your competitors. This method also has numerous pitfalls attached to it.

All-You-Can-Afford Method

An easy method is the all-you-can-afford or judgement method. Strictly speaking, these are not identical, but there are similarities. All-you-can-afford will generally be based on an executive's or group of executives' assessment of the financial situation and the need for promotion. Similarly, the judgement method relies on managerial opinion. Either of these methods may work quite well in a fairly stable promotional environment and where the decision-makers have a great deal of experience and success in the industry. These methods are most dangerous in situations that are highly competitive and volatile from a marketing perspective.

Task-Objective Method

The best method for allocating budgets is the task-objective method (or the objective and task method). This approach, however, requires a fair amount of promotional expertise and insight. It requires that a decision first be reached concerning the objectives that are to be achieved by the promotion. Then the tasks that will be required to accomplish those objectives are identified; finally, the budget is set to accommodate carrying out those tasks. This method also requires that a decision-maker learn from each attempt to reach an objective and incorporate that knowledge into the next attempt.

SUMMARY

The promotion element in the marketing mix is arguably the most glamorous, exciting aspect of marketing. Certainly it is the area that most people think of when they think of marketing. Good promotion is not easy to accomplish; it is based on a model of communication that takes into account the sender, the receiver, the medium of transmission, and the encoding and decoding processes.

Good communication also takes into account where the audience is in terms of the process of adopting the product: innovators, early adopters, early majority, late majorit, and laggards. Sometimes push strategies are necessary to get channel members to participate in communicating about the product. At other times, pull strategy calls for communicating directly with the target market.

The promotional mix is made up of both personal communications, primarily personal selling, and non-personal communications, which includes advertising, sales promotion, publicity and public relations. However, it is not easy to cleanly separate these various forms of promotion in practice, and an attempt should always be made to successfully integrate the various forms of marketing communication.

Promotional budgets should be set to accomplish specific goals that marketers have agreed upon and plan to carry out. The various methods for setting advertising budgets include the percentage-of-sales, competitive parity, all-you-can-afford, and the task-objective method. Each of these has its adherents, but the task-objective method is the most logical.

FURTHER READING

Edwards, Paul L. 1986. 'Sales Promotion Comes into Its Own.' *Advertising Age* (28 Jul.): 65.

Guiltiman, Joseph P. and Gordon W. Paul. 1988. *Marketing Management,* 3rd ed. New York: McGraw Hill Book Co., Chapter 13.

Pride, William M. and Ferrell, O. C. 1991. *Marketing,* 7th ed. Boston: Houghton Mifflin Co., Chapter 14.

Quelch, John A. 1983. 'It Is Time to Make Trade Promotion More Productive.' *Harvard Business Review* (May/Jun.): 130-136.

Stern, Aimee L. 1987. 'The Promo Wars: Sales Promotions Are Simpler and Usually Cheaper Than Ad Campaigns, and Consumers Love Them.' *Business Month* (Jul.): 44-46.

Yonovich, B.G. 1987. 'Scanner Research May Revolutionize the Approach to Consumer Promotions.' *Marketing Week* (11 May): 6-7.

17 Personal Selling

At a recent meeting of an intermediate-sized medical equipment company in Dallas, Texas, a discussion was held that pitted the marketing manager against the comptroller of the company. The discussion centred around the cost of the salesforce. Cost analysis revealed that each sales call cost the company $186.24, regardless of whether the call resulted in a sale.

The comptroller argued for fewer salespeople, less face-to-face contact with customers, and the use of more telephone calls. The marketing manager guaranteed that business would be lost and years of customer relationship-building would be wasted. Who was right?

To answer that question, you need some background on the nature of personal selling, how it functions as a part of the marketing programme, and the pros and cons of using a salesforce. The important thing to remember is that each situation is different from all others, and each must be evaluated on its own merits.

What is Personal Selling?

Personal selling is the most expensive method of promoting a product, and companies spend more on their salesforces than on any other element in the promotion mix. In fact, recent estimates suggest that an average sales call can cost a company more than £200. Not only are sales calls expensive, but companies additionally spend thousands of pounds on salesforce recruitment, training, compensation and motivation. So why use personal selling rather than other forms of promotion – say, advertising?

Personal selling has the advantage of bringing salespeople face-to-face with potential buyers. Sellers can do on-the-spot 'market research' to determine the needs of customers and the benefits they are seeking. The salesperson can then tailor a unique message to that particular customer. Thus personal selling allows a company to target each individual customer with a message that fits the customer's situation, interests, beliefs and needs. This kind of personalised touch can have dramatic impact on increasing a company's sales volume.

However, because personal selling is so expensive, the costs must be justified by the sales returns. That is, using a salesforce must be profitable as well as effective. What kinds of market conditions call for the use of, and investment in, a salesforce?

Personal selling makes the most sense when a company's customers are concentrated in specific geographical areas and are few enough in number that they can be reached by the salesforce in a reasonable period of time. The product is most likely to be expensive, with technical aspects and/or custom design that requires individual attention. Alternatively, the product may be less expensive and less technically complex but have a variety of specifications and/or models and must be purchased in sufficiently large volume so as to again justify the investment in the salesforce.

Salespeople as Professionals

Salespeople perform an important role in customer satisfaction because for most customers the salesperson *is* the company. For this reason, the vocation of 'salesperson' has become increasingly professional over the past few years. The old image of Willy Loman in Arthur Miller's *Death of a Salesman* or Abbott and Costello's vacuum-cleaner salesman has fallen by the wayside.

Today's salesperson, far from the back-slapping, fast-talking, slightly unethical panhandler of the past, is regarded by his or her company as a vital force in customer satisfaction, market information, and company revenue-generation and growth.

Consequently, jobs in selling are very attractive for graduates today. More than 60 per cent of marketing graduates find their entry level positions in sales. And no wonder. Sales jobs often provide the highest potential for earnings and for future promotion of any of the jobs available. Perhaps most important, a sales job puts the future marketing manager in touch with both the market and the salesforce. Further, sales jobs are expected to remain plentiful for the rest of the twentieth century.

Good salespeople today do not try to 'sell' to the customer; rather they help the customer buy. Therefore they must be well-prepared with knowledge about customer needs and desired benefits, the selling company's policies and procedures, competitors' strengths and weaknesses, and general market conditions. Salespeople are in the business of providing needed information and assistance to their customers; they are also in the business of establishing long-term relationships built on mutual trust and benefit.

Today's successful salespeople are problem-solvers who keep the customers' best interests in sight, while also trying to meet the goals of the selling company.

Types of Salespeople

When we think of salespeople, we often think of retail or inside salespeople, because these are the most visible to the general public. But less visible is a much larger salesforce that is responsible for bringing the product to the retail level in the distribution channel.

Consider, for example, a personal computer that you might purchase from a local computer store or discount outlet. To make the computer, the manufacturer had to order various chips, circuits and boards, along with the box that houses the computer. All of these components came via some salesperson. In addition, any capital equipment that was needed to mould parts, complete assembly, or to test the final product was also purchased from a salesperson. The computer manufacturer may have bought secretarial services from an employment agency, purchased advertising from various media, and hired an accounting firm to audit its financial statements. Then the computer manufacturer sold the computer to a wholesaler, distributor, or possibly directly to retailers. The wholesaler would purchase transportation and warehousing space, as well as a range of services previously mentioned (e.g., secretarial, accounting, etc).

There are three broad classifications of salespeople based on the functions that they perform: order-takers, order-getters and support personnel.

Order-Takers

Order-takers serve customers who know what they want, although salespeople may (and should) make suggestions when appropriate. Order-takers can be *inside* or *field.* Inside order-takers often work for retailers, but they can also work in sales offices, receiving orders by mail and telephone.

Field order-takers travel to customers and generally visit buyers on a routine basis.

Order-Getters

The order-getter's job is to inform prospects about the product and persuade them to buy. The order-getter's function is to increase the firm's sales by selling more to current customers and by finding new customers.

Support Personnel

Support personnel provide technical and advisory assistance, but they may also become involved in order-taking. Actually there are three common types of support personnel: missionary salespeople, trade salespeople and technical salespeople.

Missionary Salespeople

Missionary salespeople perform an indirect type of selling. These salespeople call on their company's customers to assist them in doing a better job of selling the company's products. A representative of health and beauty aids may call on grocery stores to monitor stock movement and oversee special promotions.

Trade Salespeople

Trade salespeople also take orders, but their primary function is to restock shelves, set up displays and special store promotions, and generally help their customers sell more products. Trade salespeople often represent food manufacturers and distributors.

Technical Salespeople

Technical salespeople give technical assistance to their company's customers. They help design and install systems, make minor repairs, and advise on usage and maintenance. However, technical salespeople can be critical in the selling process. When GTE implemented its far-reaching conversion programme to install new, updated equipment with its business customers, the link was the technical support team. These individuals were called in when a business customer experienced equipment problems. Technical support personnel were then able to advise the customer on the expense and difficulty of maintaining obsolete equipment, as well as on the fact that repair parts for many older systems were no longer available. They then were able to recommend the new Installed Base Program that was being offered by GTE with special trade-in allowances for GTE's current customers.

The Personal Selling Process

A successful selling process is based on how people buy, whether they are business buyers or ultimate consumers. While the process may differ slightly in each situation, authorities generally agree on the basic steps that are involved:

1 Prospecting and qualifying.
2 Pre-call preparation.
3 Approaching.
4 Making the presentation.
5 Handling objections.
6 Closing.
7 Following up on the sale.

Prospecting and Qualifying

A *lead* is a potential prospect, and prospects are potential customers. Salespeople start the prospecting stage of the selling process with leads, a person or organisation that might be interested in the product. The next step is to *qualify* the lead; that is, determine that the prospect has four critical characteristics. These are:

1 The need or desire for the product.
2 The financial ability to buy.
3 The eligibility to buy.
4 The authority to buy.

If qualified, the lead then becomes a prospect. Prospects only become customers when they actually buy. For example, residential real estate salespeople usually qualify buyers by asking them questions about their ability to make a downpayment and to make monthly mortgage payments.

The amount of prospecting that must be carried out depends on the situation of the selling company. Some markets consist of only ten or 20 major buyers. In such a case, the need for prospecting is almost nil. But prospecting by firms that market such products as office equipment, life insurance, or cemetery plots and services is likely to be complex and ongoing, with a great deal of time and money invested in prospecting.

Companies that require ongoing prospecting may tap many different sources to develop their leads. Past company records, friends, suppliers, competitors, newspaper announcements, trade publications and professional contacts are only a sample of sources to investigate. While prospecting may be tedious, the salesperson without qualified leads is virtually at a standstill. Therefore it behoves salespeople to maintain a pool of prospects much larger than the number of customers they call on.

Pre-Call Preparation

Successful salespeople engage in pre-call preparation before making a sales call. They want to be sure that they are calling on the right person, the one who has the authority to make the final buying decision. They also want to know as much about the prospect as possible.

An analysis of the customer's product needs, current situation, and even credit history can make the selling process go more smoothly. It is also important for salespeople to be familiar with a customer's past buying experience, particularly if there have been any problems. For example, David H. took over a territory that had previously belonged to a very poorly prepared sales rep. David inherited a lot of customer illwill as a result of that sales rep's behaviour. Before he could turn the territory into a profitable one and create customer goodwill, he had to solve a lot of lingering problems with existing customers.

Product knowledge is also important. The number-one complaint that customers have about salespeople is that they do not have enough product knowledge. A salesperson who is about to call on a customer with a product that he or she does not thoroughly understand is courting disaster. What if your customer says, 'Tell me what makes your brand better than this other brand that I've been using for five years?' Will you have an answer?

What if the customer asks you to explain the advantages of various safety features? Will you be able to do that? Knowledgeable salespeople not only exhibit self-confidence, which makes the selling process more enjoyable for themselves, but that confidence tends to generate trust on the part of customers. Conversely, unsure salespeople make the customers wonder why the salesperson is so uncomfortable. Does he really believe in his product? 'Is she telling me the whole truth about this machine?' 'Will the sales rep know what to do if I have a problem later on?'

Approaching

The salesperson's initial contact with the prospect, called the approach, is a critical step. If pre-call planning has been used, the approach is more likely to be successful. Salespeople should gather as much information as possible about their customers or prospects; then they are prepared with knowledge concerning each organisation's buying habits, meeting times, attitudes and opinions, and even communication style.

First impressions are important, because they are often lasting impressions and are difficult to overcome if customers see the salesperson in a negative light. Since establishing long-term relationships is a priority with most companies, it is best to take your time and get to know your prospect before you jump into your presentation. Ask a lot of questions so that you understand your prospect's situation, needs and priorities. Listen for opportunities of which you may not have been aware. Using a mutual acquaintance as a referral can work quite well. You have immediately established something in common with your prospect, and the goodwill that your acquaintance has with your prospect will often rub off on you. Just make sure that your acquaintance is in good standing with your prospect before you drop his or her name.

Salespeople differ in their opinions about making appointments, but, in general, it is a good idea. If you cold call on prospects – i.e., give no advance warning – you may catch them at a bad time, miss them entirely, or spend an inordinate amount of time waiting to see them. Most customers and prospects appreciate some advance warning, so that they can better plan their activities, and you are more likely to have their undivided attention.

Making the Presentation

In the late 1800s the canned presentation was developed by John H. Patterson of the National Cash Register Company. The canned or memorised presentation ensures uniform coverage of major selling points. Today canned presentations are frowned upon, because they are often poorly delivered and do not take into account the unique circumstances surrounding each customer and sale.

An organised presentation is a favourite of many companies. While an outline is used to ensure logical delivery of major selling points, the organised presentation allows the prospect to ask questions and the seller to adjust the presentation according to feedback from the prospect.

Many presentations also use demonstrations and/or audio visual aids, such as slide shows or videotapes. An advantage of these devices is that they attract and hold the prospect's attention. But they must be done professionally, and they cannot be too long. A disadvantage is that prospects may not feel free to interrupt and ask questions; consequently, the advantage of feedback is temporarily put on hold.

If salespeople use demonstrations, they should practise beforehand until the demonstration goes smoothly and works every time. Any props that will be needed should be provided by the salesperson, since the prospect may or may not have extension cords, slide projectors and adaptor plugs conveniently available. Presentations can be seriously disrupted if the prospect is forced to go and look for an item that the salesperson needs.

Certainly the more a salesperson involves the customer in the presentation, the more likely it is that the customer will buy. The national sales manager of an exercise-equipment manufacturer was recently quoted as saying that if his salesforce could get a customer to try the equipment as part of a personal demonstration, more than 75 per cent of prospects would buy. Without a demonstration, the successful sales rate was less than 20 per cent.

Handling Objections

Objections express some resistance on the part of the prospect. It is first necessary to determine whether an objection is real or simply an excuse. For example, a woman who objects to the colour of a car that she is being shown may merely be asking for assurance that the car is available in other colours. Real objections, even though they are more serious than excuses, should be viewed as an opportunity to provide the prospect with more information. Customers often bother to raise objections only if they are involved in the sales presentation – a good sign. Never respond to objections with hostility or defensiveness; you may lose a sale.

Closing

Closing the sale means asking for the order. Researchers and sales practitioners alike recognise closing as the step in the selling process that is most difficult for salespeople. For some, the possibility of rejection by the prospect is paralysing; for others, a 'no' means that all their hard work has just gone down the drain.

There are some tactics to make closing easier. Using trial closes throughout the presentation enables salespeople to 'take the prospect's temperature', to find out how interested the prospect is in making the purchase. Asking such questions as 'Which colour do you prefer?' 'When would you like it delivered?' and 'How many would you like?' enables prospects to indicate their willingness to buy without making the final commitment. By the time the process gets to the close, both parties should have essentially reached an agreement.

Following Up

Satisfying post-sale activities will often determine whether a first-time customer becomes a regular customer. In whatever way possible, salespeople should confirm that customers are satisfied. Find out whether the product arrived on time and in good condition, whether the installation procedure was timely and without disruption to the rest of the organisation, and whether the product is functioning as it should. Most of all, the salesperson should uncover any discontent that the customer is experiencing and should take steps to correct the problem.

For example, some local car dealerships make it a point to call after every service job, large or small, to find out whether the customer is happy with the servicing done on the car.

Salesforce Management

Management of the salesforce is a very important part of any business. Because a company is dependent on the salesforce for generating sales revenues, sales managers are under a lot of pressure to get high levels of productivity from salespeople.

The typical sales hierarchy begins with the salesperson at the bottom, usually in a geographical territory, reporting to a district or divisional sales manager who reports to a regional or zone manager. These then report to a national sales manager or the vice president of sales. Unfortunately, only a few report to a vice president of marketing, which emphasises again the artificial division of sales and marketing.

Establishing Objectives

Companies usually assign multiple objectives to the salesforce. A common objective would be a certain volume for a given time period – say, the third quarter. Or volume may be couched in unit sales, market share, or even in new account sales.

More and more companies expect salespeople to channel their efforts towards increasing profitability. Making a large sale may not be favourably regarded if the salesperson has negotiated away too much of the profit margin. In the past, salespeople may have been too quick to make a deal just to say they 'got the sale' and, of course, collect their commissions. But in today's competitive environment, salespeople must be more accountable than ever before with respect to the bottom line.

Sometimes the salesforce is divided into segments based on the product lines they represent and/or the type of customers they call on. Under these conditions, selling objectives may vary among the groups. For example, one manufacturer of maps and atlases has a salesforce that calls on retailers – bookstores, discount houses and supermarkets – for retail distribution of their products. Another branch of the same salesforce calls on sales promotion agencies and specialty advertising distributorships to sell their products to those who plan special promotional programmes using these items as incentives and gifts. Obviously, with these two branches serving different markets, their objectives will also differ.

Recruiting and Selecting Salespeople

One of the first questions that must be addressed, even before recruitment begins, is how large the salesforce should be. Generally, that question is addressed by estimates that relate to average workload and also by the size of the market and the number of segments that must be reached.

Many companies use the equalised workload approach to determine whether the addition of 'one more' salesperson will be profitable. An underlying assumption here is the 80/20 principle, which holds that 80 per cent of all territorial sales are likely to come from 20 per cent of a territory's prospects. Keeping this principle in mind, the sales manager will classify accounts into different sized classes, estimate how many salespeople are needed to service each account in each class, and how many hours will be involved.

Suppose Class A accounts require 25 calls per year (approximately one every two weeks) and Class B accounts require only 12 calls per year (one a month). If the company has 200 Class A accounts and 800 Class B accounts, this means that the sales manager should plan for a salesforce that can make 14,600 calls per year: (25 x 200 = 5,000) + (12 x 800 = 9,600) = 14,600. If the average salesperson in the company can make 500 calls per year, the company needs about 29 salespeople (14,600\500 = 29.2). Other analytical methods are also available, but this one serves to illustrate how salesforce size can be estimated.

It is not unusual for a company to try to cut back on the size of the salesforce during an economic recession or when the company is experiencing a decline in sales. While such tactics may be tempting to improve immediate profitability, they may prove disastrous in the long run. Not only may cutbacks reinforce the downward slide in sales, but they may also prevent the firm from rebounding when economic times improve.

Average recruitment and training costs are high, running at more than £400 per entry-level salesperson. When you include the costs of lost sales in empty territories, these costs can run as high as £35,000 to £50,000, or more. These figures illustrate the consequences of poor selection and the need for recruiting carefully.

Spotting Potential

Sales managers, sales researchers and sales trainers have long debated how to spot applicants who will be successful salespeople. While stereotypes exist concerning the characteristics needed for successful selling – outgoing, friendly, aggressive, enthusiastic, energetic – many successful salespeople seem to exhibit very different traits.

They may be quiet, retiring, relaxed and easygoing. Carl Stevens, a well-known sales educator and consultant, maintains that his research shows that only two traits can be reliably linked with sales performance: empathy (the ability to 'step into the other person's shoes') and ego-drive. Northwestern Mutual Life Insurance Company uses a test that helps them identify applicants with entrepreneurial traits. Charles Garfield, another sales educator, finds that good salespeople are goal-directed risk-takers who identify strongly with their customers – again, the suggestion of empathy.

Since theories of how to predict sales success vary, it behoves a sales manager to put together a profile of the kind of applicant best suited to his or her specific sales environments.

Screening

Sales applicants will be put through a screening process. This process may include any or all of the following: personality, intelligence or interest testing and evaluation; screening interviews; depth interviews; reference checks; credit checks and physical examinations.

Training

Some companies have formal training programmes; others use on-the-job training. Some have ongoing training for experienced personnel as well as new trainees; others do not. Some training is sophisticated and complex; other courses are basic and limited in scope. Some companies train their salespeople before putting them into the field; others put their new recruits into the field for part of the time and continue their training for part of the time.

Training can include additional testing, role playing, lectures, slide and/or video presentations, and simulation exercises. Videotaping and play-back that give trainees the opportunity to criticise theirs and others' performances are becoming increasingly popular. Some companies set up elaborate assessment centres where the intense pressure of telephone sales, sales calls and colleague feedback simulate real fieldwork in selling. Prospective employees and trainees can thus be examined to determine how well they handle pressure.

Salesforce Payment

The salesforce payment plan is an important consideration because of its impact on salesforce performance. Recent research shows that money as a motivation to increase selling efforts is effective with only a small percentage of the total sales-force. Nevertheless, inequitable or inadequate payment packages will have a negative effect on almost all members of the salesforce.

The three basic types of packages are straight salary, straight commission, and salary plus commission. Each of these has some advantages and disadvantages. Straight salary gives the company the most control over salesforce performance, but it holds little appeal for the type of individual who is motivated by incentives. And these individuals are often the best salespeople in the company.

Straight commission is based strictly on the sales volume produced by the salesperson, and it may be a fixed percentage of sales or a sliding percentage, paying larger dividends at higher levels of sales. The advantage to the company of the straight commission is that it does not have to pay the salesperson unless he or she makes a sale. The disadvantage is the lack of control that the company has over the salesperson's behaviour.

The most common form of payment is some form of salary plus commission. A small but stable salary gives the salesperson some financial security, and the commission structure provides an incentive for the salesperson to work harder. Some companies pay commission on all sales; others only pay commission on sales made after the salesperson reaches a specified quota.

The diversity of sales payment plans indicates the complexity of finding a plan that fulfils a variety of objectives. In fact, many sales managers believe that finding a payment system that will reinforce positive behaviours is their most important task.

Controlling and Evaluating Performance

A sales manager's most difficult task is to control and evaluate salesforce performance. Generally, evaluation is based on some predetermined quotas. These may be agreed between the sales manager and the salesperson, or they may have been assigned unilaterally by the sales manager. Quotas are often expressed in terms of monetary sales volume or unit volume, but they may include some specifically-targeted goals, such as new accounts sales or number of sales calls made.

An evaluation is likely to include where a given salesperson ranks in comparison with other members of the salesforce. Sales managers should also be able to assess a salesperson's strong points and weaknesses, giving praise for the former and constructive assistance with the latter.

Evaluations should be perceived as fair and equitable. Any sense of favouritism that is conveyed to the salesforce can easily result in widespread demoralisation of the entire group. Performance should be recognised and rewarded accordingly. Companies that 'reward' top performers' success by dividing their territories and giving half to someone else are, for all practical purposes, slitting their own throats.

SUMMARY

The cost of maintaining a salesforce is considerable. Not only salary and commmissions but the cost of each sales call itself, more than £120 on average, must be taken into account. Furthermore, the logistics of allocating these expensive resources are complex. Salespeople must be deployed where they do the most good, and they must be carefully selected and adequately trained to do the job once they are placed in the field. All of these activities are expensive and time-consuming.

However, the pros of having a salesforce far exceed the cons if the salesforce is well-managed. There is no substitute for face-to-face contact with your customers. You can explain your product in depth, answer questions and objections that the prospect raises, and get immediate feedback as to what the prospect is thinking. Remember, the salesforce is the revenue-producing arm of the organisation and without it all other functions are virtually useless.

The selling process involves several basic steps: prospecting and qualifying, pre-call preparation, approaching, making the presentation, handling objections, closing and post-sale follow-up. Each stage is important for making the best impression on the customer and for ensuring customer satisfaction at the completion of the sale.

Selecting and recruiting the best salespeople is a topic that has received much attention. Obviously some salespeople are better than others, but how can a manager know which ones before they are hired? Managers often use the screening phase of hiring to evaluate a possible employee's personality, intelligence, interests, and even entrepreneurial ability. The training component of hiring is also very important. In this stage the new salesperson learns the company's product, its markets, and its policies and procedure.

Payment of the salesforce is often linked to productivity. While a combination plan of salary plus commission is the most common, different companies will put together packages that best meet that company's particular sales goals.

FURTHER READING

Assael, Henry. 1985. *Marketing Management.* Boston: Kent Publishing Co., Chapter 14.

Boone, Loiuse E. and Kurtz, David L. 1992. *Contemporary Marketing*, 7th ed. Ft. Worth, Texas: Dryden Press, Chapter 18.

Coleman, Lynn G. 1989. 'Salesforce Turnover Has Managers Wondering Why.' *Marketing News* (4 Dec.): 6.

Dalrymple, Douglas. 1985. *Sales Management: Concepts and Cases.* New York: John Wiley & Sons.

Greenburg, Charles. 1990. 'Direct Response Can Become a Potent Sales Management Tool.' *Marketing News* (5 Mar.):15.

Kotler, Philip. 1991. *Marketing Management,* 7th ed. Englewood Cliffs, New Jersey: Prentice Hall, Chapter 24.

Parker, Richard M. 1989. 'How to Find Salespeople Who Know How to Sell.' *Sales & Marketing Management* (Mar.): 76-78.

Shank, Matthew and Lunnemann, Cynthia. 1990. 'Proper Pay and Rewards Help Retain Salesforce.' *Marketing News* (5 Mar.): 7.

18 Advertising, Public Relations and Sales Promotion

Hundreds of thousands of dollars are spent each year for advertising spots on the Super Bowl. For example, in 1992 30-second spots were sold for $850,000 each. And these media costs do not include the cost of production.

What do Coca-Cola, Pepsi, Miller Brewing Company and General Motors know about advertising that would induce them to spend that much money on a few seconds of television time? The truth is that some sponsors believe these spots are the most effective placements they can make, because millions of viewers will see and hear their commercial messages.

Why use advertising? And what can it do to justify enormous expenditures for something that is gone in just a few seconds? In this chapter we will define advertising and look at its strengths and weaknesses. A look at the process of creating an advertising campaign gives us some idea of the work involved in creating good advertising. The chapter also includes a brief discussion of public relations and the different elements that are used in sales promotion.

What is Advertising?

Advertising is a non-personal form of communication that is paid for by an identified sponsor. Various media can be used for transmitting the message, which is primarily intended to be persuasive. Advertising can address aspects of goods, services and ideas. Advertising differs from personal selling in that messages are not delivered face-to-face; they are transmitted through some form of mass communication, such as television, radio or magazines. Advertising reaches very large groups of people, while selling is generally confined to one individual or a small group.

Advertising is paid for by the sponsor, so that the audience is aware that the message is a biased one. Consequently, advertising may not be as believable as publicity, which gives the impression of objectivity.

An advantage that advertising has over personal selling, in addition to reaching larger audiences, is that the costs per person reached are much lower than for personal selling. However, the total cost for advertising can be very high. For example, in 1991, Procter & Gamble Company spent more than $2 billion on advertising.

Who Uses Advertising?

Just about everybody. Political candidates use advertising to solicit votes; Madonna uses advertising to announce her concerts and to get people to buy tickets; Lever Brothers use advertising to sell washing powder. Although each of these examples relates to business-to-consumer advertising, we saw in Chapter 16 that businesses use all forms of promotion, including advertising, to reach other businesses.

Under What Conditions?

Advertising is useful for reaching large audiences that cannot be contacted individually. Advertising works well when a company plans to communicate the same message to everyone in a particular market segment and when the message is fairly simple and uncomplicated.

To Accomplish What Objective?

The range of possible advertising objectives is similar to that of promotion objectives in general. Advertising can be used to stimulate demand, both primary and selective. This type of advertising is important in new product introduction and while the product is still in the growth stage of the product life-cycle. Stimulating demand is probably the objective that most people think of when they think of advertising.

As we have also seen, promotion must be geared to the stage of product adoption and the stage in the product life-cycle. As a result, for products that have achieved widespread acceptance and are in the mature stage of the product life-cycle, reminder advertising is very common. This advertising simply says to the consumer 'Remember that Brand X is still on the market and remember these qualities about Brand X that you like so much.'

Reinforcement advertising is designed to eliminate post-purchase regret. Reinforcement advertising says to the customer 'Yes, you did the right thing in purchasing Brand X. And here are some reasons that you can cite if you ever have any doubts about your decision.' Research shows the powerful nature of reinforcement advertising: more people pay attention to car advertising *after* they buy a car than before they buy it.

Advertising can be used to support the efforts of the salesforce. In channels of distribution, resellers are often interested in the amount of advertising that a manufacturer is doing with the final consumer. This pull strategy makes it easier for a reseller (a retailer, for example), to move the product once it is purchased from a supplier. Consequently, when the salesforce calls on distributors, wholesalers and retailers, it is important to show them advertising that will stimulate demand in the marketplace.

Advertising can also be used to generate leads for the salesforce from responses to advertising messages. Sometimes advertising can prepare a prospect for the salesperson's call so that the time spent is more productive for both parties.

Finally, advertising can be used as a defensive measure. It can help reduce seasonal sales fluctuations and may simply be used to offset the effects of a competitor's advertising.

Developing an Advertising Campaign

The process for developing an advertising campaign is fairly uniform. Regardless of who is in charge, the advertiser or an ad agency, and regardless of the size of the budget, essentially the same steps must be followed.

Identify and Research the Target Audience

Several groups of variables must be explored with respect to the target audience. Demographic variables determine the size of the audience, location, gender, education, income, size of family, stage in family life-cycle, and other objective characteristics. Next, lifestyle variables, such as attitudes towards important issues, spending priorities and favourite activities should be examined. General perceptions, attitudes and preferences concerning the product category should be considered, as well as more specific attitudes toward the advertiser, the brand and its competitors. Media usage, such as which programmes are watched and which magazines are read, is also extremely important for making media decisions later on. Finally, usage patterns should be established giving clues as to when and under what conditions this brand is purchased and used.

Time and budgetary constraints may inhibit the amount of information that an advertiser can reasonably collect. However, the more that is known about the audience the less likely it is that the advertising will prove to be inappropriate and ineffective.

Set Objectives

Advertising objectives can really be divided into two types: communication objectives and sales objectives. Communication objectives include reinforcement, reminder, persuading, and adding emphasis, for example to a new product benefit.

Sales objectives are more concrete than communication objectives but are difficult to isolate and link with a particular piece of advertising. Sales objectives really include any kind of action on the part of the audience: buying the product (obviously), visiting the store, returning an enquiry card, or making an appointment with a sales representative. The problem is that it is difficult to determine whether these actions take place as a direct result of advertising or whether they can be attributed to a series of factors. More will be said on this subject later.

Whatever objectives are set, they should be compatible with the overall marketing mix, the stage of the product life-cycle, the attitudes and wants of the market, and the overall objectives of the company. And, as with all promotion objectives, advertising objectives should be concrete, should involve a specific time period and should be measurable.

In an advertising campaign, the platform is the issue or issues that the campaign will address. For example, let's assume you are putting together a campaign for a sports car. You might talk about the luxury aspects of this car – leather seats, climate control, and AM FM stereo plus compact disc player – or you might talk about performance issues, the size and horse power of the engine, fuel injection, and rack and pinion steering. How would you decide? You should look at what you found out about your target audience and what attributes are most important to them. These are the ones that you emphasise in your advertising. The 'hot buttons' or key attributes for one market segment may be irrelevant to another.

It is best to confine your platform to only one (or at the most, two) major issues. Otherwise you will confuse your audience, and they will be less likely to remember anything you said. Advertisers should always remember that they are far more involved in their advertising than their audience is going to be; therefore the axiom is to keep it simple!

Determine the Budget

In Chapter 16 we discussed various methods for setting the promotional budget. That discussion applies equally to advertising. To briefly review, the best method of determining the advertising budget or appropriation is to look at your objectives, decide on the tasks needed to accomplish those objectives, and estimate how much that will cost.

If, as is often the case, the objectives are so ambitious that the tasks required to reach those goals would be impossibly expensive, then it is time to modify the objectives. Pare them down to something more realistic and prioritise the objectives, concentrating on the most important ones first. A common mistake that companies make is to try to do too much with their advertising budgets. They spread advertising money too thinly, and the advertising accomplishes none of the objectives that were set.

Develop the Media Plan

The first step in the media plan is to determine which of the major media to use. These include newspapers, television, magazines, radio, direct mail and outdoor. Each of these has some advantages and some disadvantages, which are important in making the right selections.

Newspapers

Newspapers offer flexibility and timeliness. Messages can be tailored to certain geographical areas and to specific events. Newspapers give good local market coverage, but their message is very perishable. That is, newspapers have a 'shelf life' of only 24 hours. The reproduction quality is quite poor, especially for products that rely on visual appeal, such as food.

Television

Television can be a highly-effective medium because it combines sight and sound, offers large audiences, or high reach, but it has some important disadvantages as well. Television is highly perishable. A 30-second spot lasts just that long, 30 seconds. After that it is gone, and if the audience missed it the advertiser has lost a lot of money. Which brings us to television's second disadvantage: its entry level is expensive. Television is also experiencing higher and higher levels of clutter with more and more fragmented audiences as a result of multiple cable channels, a condition that makes TV increasingly expensive per person reached.

Magazines

Magazines offer the advantages of geographic, demographic and some lifestyle selectivity. They also offer high-quality four-colour reproduction, especially important for products with a lot of visual appeal. Magazines offer long life because they are often re-read, and they have the additional advantage of a 'pass-along' rate to increase the size of the audience reached.

Magazines do require a fairly long lead time (this is the time between the decision to place an advertisement and its appearance in the magazine), often two to three months. There will be some wasted exposure, and generally placement, in terms of page position, cannot be guaranteed.

Radio

Radio is relatively inexpensive. It offers good demographic and geographic selectivity, and is a popular medium. However, the message is perishable. Radio also has the disadvantage of being purely an audio medium, and people only give it marginal attention. Therefore intrusiveness depends on frequency of exposure, which can run up the cost of radio considerably.

Direct Mail

Direct mail is the one 'mass' medium that can be personalised. With the advent of database marketing it offers extremely good demographic, geographic and psychographic selectivity. It is, though, fairly expensive per person reached, and it suffers from a negative 'junk mail' image.

Outdoor

Outdoor advertising refers to billboards and, in some metropolitan areas, transport. Geographic flexibility, low cost, high frequency and little immediate competition are the advantages of outdoor advertising. The disadvantages include little creative flexibility, limited audience selectivity and very brief exposure time.

Non-Traditional Media

A large assortment of non-traditional media have emerged in recent years. Space for advertising is being sold inside video cassette rental boxes, on the backs of supermarket cash receipts, and on the sides of cross-country trucks and trailers. In Great Britain the Boy Scouts sell sponsorships of merit badges, and in the United States most major football games have sold advertising sponsorships in their names.

Selecting the Media

Once the decision has been made as to which of the major media to use, the next question is which vehicles within the medium are most appropriate for a given ad campaign. For example, if an advertiser decides to use magazines, which ones should be chosen? Subscribers to *Good Housekeeping* are very different in their make-up from subscribers to *Top Gear*. The vehicles chosen, whether magazines, television programmes or newspapers, should be those that reach people with the same characteristics as those of the target audience.

The next decision involves the trade-offs of reach and frequency. Generally, the more of one you get, the less of the other you get. The more reach, the less frequency, and vice versa. Trade-offs are made by considering the nature of your audience, the objectives that you hope to attain, and the nature of the medium you have chosen to use. For example, the more perishable the medium, the more frequency you will have to have to make an impression on the audience.

The nature of the message is also a consideration. A message announcing a sale by a local retailer should use radio and newspapers. The introduction of a new car requires television and magazines.

The advertiser also must select the scheduling for the ad campaign. Continuity means that ads will be scheduled on an ongoing basis; 'pulsing' means scheduling at regular intervals throughout the advertising period. 'Flighting' suggests intense media coverage at certain times and no advertising scheduled at other times.

Develop the Creative Execution

The advertising platform is a statement of what to say in an ad campaign, but it does not specify how to say it. The 'how' is in the hands of the copywriter and the art director for the advertising project.

Good advertisers and ad agencies rely on the research they did with the target audience to assist them in coming up with a campaign theme, words to use, and images to portray in the advertising. Many techniques can be used. For example, a campaign that uses television might select a 'slice of life' execution or a testimonial by a highly-credible spokesperson. Radio commercials may use a straight announcement or a dramatisation. Magazines may present the solution to a customer problem, and direct mail might persuade the customer with lots of technical information.

Copy

Whatever media is used, the copy (or words that are used to persuade) should reflect the campaign objectives, the characteristics of the target audience, and the benefits the audience desires. Copy should be easy to read if in print and easy to understand if spoken. The style should be clear, get to the point, and focus on the needs and wants of the audience. Remember, copy is written for customers, not for company executives.

Illustration

The illustration used in a print ad can be either a photograph or original artwork. Occasionally, the copy graphics themselves provide artistic interest, but this approach is not common. Photographs generally work better than drawings because the audience finds them more interesting.

Remember, the first step in moving audience members through the AIDA sequence is to get their attention.

Movement from scene to scene in television commercials should use smooth transitions and be visually stimulating without being overwhelming. Sometimes advertising becomes so creative that the message is obscured by the interesting execution. You want to grab attention, but you also want your *product* to be remembered, not just the execution.

Layout

Layout refers to the way the elements are arranged in a print advertisement. There are five distinct elements in a print ad: headline, subheadline, body copy, illustration and signature. Eye movement should be smooth, usually following an S, reverse S, Z, reverse Z, C or reverse C pattern. The most important element in the ad should be at the optical centre, about two thirds up from the bottom of the page. The headline should be attention-getting, perhaps offering a benefit to the reader. The subheadline should direct attention to the body of the ad. Copy should include a call to action and end with the signature, usually at the lower right corner. The illustration should epitomise the message of the advertisement.

Evaluate Advertising Effectiveness

Since there are broadly two kinds of advertising objectives, there are accordingly two types of testing for advertising effectiveness. In one case, the communication effects are tested; in the other case sales results are evaluated. Copy-testing to assess communication effects includes several techniques. *Direct rating* asks members of a consumer panel to view alternative ads and to rate the ads according to how well they attract attention and how consumers react to the ads. In a *portfolio test*, respondents are exposed to a number of advertisements. The respondents are then asked to recall the ads and their content, sometimes aided and sometimes unaided by the interviewer. *Laboratory tests* are predicated on the theory that highly-involving ads produce some sort of physiological response in the viewer. Various physiological measurements may be taken: blood pressure, eye movement, pupil dilation, perspiration and heartbeat.

Recall tests are administered to determine how much of an ad is remembered by respondents. Those who have been exposed to the advertising are contacted and interviewed after the advertising. Recall scores are given a great deal of credence in the advertising industry; a poor recall score can cause an advertiser to scrap an expensive campaign.

Recognition tests ask respondents to point out advertisements that they remember seeing. These tests are often used with magazine advertising and give advertisers an idea of which headlines, illustrations, and copy appeals work best.

Because of the long time between the audience's exposure to the ad campaign and subsequent sales of the product, it is nearly impossible to prove a direct cause-and-effect relationship between advertising and sales. How many sales are caused by an ad campaign that increases brand awareness by 30 per cent or enables five percent of the audience tested to recall the brand's slogan? If a competitor raises prices at the same time as an ad campaign is launched, what proportion of increased sales can be attributed to the ad campaign and what can be attributed to the competitor's price increase?

The exception to this is advertising media that directly connect advertising and sales, such as a direct-mail campaign or direct-sales solicitation via television.

Public Relations and Publicity

Public relations is a broad set of activities designed to gain favourable attitudes towards a company, its image and its brands on the part of customers, vendors, stockholders, governmental agencies and the general public. As mentioned in Chapter 16, public relations may include such diverse activities as press conferences, special events, publicity/news releases, sponsorship of a charitable fundraising programme, and others.

Publicity, a subset of public relations, differs from advertising in that while advertising tends to be informative and persuasive, publicity is primarily informative. Publicity is usually prepared in the form of news releases by the 'advertiser', but since the advertiser pays nothing for the time or the space, publicity is largely at the discretion of the media. Publicity may have more credibility among audience members because it is perceived as impartial and unbiased, but a firm cannot control how often it will be used, where it will be used, how the company/brand will be portrayed, or even whether it will be used.

In addition to the standard press release or news release, some companies prepare an article for publication, or a captioned photograph with a brief explanatory paragraph. A press conference is called to announce a major news event or to address a topic that is critical to the company.

Good public relations programmes can save a company a tremendous amount of money that would otherwise have to go into advertising or sales promotion. However, a good PR programme does not just happen; it must be planned by knowledgeable PR experts and must be maintained on an ongoing basis. It is difficult, at best, to put together a credible response to a product defect or package tampering if a company has no previous experience in handling the media.

Sales Promotion

Sales promotion includes a variety of promotional vehicles, each with its own peculiar strengths and weaknesses. Sales promotion is growing much faster than mass media advertising in terms of its monetary volume because of the unique strengths of some sales promotion vehicles.

In general, sales promotion tends to get the customer more involved with the product and/or the sponsoring company. Sales promotion works well in terms of inducing a change in purchasing and usage behaviour.

Finally, in many cases, sales promotion can be targeted at a specific group that the sponsor wishes to reach.

Samples, Coupons and Premiums

These can be used with either consumer or trade promotions but are most often associated with consumer promotions. Sampling is very effective for introducing a new consumer-packaged-goods product, because it enables the consumer to experience the product firsthand.

Coupons can accomplish the same objective, since they reduce the financial risk of trying an unknown brand. Both of those devices, however, have only short-term advantages. In the long run, both essentially amount to price competition, and that amounts to losing a percentage of profit.

Premiums are items given in return for something that the customer does. These induce customers to try new products or otherwise engage in new behaviour. For maximum effectiveness, premiums should appeal to the targeted audience and have some obvious relationship to the product being advertised.

Contests and Sweepstakes

Contests and sweepstakes may generate a lot of enthusiasm for a particular product or company. To the extent that customers must become involved in the contest to win, the company has got the audience's attention and interest. Unfortunately, this may not translate directly to product interest and involvement.

Specialty Advertising

Specialty advertising is imprinted promotional products. Useful items with the company's logo, address, phone number and message are imprinted and distributed to the target market. This form of advertising has the advantage of being retained and used for a very long time. It builds customer goodwill in that it is perceived as a gift. The disadvantage is that it can be expensive per person reached. However, this disadvantage can be offset if the item has a high perceived value and retention on the part of the recipient.

Trade Shows

Trade shows are held to influence members of the channel of distribution. Manufacturers often hold trade shows to exhibit new products for their dealers and distributors. Trade shows are also an excellent time to forge closer relationships between buyers and sellers. Some trade shows are held for the ultimate consumer. One example is the 'home show', where various home appliances and improvement products can be viewed.

Trade Promotions

Trade promotions, those promotions directed to members of the channel of distribution, account for more sales promotion expenditure than do those for the consumer. Manufacturers, for example, frequently offer price-offs, allowances, volume discounts, buy-back guarantees, or free goods to get onto a retailer's shelf. In-store demonstrations and free samples to consumers may then assist the retailer in moving the product and thus gain even more shelf space for the brand. It is also common for a supplier to offer 'push money', or 'spiffs', to salespeople – special commissions to induce the salespeople to push the company's brand over other brands that are in stock.

SUMMARY

Advertising, public relations and sales promotion are very powerful tools to enhance a firm's marketing effort. This chapter has given you a brief overview of these areas of promotion, and it has also attempted to convince you of the need to plan your promotions very carefully. These tools are expensive and millions of pounds are wasted each year due to poor planning.

The process of putting together an advertising campaign follows a simple outline:

1 Identify and research the target audience.
2 Set objectives.
3 Define the platform.
4 Determine the budget.
5 Develop the media plan.
6 Develop the creative execution.
7 Evaluate the effectiveness of the campaign after it has been implemented.

When you put together your promotional plan, be sure that you have clearly defined, realistic objectives. Make your media choices carefully, taking particular note of what vehicles work best with your target audience. Then design messages that are relevant and compelling for your audience.

Finally, test your results to determine whether your promotional effort has been successful. Look at communication objectives as well as sales objectives, and evaluate the results in the light of what you originally intended to achieve.

Public relations, publicity and sales promotion are additional elements that can contribute to an effective overall marketing communications strategy. Public relations includes a diversity of activities from press conferences to grand openings. A well-managed publicity campaign has the advantage of appearing neutral and credible, since the sponsor is not identified. Sales promotion devices can be very effective in generating short-term sales results and in creating long-term goodwill for the company and the brand.

FURTHER READING

Assael, Henry. 1985. *Marketing Management*. Boston: Kent Publishing Co., Chapter 13.

Baker, M. J. 1991. *Marketing – An Introductory Text*. 5th ed. MacMillan, Chapters 16, 17 and 18.

Bishop, Nancy. 1988. 'Specialty Advertising Embarks on Second Century.' *Marketing Week* (4 Jan.): 32.

Endicott, Craiq R. 1992 'Top 100 Take It on the Chin, Feel Biggest Drop in 4 Decades.'*Advertising Age* (23 Sept.): 1, 72.

Gilligan, C. and Crowther, G. 1976. *Advertising Management*. Philip Allan Publishers.

Kamin, Howard. 1978. 'Advertising Reach and Frequency.' *Journal of Advertising* (Feb.): 22.

Kotler, Philip. 1991. *Marketing Management*, 7th ed. Englewood Cliffs, New Jersey: Prentice Hall, Chapter 22.

Lamb, Jr., Charles W., Hair, Jr., Joseph F. and McDaniel, Carl. 1992. *Principles of Marketing*. Cincinnati: South-Western Publishing Co., Chapter 14.

Wilhide, Doug. 1989. 'Does This Ad Stuff Work?' *Business Marketing* (Oct.): 9–97.

Wilkie, William L., and Farris, Paul W. 1975. 'Comparison Advertising: Problems and Potential.' *Journal of Marketing* (Oct.): 7-15.

Workbook for Estimating Your Advertising Budget. 1984. Boston: Cahners Publishing Co.

19 Marketing Planning

Against an environment of entrepreneurship, the UK government launched the Enterprise Initiative Scheme in 1988. This scheme was designed to help small companies with their overall business planning. Among the various initiatives included was the Marketing Initiative, in which one of the authors was directly involved in monitoring quality control

Essentially, small companies were given a grant by the government in partial payment of a consultancy project, in which a marketing plan was developed. For the majority of these companies, this was their first introduction to marketing. Primary market research was carried out into the companies' existing situation, their customers, competitors and opportunities and threats in the market place. After analysing these, a plan of action was drawn up covering the following 12 months, giving indications of a promotional campaign, a pricing plan, any product developments or amendments required and advice on a distribution strategy.

To many companies this initiative gave them a structure around which to plan their future strategies. Others identified market opportunities for their product of which they had been unaware, whilst others fine tuned their promotional campaigns to better suit their market needs. One company, the Edinburgh Bicycle Company, grew from strength to strength after this initiative, winning a prestigious prize in marketing from the Chartered Institute of Marketing for their achievements.

The launch of this scheme by the government highlighted its recognition that marketing, as with any other business activity, must be a planned set of tasks, carried out with clear objectives in sight. In addition, to help with marketing, other initiatives covered design, manufacturing and finance. The scheme finished in 1994, but in its time helped many small companies develop in a much more structured fashion than their financial position may have allowed.

This chapter looks at the types of issues which consultants going into these companies would have faced. How should this company's planning be organised? What are the main objectives of the firm? We then look at marketing plans, the information they require in order to be properly formulated and how this is encompassed into the strategic planning dimension.

Definition of Strategic Marketing Planning

Strategic marketing planning is the process that firms go through as they decide how to allocate and manage resources profitably in the market place. As the definition indicates, strategic planning must be an ongoing activity that takes into account the mission of the organisation and its broader set of objectives.

If the organisation's mission is education, then strategies must be outlined to reflect those goals. If the mission is to build the best high-performance sports cars in the world, then plans must be formulated to enhance that objective.

Many firms have a variety of objectives. For this reason, strategic planning must be viewed as a broad activity that creates a macro framework for the organisation. From this macro framework, a number of more specific marketing plans may be developed.

In summary, the process of strategic planning leads to a macro view of the firm's position in the marketplace, which, in turn, leads to market plans designed to direct the actions towards individual target markets.

Strategy Versus Tactics

Marketers realise that strategic plans cannot, nor should they encompass a great deal of detail concerning such things as what price to charge, which magazines to advertise in, or which transportation company to use for product distribution. These are questions of tactics and should not be included in the strategic plan.

Appropriate issues for strategic plans include such basic questions as:

1 Which target markets should we pursue?
2 Should we introduce our new product one region at a time or on a national roll-out?
3 By what percentage can we increase sales of our product in Europe during 1996?

Strategic plans tend to be long-range, that is, three to five years or more, rather than short-range. In contrast, tactical plans refer to the here and now: which stores should carry our products? What package sizes should we offer? How many colours should be available in our line?

Strategic planning is carried out by upper level management, those who are naturally positioned to see and be concerned with the overall performance of the organisation. In turn, most of the tactical decision-making is done at the middle-management level, or even at the supervisory level.

Company Resources and Limitations

As upper management thinks about the strategic position of the company it makes sense to conduct an inventory of the firm's resources, including intangibles such as expertise and experience, as well as its weaknesses. During the late 1980s, many companies got 'burned' in the rash of corporate mergers and takeovers by trying to get into markets unrelated to their customary businesses.

For example, in the mid-1980s Thomas Nelson, Inc., the largest Bible-publishing concern in the United States, wanted to get into manufacturing and diversify into the secular market. So it purchased a 240,000 sq. ft. bindery and printing press and also purchased Dodd, Mead & Co., a New York publisher. By 1986 Thomas Nelson was losing $5.4 million on revenues of $72 million. Debt ballooned, and the company was in real trouble.

While this was a disappointing experience for Thomas Nelson, other companies find that their existing resources allow them to develop target markets and products that they had previously overlooked. These new ventures can prove to be extremely profitable for a business if proper caution is used in making the decision to enter a new market.

Later, after selling Dodd, Mead and the new printing assets, Thomas Nelson began producing gifts and music tapes to be sold in the same bookstores with whom the company already had a solid relationship. This venture has been extremely successful and profitable for Thomas Nelson.

The environmental factors discussed in Chapter 3, political and legal, economic, competitive, social and technological, also impact on marketing opportunities, opening up some doors and closing others. The strategic window of opportunity is used to designate a limited period of time in which the resources of the firm match the needs/wants of a particular target market.

Market-Planning Tools

A variety of tools are available for strategic planning. While these tools differ in their usefulness, each illuminates a different aspect of the firm's position in the total market environment. These tools provide insight into how well the company is performing, as well as aiding executives in evaluating potential courses of action.

Strategic Business Unit

The strategic business unit (or SBU) represents a division, product line, or even an individual product within the company that can be isolated for assessment. That is, an SBU has its own identifiable costs, competitors, customers, and a unique strategy that sets it apart from other SBUs within the company. Typically, each SBU has its own management group, although a given individual – say, an accounting representative – may be involved in more than one SBU management group.

Some companies that only produce or market one product have little difficulty in determining the profitability and performance of that product. However, for larger companies with multiple products and product lines, being able to consider each SBU individually enables management to identify those that are profitable and those that are unprofitable, those that are growing and those that are declining in sales.

Procter & Gamble is an example of a company that is organised around its

SBUs. Brand managers head up the teams that are responsible for P&G's products and product lines.

Product Portfolio Analysis

Because all products do not perform alike and because all are not equally profitable, the Boston Consulting Group in the early 1970s developed a new approach to evaluating SBUs. (See Figure 19.1). The market growth rate, plotted on the vertical axis, shows annual growth. The percentage of the market that SBU controls, its market share, is plotted on the horizontal axis. Market share gives an indication of how the product is performing relative to competitors' offerings.

The matrix, which includes all the firm's products or SBUs, depicts four situations, and each requires a different marketing strategy.

Stars have high market share and high growth. These products are performing well in the marketplace but will also require continued support. Additional investment in promotion, new distribution channels, or modernised packaging could be necessary.

Cash cows show high market share with low market growth. These are typified by products in the mature stage of the product life-cycle. Since they are producing considerable cash flow, managers often take these profits to finance new product development or the growth of other SBUs with high-profit potential.

Question marks (sometimes called 'problem children') exhibit low market share but high market growth. These have the potential to be cash cows, since they are in a high-growth market. However, for some reason they are not living up to their potential. Generally, a major cash investment will be needed to salvage these: the big question is, which ones are worth the risk?

Dogs represent low market growth and low market share. These products are generally a drain on the firm. While some may generate enough cash flow to profitably retain them, the majority should probably be phased out.

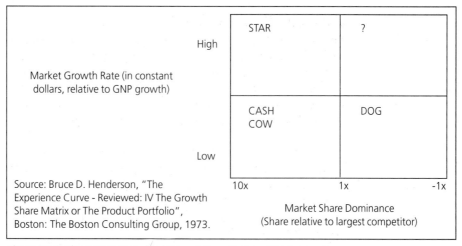

Figure 19.1 The Boston Consulting Group's Growth-Share Matrix

Profit Impact on Marketing Strategy (PIMS)

The Profit Impact on Marketing Strategy (PIMS) project is administered by the Strategic Planning Institute. Its purpose is to gather data from a variety of businesses representing more than 2,000 SBUs and approximately 600 companies in the attempt to determine what makes a business profitable. Information is collected on a number of topics, including budgeting, production processes, competitive positions, promotion and other strategic moves made by the firms in managing their SBUs.

According to PIMS findings, firms that offer high-quality products and demonstrate significant value added to the product are most profitable. Market share relative to the three top market leaders also appears to be an important factor. Vertical integration (ownership of other channel members) works to decrease a firm's costs and to increase profit, while companies in the midst of high growth industries may experience a lot of cash outflow. Not surprisingly, a cash drain results in decreased profitability, at least in the short-term.

Spreadsheet Analysis

Spreadsheet analysis answers 'what if' questions. Software programs, such as Lotus 1 2 3, VisiCalc, and Excel enable marketers to assess the impact of various decisions, given certain assumptions. For example, suppose Company ABC, a microchip manufacturer, plans to improve the quality of its product. Because an investment will be required to change engineering specifications and production processes, ABC's executives want to know what pricing level will ensure a return on investment (ROI) of ten per cent. To answer this question, we would have to have estimates of market demand, elasticity (customer sensitivity and responsiveness to price changes), costs of investment, and possible pricing points. Spreadsheets are designed to handle this kind of question.

However, for the analysis to be realistic, the assumptions must also be realistic. Faulty assumptions will lead to misleading and potentially disastrous conclusions.

Marketing Audit

A marketing audit is a systematic examination of all of the firm's marketing activities. These include objectives, target market identification and analysis, information systems and research, all marketing activities, the structure of the marketing department, and the performance of marketing investments and marketing personnel.

Just as a bank's auditors are very careful and thorough in their investigations, so should marketing auditors cover the entire spectrum of marketing decision-making and activities in great detail. Examples of questions that the auditors should answer are:

● How competent are marketing personnel in each position?
● How do we select and support members of our distribution channel?

- How closely do we evaluate the performance of our new pr/
- What mechanism do we have for obtaining customer feedt
- What do we do with that information?

You can probably think of many more questions that ne/
because the marketing audit is so extensive, it is alsc
Nevertheless, a regular, periodic marketing audit will enable a in
many of its mistakes before it is too late. The marketing audit will also encuc
marketing managers to look at new opportunities in the marketplace and to
improve current marketing mixes.

Sales Forecasting

Sales forecasting is an important tool in the planning process. Forecasts determine the size of the salesforce, production and inventory management, product
distribution, and many other aspects of the business. Accuracy is critical, since
an inaccurate forecast can get a company into a lot of financial trouble.

One way of forecasting is to use a *top-down approach*, in which an aggregate
estimate is subdivided into its individual components. These are then evaluated
for accuracy, and the final estimate may be adjusted accordingly. The opposite
approach to forecasting is a *build-up approach*. Here the analyst compiles sales
forecasts of individual components, such as customer types or sales regions, into
a composite figure that represents the total forecast.

Another way of looking at forecasting techniques is to divide them into quantitative and qualitative techniques.

Qualitative Methods

Qualitative methods include executive opinion, the Delphi Technique, salesforce
estimates and customer surveys. Each has advantages and disadvantages.

Executive opinion relies on the opinions of knowledgeable managers from
different departments within the company. This method is quick and easy.
However, estimates may be unduly optimistic or pessimistic, depending upon
how well-informed the executives are and how willing they are to voice their true
beliefs.

While executive opinion is used mostly for short-term forecasting, the Delphi
Technique is used for long-term, technological breakthrough forecasting.
Opinions are solicited from a panel composed of industry experts outside the
company. These may include outside researchers and commentators, as well as
executives. In an iterative process (that is, a series of rounds), whereby the results
of each round of opinions are subsequently reported to the panel, the experts
finally reach some degree of consensus. However, this process is complicated,
long and expensive.

Salesforce members may be excellent sources of information about future sales
because they are out in the field talking with customers directly. However, if
salespeople believe that their quotas will be based on their estimates, they are
likely to give very conservative estimates of future sales. Salespeople are also

prone to base their estimates on the very narrow experience that they have had with their own sales territories. Such estimates may not take into account broader trends.

Customer surveys work well for companies with only a few large customers. They can be prohibitively complicated if the firm has thousands or millions of customers. It can certainly be argued that customers themselves are the best judges of how much they plan to buy in the future; however, stated intentions often do not translate into actual behaviour. And sometimes customers just want to be agreeably optimistic. These surveys, too, work best for short-term estimations.

Quantitative Methods

Quantitative methods involve analysing customers' prior behaviour and purchasing patterns. In many cases, the services of a qualified statistician may be in order to ensure accuracy.

A market test, where the marketing mix has been fully developed and implemented, can represent a small scale model of what will happen in the whole market. Many companies use market tests to uncover unsuspected problems with a new product, to assess competitors' strengths against the new offering, or to get an estimate of future sales. Different test markets can also be used to test one version of the marketing mix against another, such as comparing radio advertising with newspaper advertising. These tests are most accurate in the short-term because of rapidly-changing market conditions. They are also subject to sabotage by competitors, who have a vested interest in corrupting the results.

Trend analysis relies on predicting future sales on the basis of past sales. This approach, of course, requires a fairly major assumption: that marketplace conditions will continue as they have been. For example, suppose the following represented past sales levels and yearly increases:

Year	Sales (£)	Increase
1988	1,000	0
1989	1,100	10
1990	1,320	20
1991	1,518	15
1992	1,897.50	25
1993		

What would you expect sales to be in 1993? What percentage increase would you expect? Average sales growth has been 17.5 per cent, so that is the increase that you would expect in 1993, all other things being equal. So our 1993 estimate would be £2,229.56, or last year's sales plus this year's forecasted increase. The 1993 forecast formula would be:

Last year's sales X Average sales growth

or

(£1,897.50 X 17.5%)

PLUS

Last year's sales

The calculations would look like this:

(£1,897.50)+(£1,897.50 X .175)= £2,229.56

The disadvantage of this method is that future sales may bear no relationship to past sales.

Exponential smoothing is similar to trend analysis except that this method recognises that more recent years' sales are more likely to reflect the current marketplace than much older sales data. Greater weight then is given to the most recent years; lesser weight is assigned to years farther in the past. For example. with the above data, weights might be assigned as follows:

Year	Weight
1988	.6
1989	.7
1990	.8
1991	.9
1992	1.0

Since the conditions present in 1992 are more likely to impact on sales in 1993 than are conditions that prevailed in 1988, 1992 data receives greater weight.

The Marketing Plan

Once a company has done its strategic planning, it is ready to begin putting together its marketing plan. Each marketing plan is designed to address a specific SBU with its own management team, product or product line, objectives, budget and target market. The marketing plans can be defined as dynamic blueprints for determining future actions in the marketplace.

A marketing plan is dynamic because the marketplace is constantly changing. Strategies that work today must be modified or discarded altogether tomorrow. Hence the need for flexibility and willingness to periodically review and change the plan in response to new developments.

The plan is a blueprint because it outlines marketing activities necessary to carry out the strategic plan. The marketing plan provides direction for managers that extends beyond immediate, day-to-day operations. The marketing plan is typically made up of several important sections, each of which will be addressed in order.

The Executive Summary

This section is for the busy executive who does not have time to read pages and pages of detail. The summary should be one page (or a maximum of two pages) long. It should inform the reader of the main objectives and recommendations contained in the plan.

Situation Analysis

The situation analysis describes the company's current market condition, including details on the target market(s) and competitive information. Market share, growth patterns and distribution channels should all be described.

A second component of the situation analysis is the discussion of the SBU's strengths, weaknesses, opportunities and threats. For example, Unilever with its Lever 2000 brand of soap, jumped ahead of Procter & Gamble to capture the lead in the US bar soap market. But Dial Corporation, not to be left behind, quickly began test-marketing Spirit to compete with Lever 2000. Some relevant details in this situation analysis are:

1 This is a $1 5 billion market.
2 Lever Bros. has about a 34 per cent market share, P&G has about 32.3 per cent and Dial Corp. has about 18 per cent.
3 Lever 2000 and Spirit are both positioned as a moisturising, deodorant and antibacterial cleansing soap, in effect as three-in-one bars.
4 Lever 2000's brand share of the total market averages about 8.5 per cent dollar share and 7 per cent unit share.
5 Spirit enjoys about a five per cent share in its markets.
6 Dial projects growth in the multi-benefit soap market from 10 to 20 per cent of the category within three years.

Such statements reflect the kind of necessary information and situation analysis that enable marketing decision-makers to conduct strategic planning.

Marketing Objectives

With a clear picture of the marketplace situation in mind, the management team is then in a position to choose objectives for their SBU. These objectives should be stated in concrete, specific terms and should be met within the time period covered by the plan. For example, Dial Corporation might choose an objective of achieving a national roll-out of Spirit within the next 12 months.

Strategy Selection

The situation analysis and process of setting objectives should bring the management team to the stage of setting up a strategy. Here the plan should clearly show who constitutes the target market, what form the product offering will take, which pricing policy will be in effect, and what promotion and distribution approaches will be used. For example, the plan for Spirit might include a media mix of magazines, coupons, samples and television commercials.

The plan should include quite a bit of detail so that it can be implemented by the managers in charge of various marketing areas. For example, if a field sales-force is in the plan, the size, deployment and compensation structure should be included as well as a plan for salesforce recruitment.

Budget

Here is where forecasting assists in the planning process. Forecasted sales, along with costs, enable a manager to construct a preliminary profit-and-loss statement. Thus the manager is able to evaluate different courses of action in the light of their impact on profitability.

For example, increasing the quality of a product may allow the firm to charge a higher price, but a higher price is likely to reduce the number of units that can be sold. How will increasing the quality affect revenues? How will the cost of more expensive materials plus the reduction in sales affect total revenue? How will these changes affect profits? What if Dial decides to support Spirit with a $5 million advertising budget? Will that increase sales profitably or cost more than Dial makes on Spirit?

SUMMARY

Marketing planning is critical to the successful management of the marketing function. The process of planning forces marketing decision-makers to carefully examine the marketplace, their firm's strengths and weaknesses, and the general environment. This detailed examination turns up mistakes, overlooked opportunities, better methods, and alternative strategies in the current marketing activities.

A number of tools are available to make the planning process more effective, but students should realise that these tools cannot take the place of informed and experienced judgement. The human factor is still, and always will be, essential to good marketing practice.

The marketing plan itself should be an outgrowth from planning. This plan is a detailed blueprint of the steps necessary to implement the marketing strategy. Generally, the marketing plan is a series of tactics that will result in a co-ordinated, effective marketing mix that serves the target market well.

FURTHER READING

Aaker, D.A. 1988. *Strategic Market Management*, 2nd ed. Wiley.
Abelli, Derek F. 1978. 'Strategic Windows.' *Journal of Marketing* (Jul.).
Anderson, Paul F. 1982. 'Marketing, Strategic Planning, and the Theory of the Firm.' *Journal*

of Marketing (Spring): 15-26.

Baker, M. J. 1992. *Marketing Strategy and Managment,* 2nd ed. MacMillan.

Boone, Louis and Kurtz, David L. 1992. *Contemporary Marketing*, 7th ed. Ft. Worth, Texas: Dryden Press, Chapter 4.

Chithelen, Ignatius. 1991. 'A Brush with the Devil.' *Forbes* (19 Aug.): 58-62.

Guiltinan, Joseph P. and Gordon W. Paul. 1988. *Marketing Management*, 3rd ed. New York: McGraw Hill Book Co., Chapter 15.

Haspeslagh, Philippe. 1982. 'Portfolio Planning: Uses and Limitations.' *Harvard Business Review* (Jan./Feb.): 58-73.

Hopkins, David S. 1981. *The Marketing Plan.* New York: The Conference Board.

Lyons, James. 1991. 'Border Merchants.' *Forbes* (19 Aug.): 56-57.

Norgan, S. 1994. *Marketing Management: A European Perspective*. Addison Wesley, Chapters 14 and 15.

Phillips, Lynn W., Doe R. Chang and Buzzell, Robert D. 1983. 'Product Quality, Cost Position, and Business Performance: A Test of Some Key Hypotheses.' *Journal of Marketing* (Spring): 33.3.

Pride, William M. and Ferrell, O. C. 1991. *Marketing,* 7th ed. Boston: Houghton Mifflin Co., Chapter 19.

Sloan, Pat and Bradley Johnson. 1991. 'P&G Slips on Soap.' *Advertising Age* (30 Sept.): 3, 45.

Smith, Wendell R. 1956. 'Product Differentiation and Market Segmentation as Alternative Marketing Strategies.' *Journal of Marketing* (Jul.): 3-8.

The PIMSLETTER on Business Strategy: Nine Basic Findings on Business Strategy. 1980. Cambridge, Mass.: Strategic Planning Institute: 3.

20 | Implementing and Controlling Marketing Programmes

The best strategy in the world cannot work unless it is implemented properly. Everyone in the organisation is ultimately involved in implementation. Quality products begin on the assembly line or in the plans drawn up by engineers. Prompt delivery to customers depends on inventory control and reliable transportation systems. Customer problems and special orders can only be resolved by effective customer service departments.

The point is simply that marketing implementation depends on co-ordinated efforts throughout the organisation. While executives may develop a brilliant strategy, if the average worker in the company senses no need for commitment to the plan, it will inevitably fail. And these failures will eventually be noticed by customers.

So part of marketing planning must include some way to co-ordinate 'marketing' activities with the demands placed by the organisation on other functional areas.

In Chapter 19, we discussed Dial Corporation's introduction of Spirit soap to compete in the $1.5 billion bar-soap market. Spirit, positioned as a three-in-one bar, has the jump on any new offering planned by Procter & Gamble, but P&G is a formidable competitor. Additionally, Lever 2000 already the market leader, has a big advantage.

Suppose that in the light of this situation analysis, Dial Corporation decides to spend $5 million on advertising Spirit. The finance and accounting department will have to 'okay' these expenditures. Production must be able to make and ship enough Spirit to satisfy increased demand. And distribution networks must already be set up so that products will be available to customers at the retail level.

Here is where tactics become so important to the marketing plan. Tactics, the day-to-day administration of the marketing plan, ensure that the company carries out the overall strategy as it was intended.

Planning Implementation

Like all of us, sometimes managers bite off more than they can chew or fail to fully realise the tasks required to successfully implement a plan. Network diagrams have been useful in helping managers keep track of deadlines and making sure that budgets are not exceeded. The basic premise of network diagrams is that some activities are independent and can be carried out at the same time as other activities. However, activities are dependent; they must be performed either before or after other activities. It is these interdependencies that often cause projects to fall behind when managers fail to allocate enough time for completion of all the steps involved.

Two widely known network diagram techniques, the critical path method (CPM) and the programme evaluation and review technique (PERT), have been used to assist managers in setting and meeting implementation schedules. Both depend on flowcharting and were originally developed by NASA to keep segments of the space programme on schedule.

With the help of computer software, it is now easier than ever to plot the various activities necessary for completing a project. Managers can total the time allotments for each step in each individual path/segment required for the entire project. The longest path is the 'critical' path, and this is the one that must be managed most carefully for the project to meet its deadlines. These techniques also allow planners to observe how completion of one phase of a project may be contingent upon completion of another, thus taking into account complicated interdependencies that they might otherwise overlook.

Barriers to Effective Implementation

Lack of co-ordination between functional areas within the organisation, as already mentioned, is a prime cause of failure to properly implement the marketing plan. Sometimes planners are out of touch with the rank and file workers and with customers. For example, we interviewed several salespeople for a major consumer-packaged goods manufacturer in the United States. They complained of a marketing department at company headquarters (located, halfway across the country, by the way) that constantly tried to foist unworkable promotions on the salespeople and their grocery manager customers. As one salesperson commented, 'They get those MBAs in there who have never been in the field and never talked to a grocery manager. Then they come up with these stupid ideas and expect me to convince my customers (grocery managers) to go along. No way!'

Natural resistance to change or the 'not invented here' syndrome causes some employees to upset the plan. These individuals may not understand why a procedure is being implemented; in other cases, some employees may be alienated from the organisation and wish to see the plan fail. Broadly speaking, such an attitude may reflect a lack of effective internal marketing with the company's own employees, or it may reflect the fact that the company's top management is out of touch with the realities of the marketplace.

Sometimes strategies fail because planners neglect to develop specific implementation procedures. Broad-stroke strategies have to be linked to specific instructions on how to carry out the strategies. For example, timetables, budgets, media plans and distribution contracts and schedules enable employees to determine their roles and responsibilities in implementation.

The Role of Company Structure

Whether a company is centralised or decentralised, formal or informal, will affect its ability to implement its marketing plans.

A centralised firm has all of its important decision-making under the control of a small group of executives at the top of the organisation, usually located at a central headquarters. Little autonomy is allowed at lower levels or at diverse locations of the organisation. Centralised companies tend to have common strategies and policies across divisions and locations within the organisation to present a unified front and a standardised approach to employees and customers alike.

A decentralised company is just the opposite: decision-making is in the hands of lower-level managers. In fact, the goal of the company is to have decision-making at the level of impact rather than at a level that is far removed from the consequences.

Large firms in stable industries can function well with a centralised organisational structure, but innovative companies in quickly changing markets must be able to react quickly. Such a situation calls for a decentralised organisational structure, and these companies are more likely to be able to respond to changes in the marketplace in the short-term. One could also argue effectively that information flows more freely in a decentralised organisation.

Another difference between companies pertains to the company culture's relative levels of formality or informality. Formality is appropriate and expected in some industries, for example, the banking industry. Formality denotes stability and solidarity, two attributes that are desirable when it comes to customers' finances.

Yet in some industries, one may find a mix of formal and informal companies. The advertising industry has successful agencies that are quite formal, but there are also some very successful agencies whose employees wear sweatshirts and jeans to work. Not surprisingly, centralised companies tend to have a formal culture, and decentralised companies tend to have an informal culture. One might speculate that the determining factor is the extent to which top management feels a need to control its employees' thinking and behaviour. Another factor is how much confidence top management has in middle-management decisions.

The Structure of the Marketing Function

Over the years, it has become apparent to businesses all over the world that the pivotal function of a business is to market its products. In a marketing-oriented business, as we discussed in Chapter 1, the focus is to discover what buyers want, then to produce and market those products. Consequently, in such a company, marketing will occupy a prominent position in the organisation. The vice president of marketing should be on the same level as the vice president of finance, the vice president of production and so on. (See Figure 20.1).

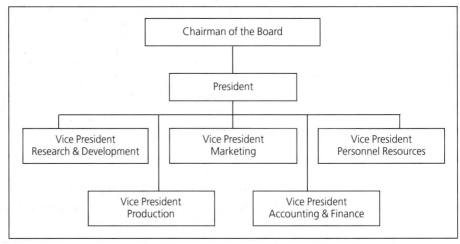

Figure 20.1 Marketing in a Prominent Position in a Typical Organisational Structure

However, the effectiveness of marketing depends not only on its place within the organisation but also on how the marketing function is organised internally. Marketing departments can be organised according to functions, products, regions or types of customers. (See Figures 20.2a-d.)

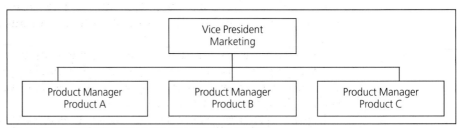

Figure 20.2a Marketing Department Organised by Product

Figure 20.2b Marketing Department Organised by Region

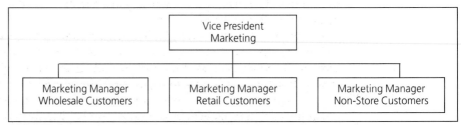

Figure 20.2c Marketing Department Organised by Customer

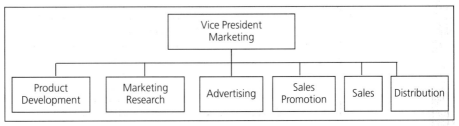

Figure 20.2d Marketing Department Organised by Function

There are no cut-and-dried rules for which of these approaches works best; that depends strictly on the circumstances of each company. Organising by products or by SBUs gives a company the ability to develop unique marketing mixes for products that require very diverse approaches. Procter & Gamble has epitomised the brand management system for many years, and other packaged-goods manufacturers follow its lead. A team is assigned to each product/SBU with representatives for the various marketing areas: packaging, distribution, research, product design, advertising, etc.

Organising geographically or by region is similar in many respects to organising by product. That is, each region or geographic division is assigned its own team of marketing personnel. Sometimes these efforts are co-ordinated by a team at headquarters, but often the needs of customers in different locations vary widely.

Sometimes the marketing function is organised by types of customers. For example, Parker Pen Company has a retail division and a division that markets to promotional agencies. These two types of customers have very different product needs, pricing needs and distribution needs.

Organising by function can be seen in a department that is divided into market research, advertising, product development, distribution and sales promotion. Obviously this approach represents a centralised company that does not want duplicated functions in different divisions or in different regional areas.

Controlling the Marketing Programme

Managers need to plan a control system that will be used to monitor progress and to notify managers of the need to make an adjustment in the marketing plan. Managers should institute a reporting system that minimises unnecessary paperwork or duplicated effort, but which gives them the data they need to make intelligent marketing decisions.

Too often, companies provide their managers with stacks of meaningless data and deprive them of the very information that they must have. Managers should think about what decisions they are called on to make and, specifically, what information they need to make sound marketing decisions.

For example, managers need to know which products are selling and how much they are selling. Which customers are buying? Everyone? Or is the 80/20 rule in evidence, where only 20 per cent of customers account for 80 per cent of sales? Or, perhaps, 20 per cent of products are accounting for 80 per cent of sales. Such conditions are overwhelming evidence that some changes must be made in the marketing mix or the product mix. But only the right kinds of information can answer the critical questions concerning where changes should be made and, equally important, what to change to.

Evaluating Performance

Marketing managers must be able to communicate with those employees below them in the chain of command who are implementing the marketing programme. Managers must also communicate with top management to ensure that marketing strategies and tactics are in keeping with the firm's overall objectives.

In addition to these, lines of communication must be established across functional areas, since marketing activities must be integrated into the plans of other departments, such as personnel, finance and production.

For these reasons, a sound marketing information system, such as was discussed in Chapter 7, is critical to the smooth working of the marketing functional area. Marketers need such a system to inform them about sales analyses, market-share data, customer satisfaction and ordering patterns, employee performance, and many other kinds of data. By co-ordinating marketing's information needs with other departments, marketing should be able to obtain vital information to keep the company's marketing strategy on track.

Such data will also enable marketers to keep track of the performance of salespeople, advertising agencies, middle-men, research, and a variety of others on whom marketing depends. Actual performance is compared with the marketing goals that have been set and the performance standards that have been established for individuals, departments or agencies. If a discrepancy is noted, corrective action can then take place. Sometimes standards have to be lowered because they were set unrealistically high. At other times, a given salesperson or product may not be living up to reasonable expectations. And on other occasions, discrepancies between desired and actual performance may simply be the result of uncontrollable factors in the environment that no one could have anticipated.

While numerous control methods exist, we will discuss specific methods of sales analysis and methods of cost analysis, giving the advantages and disadvantages of each.

Sales Analysis

Sales is probably the most frequently used measurement of performance. Sales data are important to a company because sales reflect the success or failure of the marketing mix. Sales can be expressed as pound (or some other currency) volume, unit sales or market share. Each of these can be useful, but only when measured against other data that provide a frame of reference.

For example, suppose you sell £1.5 million worth of widgets this year. Is that good? Is it disappointing? The answer depends, for example, on what you sold last year. If you sold £2.5 million last year, you lost 40 per cent of widget revenue, and you are probably in trouble; but if you sold £750,000 last year, you have doubled your sales. Now you are overjoyed!

Consider the impact of looking at unit sales. Suppose you sold 750,000 widgets at £1.00 each last year. But this year your cost of materials doubled, so you had to sell your widgets at £2.00 each. Now that £1.5 million doesn't look so impressive. You doubled your revenues, but you sold the same number of units as last year.

Now let's look at market share. Suppose that last year your £750,000 in sales represented a ten per cent share of the total widget market. This year sales of widgets industry-wide were up by 20 per cent. That means that your 750,000 widgets this year only represent 8.3 per cent of the market instead of last year's ten per cent. Now you are no longer breaking even; it is evident that your position in the industry is slipping. You need to take some sort of corrective action before the situation worsens.

Cost Analysis

Sales is certainly an important measurement of marketing success, but there is also another side to this coin: marketing costs. Although marketers understandably focus on increasing sales, the final profitability of the firm is dependent as much on controlling costs as it is on making sales. Marketers have often been accused of wanting to make a sale regardless of the cost, and there is probably some justification for this charge. Nevertheless, astute, professional marketers today understand the need for analysing strategies and tactics in the light of the bottom line rather than just in terms of gaining more sales revenue.

For example, in advertising people's briefs one company relied on the attention-getting power and the reference group influence of a celebrity sports star to advertise its product. Another company produced a similar magazine advertisement using unknown male models that suggested youth and fitness. The first company obviously paid a lot more money for the celebrity endorser. Was it worth the extra cost? Only if the net increase in sales resulted in profits that were higher than if the company had used an unknown model. In other words, to use the celebrity profitably, sales would have had to rise enough to pay for the celebrity endorser plus all of the other costs normally associated with marketing the product.

Reward Systems

There is a saying, 'Tell me how I will be rewarded and I'll tell you how I will behave'. Reward systems can work for or against successfully implementing and controlling a marketing programme. If salespeople make a larger commission on Product A than on Product B, which one will they try harder to sell? If a marketing manager is rewarded on short-term sales rather than on long-term brand-image building, is she more likely to choose sales promotion or mass media advertising to promote the product?

While numerous writers today deplore the short-term thinking of American business, executives continue to devise reward systems that encourage employees to focus on short-term goals because that is how they are rewarded.

One company was concerned about why sales were slipping consistently in a growing market. When the president of the company was challenged in a seminar to examine the root cause of the drop in sales, he found that he was the root cause. That is, he was rewarding the vice president of sales for staying within his prescribed budget. Therefore the VP had instituted a hiring freeze, resulting in sales territories that were vacant or too large to be covered by one salesperson. Customers were not being serviced adequately and were taking their business elsewhere. No wonder sales were dropping!

SUMMARY

In this chapter, we have looked at the different processes of implementing and controlling the marketing plan. We saw that managers need an implementation plan that consists of short-term tactics that will be carried out on a day-to-day basis. We looked at the role of company structure, whether it is centralised or decentralised, formal or informal, in determining the approach to implementation.

Finally, we saw how marketers should organise the marketing function internally to facilitate the working of the marketing plan. The unit may be organised around customers, geographic regions, products, or even a combination of these variables.

Controlling the marketing programme means that management must monitor performance, evaluate it, and take steps to improve it where there is a discrepancy between goals and actual outcomes. Monitoring sales and costs are two areas that are most important in evaluating a marketing programme's success. To bring employees' behaviour in line with the objectives of the company, a reward system must be designed and implemented that makes it in the best interest of employees to meet the expectations of marketing decision-makers.

FURTHER READING

Alexander, L. D. 1985. 'Successfully Implementing Strategic Decisions.' *Long Range Planning* (Jun.): 92.

Assael, Henry. 1985. *Marketing Management*. Boston: Kent Publishing Co., Chapter 20.

Jaworski, Bernard. 1988. 'Toward a Theory of Marketing Control: Environmental Context, Control Types, and Consequences.' *Journal of Marketing* (Jul.): 23-39.

Lamb, Jr., Charles W., Hair, Jr., Joseph F. and McDaniel, Carl. 1992. *Principles of Marketing*. Cincinnati: South-Western Publishing Co., Chapter 19.

Lorange, Peter and Murphy, Declan. 1984. 'Considerations in Implementing Control.' *Journal of Business Strategy* (Spring): 27-35.

'P&G Rewrites the Marketing Rules.' 1989. *Fortune* (6 Nov.): 34-48.

Pride, William M. and Ferrell, O. C. 1991. *Marketing Concepts and Strategies*, 7th ed. Boston: Houghton Mifflin Co., Chapter 20.

Zeithaml, Valarie, Berry, Leonard and Parasuraman, A. 1988. 'Communication and Control Processes in the Delivery of Service Quality.' *Journal of Marketing* (Apr.): 35-48.

21 International Marketing

Marketing in a foreign country has all the complexities of marketing in the domestic market, and more. In addition to the obvious barriers of language and foreign culture, there are economic, political and environmental differences with which to deal.

Nevertheless, US companies are increasingly finding ways to open up new marketing opportunities for themselves internationally. While only a small percentage of domestic companies have international divisions or other interests, the trend is certainly in that direction.

To some extent, international expansion is a defensive posture for US businesses. In the past few years, we have seen the invasion of many powerful foreign competitors into the US domestic market. Toyota, Panasonic, Nestlé, BMW, Sony and Volvo have become household names. If US companies wish to remain viable, they too must seek out new markets for their expertise. And some have. In other countries, US companies such as Dow Chemical, Coca-Cola, Ford Motor Company and McDonald's have huge markets.

In this chapter we will look at various avenues available for firms to become involved in international marketing. We will examine the strategies used by multinational corporations to establish an international presence, and we will investigate how they research these foreign markets to develop strategic marketing plans. We will take a look at some of the major trade areas by regional grouping, and, finally, we will briefly touch on some of the most dominant problems in embarking into international markets.

Levels of International Involvement

Not all companies maintain the same level of involvement in international marketing. Some want to proceed cautiously and conservatively; other companies are comfortable with fully-fledged commitment. It is often the case, however, that a company begins with a low level of involvement and gradually works up to direct investment in a foreign country as its experience broadens and the relationships with foreign nationals grow.

Exporting

The easiest and safest way to enter a foreign market is through some form of exporting. Exporting allows a company to continue doing business in its customary manner. All products are still produced domestically, and the company has little or no investment abroad. In some instances, however, a company may get into exporting involuntarily. For instance, a foreign customer may place an unsolicited order.

Exporting can be indirect, that is, the company has an arrangement to supply products overseas through international middle-men. These 'experts' in cutting through foreign regulations know how to sell products in markets that may be unfamiliar to domestic producers. Often a company uses this outlet for disposing of excessive inventory or obsolete products, but the firm's marketing mix remains basically unaltered.

Direct exporting means that the company is now handling its own sales or an overseas sales branch. The company is now able to maintain more control over its foreign markets. This approach involves more risk and investment; however, it eliminates loss of revenue that goes to middle-men when using indirect exporting.

Joint Ventures

Joint venturing, as the name implies, is an arrangement in which the domestic firm has entered into an agreement with a foreign firm for their mutual benefit.

Licensing is a fairly low-risk method for entering into a joint venture. Licensing means that the domestic company sells a foreign firm the rights for a fee or royalty. The licensee takes most of the risk, but the licensor gives up quite a bit of control over quality. Another problem for the licensor is that if the licensee is very successful, the licensor has given up most of the profits.

Sears used the method of *contract manufacturing* as a means of opening up stores in Mexico and Spain. Sears simply contracted with local producers to manufacture many of the products that would be sold in the stores. This approach may be very desirable where labour problems exist or where government officials must be bribed to ensure co-operation.

A similar situation might call for *management contracting*, an approach in which the domestic firm supplies the management expertise to a foreign company that puts up the capital. In effect, the domestic firm is selling its managerial know-how rather than a tangible product or component. As with the other methods, the biggest disadvantage with management contracting is that the domestic company may lose profits that it could be making for itself in a foreign market. Sometimes, though, the many cultural and political factors in a foreign country make ownership prohibitive.

Joint Ownership

Joint ownership ventures occur when a domestic firm enters into a full partnership with a foreign company. In this case, the two organisations share ownership and control of the business. Often a domestic company must enter into this type of arrangement because many countries prohibit foreign ownership of businesses and/or limit how much capital can be removed to another country. In these situations, cultural differences can be significant factors in whether the two organisations can get along together.

For example, many American companies operate strictly according to specified schedules and timetables; many Latin American companies prefer to conduct business in a more leisurely manner. And while personal relationships are absolutely crucial to Latin American businesspeople, Americans are often content to make the 'best deal' regardless of personal feelings.

Wholly-Owned Subsidiaries

A wholly-owned subsidiary is one where the domestic firm completely owns and operates the foreign entity, usually manufacturing or assembly facilities. This situation can work well if the foreign country is politically stable and offers a very profitable opportunity. The domestic company can also benefit from increased flexibility. For example, products that are labour-intensive to produce can be moved to a manufacturing facility where labour costs are low compared with domestic wage scales.

The risk, of course, lies in the possibility of devalued currencies, political or social unrest, or nationalising of foreign investment by the host country. In many cases, however, the potential profits outweigh the risks.

Multinational Corporations

We have seen that exporting is the lowest level of involvement in international business. Joint ventures represent more involvement, and the wholly-owned subsidiary represents even more investment and risk-assumption in the international arena. However, the multinational corporation is the most extensive form of international involvement that a company can make. A multinational corporation is a company that does business in other countries besides its 'home' country.

Multinationals own their assets in foreign countries, they operate out of more than one foreign country (hence the prefix 'multi'), and they take a global approach to doing business. No longer do these companies see themselves as 'American' or 'British'. They view themselves as truly operating in a worldwide marketplace.

Many of these companies are US-based. Some of the largest include General Motors, IBM, Exxon, Ford and Mobil Corporation. Others are based in Europe and Japan, such as Royal Dutch Shell, Nestlé, Unilever, Foreign Sony and Panasonic. These companies look at the rich US market, and they devote considerable resources to establishing a successful marketing base in the United States.

International Marketing Strategy

Successful multinational firms approach marketing in just the same way as a successful domestic firm approaches marketing. They look for unsatisfied needs that dovetail with the firm's resources and expertise and find a way to fulfil those needs profitably and within the firm's overall objectives.

In this section we will look at intelligence-gathering and ways to approach international marketing strategy. These include whether to use a global or a multinational strategy and standardised or differentiated marketing mixes. We will also examine ways in which firms can vary the four elements of the marketing mix – product, price, promotion and distribution – to achieve differentiation.

International Marketing Information

As with all domestic marketing, the international strategy must begin with marketing intelligence, good information on which to base the strategic decisions that must be made.

The place to begin is with secondary data. Sources of information include government publications (the Department of Trade and Industry in the UK has many country-specific reports), international organisations such as the United Nations or OECD and foreign governments themselves. Your own embassy based in the foreign country can often provide a good starting-point, as can international trade organisations. Primary data collection, as discussed in Chapter 7, would be the obvious next step. Here again, language difference, privacy customs, literacy rates and willingness to co-operate in the data-gathering stage will not always be easy obstacles to overcome. In fact, you can count on considerably more difficulty in the international arena than you would find in the domestic arena.

Since the main thrust of primary research is to uncover customer behaviour patterns that differ from domestic patterns, it makes a lot of sense to use as an informant a well-educated national from the country in which you are interested. Often such an individual, or panel of individuals, can save you time, money and embarrassment by explaining local customs, helping you cut through government red tape, and translating for you.

Assessing Foreign Environments

Just as we examined the uncontrollable factors in marketing in the home market, so we should be cognisant of the uncontrollable factors that operate in international markets.

Economics

Economic conditions dictate that the product must not only fit the needs of the market but that it must be sold where there are sufficient levels of income to support sales of the product.

Developed countries, such as the United States, Canada, Great Britain, Japan and most of the nations of Western Europe, have mixed economies. Private enterprise exists alongside a public sector. In developing countries, the economic base is moving from an agricultural to an industrial economy. Some countries have already made the transition, such as Australia, Israel and Venezuela. Others are still in the process, such as Pakistan, Sri Lanka and India.

International marketers must also look at income distribution. If the majority of a country's disposable income is held in the hands of relatively few individuals, such as in Kuwait, the number of possible customers is too small to warrant entry into the market.

Political and Legal Posture

The important consideration here is how long present conditions will continue. That is, entry into a new country may look attractive today, but what are the indications that today's political stability will endure?

Billions of dollars were lost in the Middle East by oil-drilling companies because of bombings throughout the eight years of the Iran-Iraq war. Holiday Inn took severe losses in Lebanon during the 1978–1981 war.

Even friendly countries can change marketing conditions by imposing quotas (limits on how much of a product is allowed to enter the country) and duties (special taxes on imports). However, the worst-case scenario for a foreign company is expropriation, or when a company is taken over by the host country.

Different countries have differing attitudes concerning foreign involvement in their economies. For example, until recently, doing business in India involved such massive regulation, tariffs and red tape that many companies refused to even attempt to tap into this marketplace. Even Coca Cola eventually decided to dissolve its interests, although it is now looking at India with renewed optimism.

Culture

The most obvious adaptation that marketers must make to successfully enter a foreign market is to learn the language, yet many companies have failed to do just that. However literal, translations are insufficient to address the differences between peoples. Understanding the culture and the context in which words and images appear is just as important as the words. Such cultural knowledge must accompany strategic and tactical planning.

For example, consider the following: when Hertz used its American slogan 'Let Hertz put you in the driver's seat' in Germany, the meaning conveyed was, 'Let Hertz make you a chauffeur.' Not an attractive concept to a country that is still very class-conscious.

The 3M Company confused the Japanese by claiming that Scotch Brand Cellophane Tape 'sticks like crazy'. To the Japanese this meant that it sticks foolishly.

Other examples abound concerning differences in customs. Arabs consider their left hands dirty and offensive; they never eat with their left hands. In Japan, white is the colour signifying death and mourning – not weddings, cleanliness and purity as it does in the Western world. And in Italy a favourite snack is a chocolate bar between two slices of bread.

Marketing Mix Strategies

There are, however, two broad alternative approaches to developing an international marketing strategy. A global marketing strategy sees the world as one large and basically homogeneous marketplace. Modifications in existing marketing mixes would be minimal and, obviously, the investment would be much less than if the firm were customising marketing strategies for individual countries and/or cultures.

The global strategy works best for products that have universal appeal for certain types of market segments. For example, McDonald's restaurants have a fairly standardised marketing strategy, regardless of the country in which they are doing business. Granted, there are some modifications, such as changes in menu items and pricing, to account for transnational differences, yet the basic marketing strategy remains constant.

Benetton is another example of global marketing. This company markets sportswear to the young, avant-garde segments of society in Westernised countries. Other than changing the language used in their advertising, Benetton uses very little differentiation across countries.

By contrast, multinational marketing strategies are practised by most companies that operate in more than one country. Not surprisingly, different cultures usually require changes in the marketing mix, with customised approaches for each. Sometimes these customised approaches mean far more than just adapting your own way of doing things.

For example, Imperial Margarine's crown symbol would not work well in Germany because German people have a tradition of being anti-monarchical. Thus considerably more adjustment would have to take place in the marketing mix than merely translating Imperial advertisements into German.

Standardised Versus Customised Marketing Mixes

In general, there are two ways to approach marketing in the international arena. One way is the standardised approach, in which all aspects of the marketing mix remain essentially the same. This approach is workable when there is good reason to believe that the product is viewed and used in the same way across cultures. An obvious example of such a product is Coca-Cola, for which the product and promotion strategies tend not to vary measurably worldwide. The standardised approach to the marketing mix goes hand-in-hand with a global marketing strategy.

The second approach involves some type of customisation of the marketing mix. Sometimes the product must be adjusted or even dramatically changed; under other conditions, the promotional message or the media used must be altered. And, of course, sometimes nearly all aspects of the marketing mix require adjustment.

SUMMARY

International marketing means venturing into uncharted waters for many businesspeople and, thus, incurring risk. Many products fail in the domestic market; how much more likely it is that marketers will make serious mistakes in the international marketplace!

To assess the risk and the potential for success in international markets requires attention to the same kinds of variables that we would look at in developing a domestic marketing effort.

Marketing intelligence and research are critical domestically: they are even more important internationally. Because of unique beliefs, religious practices, language, cultural patterns, holidays, values, etc, the number of variables increases. Knowledge that we take for granted here in the domestic market must be acquired in order to understand a foreign culture.

Even more unsettling is the fact that, for the most part, data are much more scarce in foreign markets than in the Western World.

Companies can adopt a global strategy in which the marketing mix remains virtually unchanged from one country to another. A second option is to adopt a multinational strategy in which marketing strategies and tactics are tailored to very specific markets in which the firm will be operating.

Tailoring a marketing mix to a specific country can involve changing the product, the promotion, or even all aspects of the marketing mix. No matter which route a company chooses, the need for careful planning in the international area is imperative.

FURTHER READING

Boone, Louis E. and Kurtz, David L. 1992. *Contemporary Marketing*, 7th ed. Ft. Worth, Texas: Dryden Press, Chapter 3.

Calof, Jonathan L. and Lane, Henry W. 1987. 'So You Want to Do Business Overseas?' *Business Quarterly* (Winter): 52-57.

Cundiff, Edward and Mary Tharp Higler. 1988. *Marketing in the International Environment*, 2nd ed. Englewood Cliffs, New Jersey: Prentice Hall.

Faltermayer, Edmund. 1990. 'Is Made in the U.S.A. Fading Away?' *Fortune* (24 Sept.) 62-73.

Hager, Bruce. 1990. 'Can Colgate Import Its Success from Overseas?' *Business Week* (7 May.): 114-116.

Kotler, Philip. 1991. *Marketing Management*, 7th ed. Englewood Cliffs, New Jersey: Prentice Hall, Chapter 15.

Lamb, Jr., Charles W., Hair, Jr., Joseph F. and McDaniel, Carl. 1992. *Principles of Marketing*. Cincinnati: South-Western Publishing Co., Chapter 22.

Levitt, Theodore. 1993. 'The Globalization of Markets.' *Harvard Business Review* (May/Jun.): 92–102.

Terpstra, V. *The Cultural Environment of International Business*. South-Western, 1978.

Snyder, Adam. 1990. 'Global Marketing: We Are the World.' *Superbands 1990: A Special Supplement to Adweek* (Aug.): 59–68.

Young, S., Hamill, J., Wheeler, C. and Davies, J.R. 1989. *International Market Entry and Development*. Harvester Wheatsheaf.

22 Services and Non-Profit Marketing

The growth of services around the world has been phenomenal in the past 20 years. In many ways marketing services – both for profit and non-profit services – is exactly like marketing tangible products. However, there are also some differences and some special considerations.

In this chapter, we will first focus on marketing for-profit services, citing the unique characteristics of services and the opportunities that services present to marketers. Next, we will examine the growing importance of using marketing in the non-profit sector, and how effective strategies can be built by non-profit organisations.

Characteristics of Services

Products are a combination of tangible and intangible features. For example, a package of your favourite biscuits is almost entirely represented by the good itself. On the other hand, although your education is almost entirely a service, it does have some goods associated with it, such as your degree.

Many products are a combination of goods and services. For example, an airline ticket not only includes transportation from one place to another, it also includes a meal served to passengers while they are on the plane.

In the following sections, we will look at some products that are mostly services and some characteristics that are unique to services.

Intangibility

The first of these is intangibility. An intangible product is one that cannot be seen, touched, tasted, smelled or possessed. It is the intangible nature of services that often makes it difficult for customers to understand exactly what the service represents.

With services, then, buyers look for indicators of service quality and attributes. For example, a clean business location may suggest that the service company is conscientious and takes pride in the way it is presented to its customers. Uncluttered, straightforward advertising implies honesty and truthfulness.

Inseparability

The second characteristic is inseparability, which means that services are produced and consumed at the same time. Dental work cannot be examined before it is performed; a dance lesson cannot be tried out before purchasing. And since the service provider and the consumer are usually both involved in the production of the service, it is impossible to know the exact outcome until the service has been performed. For example, it is difficult to predict how a new hair-style will look.

Of course, another aspect of inseparability is that consumers may have a very strong interest in who performs the service. A heart operation done by a cardio-vascular resident has less value than one done by a well-known cardiovascular surgeon. In fact, preferences may even dictate the value of a service to the customer.

Perishability

The next characteristic of services is perishability, which means simply that services do not have a shelf life. They cannot be stored for consumption at some later time. It is impossible to inventory services. And this time-dependency of services is a great weakness in the process of marketing.

Your psychiatrist may charge you for a missed appointment if you do not notify her far enough in advance, because she loses income when she is not seeing patients. Therefore, she must have adequate notice in order to schedule someone else in your time slot.

For the same reason, airlines overbook flights. Unfilled seats cannot be stored and pulled out later to compensate for a flight that is not filled to capacity. Overbooking results from the fact that many passengers book a flight and then do not arrive for it. The airline is merely trying to ensure maximum revenue for each flight that takes off.

Some companies use strategies that equalise the supply and demand for their services. Airlines schedule more flights during peak travel periods. They are addressing a shortage by increasing the supply of services.

Other strategies for addressing either lack of supply or too little demand include running a sale, hiring part-time help, or offering a variety of pricing levels.

Variability

The final characteristic is variability. Since people perform services, the outcomes may be different from one customer to another. Consistency may be difficult to achieve, which can lead to customer dissatisfaction.

Attempts to standardise services are met with varying degrees of success. Restaurant chains try to standardise menus and personnel training, along with decor and atmosphere, to ensure that patrons at multiple locations will receive essentially the same products.

On the other hand, some companies tout customisation as a benefit to the consumer. Financial services, for example, are a product that requires recommendations and investments to meet the customer's specific income, family and stage of life.

Classifying Services

Services can be targeted towards consumer markets, business markets, or both. For example, car washes can be used by consumers for family cars or by companies for their fleets. As shown in Figure 22.1, these services can be performed primarily by people or by equipment. Repairs, barber shops and day-care centres rely on people; dry cleaning, health clubs and tanning salons rely on equipment to perform the services.

Another way to classify services is according to the degree of skill required to perform the service. Among services done primarily by people, professional

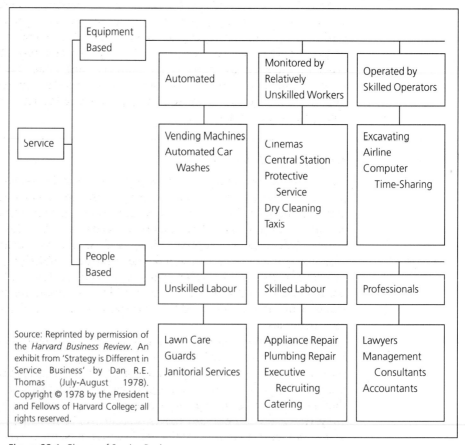

Figure 22.1 Classes of Service Business

services, such as legal counsel, accounting and management consulting, depend on high levels of skill. These individuals are also more highly regulated than others, because they perform complex tasks for customers.

Services that reflect high levels of performance from equipment include such businesses as airlines, computer maintenance, and excavating. In contrast, cinemas, dry-cleaning services and taxis involve less risk for the customer and, commensurately, call for lower levels of skill from those who provide the services.

Marketing Strategies for Services

The marketing concepts that we have covered so far in this book are equally applicable to services and goods. The marketing concept encourages businesses to find unmet customer needs and to develop and maintain a satisfying marketing mix for viable customer targets.

Nevertheless, it has been typical for many service businesses to lag behind goods marketers in the implementation of the marketing concept. Many service businesses are represented by small operations that do not have the time, money, or, perhaps, the expertise to embark on a sophisticated marketing programme. In other cases, such as professional services, marketing has traditionally been frowned upon. The medical profession, banking and accounting are three groups that have been slow to adopt marketing practices, although the situation has been changing over the last decade.

Differentiation

Like some goods, some services are perceived to be essentially alike. Such a perception on the part of customers reduces the firm's marketing tactics to simple price competition. Yet astute service marketers realise that true functional differentiation and/or image differentiation is the best way to build a loyal clientele.

One differentiation approach is to add innovative features to the product offering. American Airlines led the way in establishing its frequent-flyer programme to provide added value to its best customers, business travellers. Some colleges and universities have tried to compete for limited numbers of students by offering weekend MBA programmes and special on-site programmes for businesses.

Another good example of innovation is the introduction by the University of Strathclyde of an MSc in International marketing, so creating a differential advantage in the short term. This option had not been available in Scotland prior to this introduction. Many other institutions nation-wide followed this lead by introducing this 'dedicated' type of degree. Innovation in the service sector is easy to copy. However, the company that is first can establish a reputation for innovation and customer responsiveness that will keep its customers coming back.

Another strategy is to establish compelling brand images for services through symbols and branding. British Airways with its 'Fly the Flag' and 'The World's

Favourite Airline' slogans, attempts to differentiate itself in the minds of consumers in the area of customer service. This campaign has been very successful and the majority of travellers perceive this airline as a good quality and reliable service company.

Quality

Service quality is more difficult to define and monitor than goods quality. For example, it is more difficult to predict and assess customer satisfaction with a tennis lesson than with a tennis racquet. Yet the most powerful competitive weapon in the hands of service companies is to consistently deliver higher quality than their competitors.

To determine exactly what the level of quality should be, a service company must first establish a baseline measurement. That baseline should be the minimum acceptable quality as perceived by the customer. Although no company can satisfy every single customer on every dimension, it is equally true that unless most customers' expectations are met, the firm cannot survive. Therefore, the first stage in setting standards of quality is to determine the average customer's expectations.

The best companies, then, set goals to exceed expectations. Such companies have a long-standing commitment to quality; they want to be known as 'the best' rather than simply adequate. Top management is typically involved in setting high standards of performance, and an effective monitoring system is in place to warn executives if the company is going astray.

Monitoring can be accomplished in a variety of ways. Customer satisfaction surveys, 'mystery shoppers' and customer complaints are just a few examples of how management can obtain perfomance feedback.

Finally, the best service companies are committed to their employees as well as to their customers. In marketing services, even more than in marketing goods, the employee who comes in contact with the customer *is* the company to that customer. Consequently, service companies want their employees to feel good about the company; such job satisfaction will be reflected in the way employees treat customers. Companies use rewards, good remuneration packages, and an environment of employee support to achieve the best representation in the marketplace.

Productivity

Since businesses are constantly facing rising costs, they are also constantly challenged to increase productivity. Otherwise, profits fall. There are several ways to increase productivity. One is simply to hire more people to perform the service. However, this decision should be dependent on whether increased revenue will also cover the increased costs of new employees and still allow the company to make a profit.

Another option is to screen applicants more carefully and hire only very skilled workers, those who can turn out more production and still maintain the quality of the product.

An additional option is to purchase new technology that assists employees in raising individuals' productivity. Here again, since new technology represents additional costs, good forecasting will be necessary to assess whether these acquisitions will be a profitable investment for the business.

Some services can become more productive simply by targeting customers who spend more on the services. Many US ski resorts are currently targeting the European and Japanese markets because foreign visitors take longer holidays and spend more than domestic skiers. The Europeans average about $200 to $250 a day, compared with $150 for Americans; the Japanese average at least $400 a day.

Marketers should bear in mind that too much productivity can result in a loss of quality. Large volume often allows mistakes to go unnoticed; hence the need for ongoing quality control.

Another pitfall can be the loss of customisation. As a firm's volume increases, standardisation becomes much easier to control than customisation. Standardised services are also usually faster to produce. In such cases, the loss of customised service can mean the loss of competitive advantage, and this is an important aspect to consider. Remember, large size and more sales do not necessarily equate with more profit.

Marketing Mix Variables

As with goods marketing, the marketing of services requires the identification and analysis of the target market. The market may be analysed on any of several dimensions: demographics, lifestyle, product usage patterns, or benefits sought. Each element of the marketing mix should then be developed with a view to maximising customer satisfaction with the offering and being able to maintain that offering at a profit.

Product

As we have already mentioned, consumers can evaluate goods based on their tangible attributes and their functional qualities. Nevertheless, it is not as easy to evaluate services. One way to overcome this problem is to associate certain tangibles with the service to give customers a handle for evaluating the service.

For example, Greyhound Lines, Inc. remodelled their terminals to give them a clean, modern appearance; the company also updated their ticketing system to reduce travellers' waiting time. These changes helped Greyhound overcome some negative perceptions with respect to its service. Customers had perceived bus terminals as dirty and crime-ridden; they also resented spending a lot of time in the terminal while waiting to buy tickets. Such changes represent tangible cues that send positive messages to Greyhound's customers about the quality of the service.

Service-providers can be trained to offer tangible evidence about the quality of the service. US ski resorts believe that they offer some advantages that make them superior to foreign ski resorts. For example, they offer facial tissues at the lifts and ski patrols on the trails. They have also invested in trail-grooming equipment, snow-producing equipment and high-speed lifts to ensure optimal snow conditions and minimal loss of ski time.

Ski resorts in the western US have enhanced their product value with the 'Western' image. The concept of the Wild West is very salable abroad, and foreign visitors are intrigued by barbecues and cowboys.

Price

In some respects, pricing services does not differ from pricing goods. That is, the service marketer must consider the size of the target market, the demand for the service, and the costs of producing the service to determine projected profit. Price can then be set accordingly.

However, in other respects there are some differences. For example, since services are intangibles, customers must often rely on price to determine quality. Up to a point, higher prices would suggest better quality service to the customer.

Another pricing practice in the service sector is to group services and sell them as a package to the customer. One example is a hotel that sells a weekend package for two, complete with two nights' lodging, complimentary breakfast and one round of golf at a nearby country club. Because the ratio of fixed costs to variable costs is high in services, this type of pricing tactic can be very effective and profitable. Also, because the customer perceives added value to the service, grouping services is an excellent way to increase usage among current customers and add customers to the pool.

Recent trends in the marketplace have caused the pricing element of the marketing mix to take an active role rather than a passive role with respect to marketplace competition. One example is deregulation among airlines. Airline passengers today face a bewildering collection of fare categories and discounts – not to mention the multitude of restrictions that accompany them.

Some services do lend themselves to price negotiation. For example, some financial, legal, or medical assistance services allow the customer to consider various options. Car repair, beauty consultation and physical fitness programmes can also represent variable pricing depending on customers' wants and needs.

Service marketers should keep in mind their company's objectives and their marketing objectives when setting a pricing policy for services. As with goods, services pricing should take a portfolio approach, with each offering making a significant contribution to the firm's overall profitability and competitive posture in the marketplace. Some products may be very profitable, some may serve to raise demand during off-peak fluctuations, and some may serve as loss leaders to attract new business.

Promotion

One way to make intangible services more tangible to customers is to provide tangible cues that relate to the service that is being promoted. Many companies choose to use celebrities to promote their services. If it is, for example, financial services, they are likely to pick someone who represents reliability and trustworthiness to the target audience. If, however, they want to promote their service as being for young, fun-loving people, they may use a sporting hero instead.

American Express also uses spokespersons; recently, however, its strategy has been to feature well-known cardholders. By using a variety of individuals, American Express suggests that 'everybody who is anybody' holds American Express cards.

In the insurance industry in the UK, Prudential uses a rock and Legal and General use an umbrella as their symbols of security and reliability. All of these symbols are designed to communicate subtle but strong messages about the coverage provided by these insurance companies.

Another way to use promotion to make services more tangible for customers is to feature some object that represents the service. For example, a tanning salon may show its tanning booths, a hotel may show guests relaxing by the swimming pool or enjoying a fine meal, and a financial planner may show his clients living in a desirable retirement community.

Personal selling is often an important element in the promotion mix for services. Face-to-face communication allows buyers and sellers to interact and obtain immediate feedback from each other. Sales personnel use this opportunity to reduce customer uncertainty, better explain product benefits, and enhance the image of the service company.

Customers generally seem to prefer word-of-mouth communication about products, especially concerning services. Service firms should do everything possible to stimulate positive word-of-mouth testimonials among their customers. A service firm can offer discounts, bonuses or gifts to customers who bring in new business for them.

Distribution

Generally, you can assume that the distribution channel for services will be shorter than that for goods, because services are perishable. They cannot be stored, transported or inventoried.

Another characteristic is that convenience is of paramount importance to consumers of services. Because of the now widespread availability of ATMs, the importance of convenient locations for banks has somewhat lessened. Nevertheless, location is still probably the number one criterion for consumers of a variety of services, including financial institutions. A factor related to convenience is scheduling. For airlines, doctors, dentists, buses and many other services, customers want to know that these are available at desirable times of the day and week and also when the customer desires to use them.

Two major decisions must be made by services marketers when determining their distribution strategies. First, the distribution objectives must be set. For example, the number of outlets and the intensity of the distribution of those outlets must be decided. Too many outlets means that unnecessary costs are incurred that may prevent the company from achieving a profit. Too few outlets means lost opportunities for sales. The market analysis that is done in the planning stages should provide the information necessary to make wise distribution decisions.

The next issue is whether to distribute services directly to end-users or indirectly through other channel intermediaries. Simple distribution systems are generally preferred for services. Many services require direct marketing to the ultimate consumer, such as medical, dental and legal services. Others, such as the airlines, have developed very effective distribution through independent intermediaries, such as travel agents, hotels and tour managers.

Non-Profit Marketing

The Heart Association solicits donations for research. The Red Cross persuades donors to give blood. Universities try to increase the number of high-calibre students they attract. These are all examples of non-profit marketing.

Sometimes called non-business marketing, this branch of the marketing discipline focuses on marketing by individuals or organisations whose goals are something other than ordinary business goals of profit and return on investment.

Another branch of non-profit marketing concerns the marketing of social causes and organisations, including groups such as the National Organisation of Women (NOW), the Conservative and Labour Parties, and recycling programmes. Their tactics differ, but these groups and others like them need and use the principles of marketing that apply to traditional business entities.

Specifically these groups need to do the following:

1 Identify their target market – clients, patrons, members or sponsors.
2 Set objectives that are in keeping with the overall goals of the organisation or group.
3 Develop and maintain a satisfying product, usually a service. The possibilities range from a library offering reading seminars to a police department offering self-defence training. It could include colleges soliciting students and political candidates soliciting votes.
4 Decide on a pricing policy and set the charges. Often these prices are not expressed in financial terms. The 'price' may be a fee, donation, tuition, fine, vote, fare, rate, or simply attendance at an event.
5 Set up a distribution system. This includes scheduling events, deciding where to hold the events or programmes, and making any contractual agreements with other suppliers. For example, when the 'bloodmobile' comes to campus to take blood from students and staff, the Red Cross must schedule a time, provide the on-site facility, and make arrangements with the university administration.
6 Communicate availability of the product to the group's constituencies through brochures, signs, public service announcements, advertisements, publicity releases and word-of-mouth.

Although many non-profit organisations carry out these activities, they often do not realise that they are engaging in marketing practices. However, larger, more successful non-profit institutions, such as Oxfam or UNICEF, have embraced marketing as a means to accomplish many of their goals.

SUMMARY

Services marketing differs from goods marketing in several ways. It involves intangible products that may not be comprehended by customers as easily as tangible products. Services are inseparable from the providers that offer them, and they are perishable. They also vary from one purchase to the next.

Services are sold in both the consumer and the business-to-business sectors. The amount of equipment needed to provide the service and the level of skill required from service-providers differs widely.

Service marketers need to find ways to enhance their competitive positions in the marketplace. This can be done through differentiation, better quality and increased productivity. The key in any case is to match the service offering to the needs and resources of the target market. Consequently, each element of the marketing mix must be carefully evaluated to provide customers with the most appealing bundle of product attributes, prices, promotion and distribution.

Executives and managers who run non-profit organisations also engage in marketing, although they may not always recognise that that is what they are doing. Nevertheless, such groups as Enable, The Liberal Democratic Party and Save the Whale, as well as a plethora of charitable and community organisations, identify target markets and present marketing mixes for their constituencies.

FURTHER READING

Assael, Henry. 1985. *Marketing Management*. Boston: Kent Publishing Co., Chapters 22 and 23.

Bateson John E.G. 1989. *Managing Services Marketing*. Hinsdale, Illinois: Dryden Press: 4.

Berry, Leonard L. 1980. 'Services Marketing Is Different.' *Business* (May/Jun.): 24–29.

Cowell, D. 1987. *The Marketing of Services*. The Marketing Series, Chartered Institute of Marketing. Heinemann.

Fine, Seymour H. 1990. *Social Marketing*. Boston: Allyn and Bacon.

Heskett, James L. 1987. 'Thank Heaven for the Service Sector.' *Business Week* (26 Jan.): 22.

Lamb, Jr., Charles W. and Cravens, David W. 1990. 'Services Marketing – Reaching the Customer and Creating Satisfaction.' *Business* (Jan./Mar.): 13–19.

Pope, N.W. 1979. 'Mickey Mouse Marketing.' *American Banker* (25 Jul.): 4, 14.

Pride, William M. and Ferrell, O. C., 1991. *Marketing*, 7th ed. Boston: Houghton Mifflin Co., Chapter 22.

Rados, David L. 1981. *Marketing for Non-Profit Organizations*. Boston: Auburn House.

Zeithaml, Valarie A., Parasuraman, A. and Berry, Leonard L. 1985. 'Problems and Strategies in Services Marketing.' *Journal of Marketing* (Spring): 33–6.

23 Marketing and Society

It is now considered totally irresponsible for any company to alienate all or part of its target market. Legislation on what is and is not acceptable is now much more stringent and the public will react directly by ceasing to purchase from that particular company.

Perrier Water of France had to completely withdraw their product from the marketplace throughout Europe when it was discovered that there were traces of mercury in the water. Perrier acted quickly and decisively, correcting the situation and although they lost sales in the short term, their long-term image was that of a caring company.

Benetton also succumbed to social pressures against their controversial adverstisements showing new-born babies. Although they created awareness for the company, they were not considered acceptable by a large proportion of their audience.

Some companies, like Benetton, may decide to run the risk of alienating some consumers in order to create product awareness, but in a society which is increasingly aware of its rights and not averse to making its feelings known, this is a very risky strategy to adopt.

'Vaporware' is the derogatory term used for software products that have been announced but are not available. 'Marketecture' describes what a software company does when it markets by promising customers a future strategic direction. These tactics have become so annoying to customers that a coalition of 17 software companies and a committee of the Computer Software & Services Industry Association has written a white paper to condemn these practices.

Are consumers willing to pay more for environmentally-safe products? And what exactly constitutes an environmentally-safe product? Words like 'biodegradable' and 'environmentally-friendly' have been bandied about for years. But the evidence shows that although most consumers say they are concerned about the environment, they have not yet shown a marked preference for products made by environmentally responsible companies.

Marketers are in the business of finding unmet needs and creating a marketing mix to satisfy those needs and, in the process, creating a profit for the firm. This sounds like a relatively easy procedure. But, as the examples illustrate, marketing is much more complex than the casual observer may realise.

The preceding scenarios offer just a few examples of the social impact of marketing. The purpose of this chapter is to examine social criticisms of marketing, looking at both the pros and cons of each argument. We will also discuss some of the ways in which society and marketers themselves are seeking to improve marketing's record on social responsibility.

Criticisms of Marketing

Consumers, society as a whole, and even other businesses, express concern about the impact marketing has on individuals and groups. These concerns have given impetus to various kinds of responses in the past: consumer action groups, government regulation, and industry regulation of itself. If we examine the source of most of these actions, we will find that they arise in response to fairly specific abuses. One axiom to remember is that if business will not act in a socially responsible way, someone will take action to see that it does. And, unfortunately, the actions may be excessive or not very well thought out. Certainly the ideal is for business to regulate itself.

In the following section, we discuss some of the criticisms of marketing that have been most prevalent over the years.

Higher Prices

The concept that marketing activities cause higher prices is not new. After all, it stands to reason that someone must pay for product development, attractive packaging, advertising, and delivery of the product to the customer.

One of the favourite scapegoats, as we discussed in Chapter 10, is the middleman. Critics insist that there are too many middle-men and/or that intermediaries are inefficient, poorly-managed, or provide unnecessary services. Remember, however, that someone must perform the distribution services. If they are not performed by intermediaries in the marketing channel, then the activities must be performed by the customer.

Advertising is frequently criticised as adding to the cost of products. Marketers admit that many ads are ineffective, not to mention misleading, annoying and sometimes in bad taste. But the use of advertising can, and often does, lower prices.

Good advertising – the kind that is well thought out, and carefully planned and executed – is an efficient and effective method of informing large numbers of consumers at a relatively small cost per person reached. Advertised products that satisfy consumer needs lead to greater demand for the products, which, in turn, leads to economies of scale in manufacturing, distribution and sales. Because the savings generated from these economies of scale often exceed the costs of advertising, prices may actually be lower. Recall, for example, the dramatic drop in the price of calculators in the late 1970s as demand rose and the number of competitors increased. Within two years, the price of a simple calculator fell from approximately £30 to less than a third of that cost.

Deceptive Practices

Deceptive practices occur in several areas of marketing. Some products promise to deliver far more than they actually can. Some advertisers make claims that cannot be substantiated. And sometimes deceptive 'bargain prices' are promoted. Within marketing, several versions of each of these practices can be found.

Some industries also seem to be more prone to abuse than others. Bad practices tend to flourish where the consumer does not have the means or expertise to fully judge the value of the service being performed. If your car mechanic claims that your car needs a new air-conditioner compressor, can you determine whether that diagnosis is accurate or whether the compressor belt simply needs to be tightened?

Unfair Sales Tactics

Salespeople are often targeted as offenders when it comes to questionable marketing practices. Salespeople may use high-pressure sales styles that convince people to buy things they do not need or cannot afford.

To counteract such abuses, the law requires a three-day 'cooling off' period in which customers can re-evaluate their buying decisions and change their minds if they wish.

In the US some communities have Green River Ordinances that prohibit door-to-door sales. However, other problems may surface in selling. For example, an industrial salesperson may promise a buyer delivery of vital parts within two weeks, knowing full well that the production schedule would allow shipment in no fewer than four weeks. Such misrepresentation will eventually cost the salesperson's company many customers and may cost the salesperson his or her job.

Reputable companies do not tolerate, much less support, such practices. They know that in the long run they will lose their customers and their good names. For this reason, customer satisfaction should be constantly monitored to ensure that these abuses are not creeping into a firm's marketing system.

Unsafe/Poorly Made Products

Some products lack the functional value that consumers have a right to expect. Cars that break down within the first few months of driving, cereals that have no nutritional value, and air-cleaners that really do nothing for air quality are just a few examples that have made the news in the last few years.

Although most manufacturers want to produce a quality product, some conditions work against them. Inadequate quality control occurs frequently when a company experiences rapid growth and does not have enough time to adjust control mechanisms to cope with increased output. Sometimes poorly trained and/or motivated employees simply fail to perform their tasks correctly. When the costs of raw materials and component parts rise, a company may try to use lower quality parts to keep costs in line. This strategy may also result in a product of inferior quality. For example, several years ago, many fast-food restaurants changed from using real cheese on their burgers to using cheese food. Although many customers did not notice the difference, others complained about the change in flavour.

Planned Obsolescence

Some critics believe that marketers produce and sell products that they plan for customers to have to replace within a short period of time. The fashion industry has been cited most often for this alleged abuse, being charged with changing clothing styles each year so that people (usually women) feel compelled to buy new 'wardrobes'.

However, other industries have also been targeted. The car industry has been accused of failing to offer available technology that might lengthen the life of a vehicle. Others have been cited for using inferior materials and workmanship. Hence, the rise of Japanese product sales over the past decade or so.

Marketers do have some responses that are not entirely without merit. First, they argue that style and function preferences change and that many new product offerings are in response to changing consumer wants. Marketers also point out that in many fields, technology is changing rapidly; it takes time and investment to develop new product features and benefits. Finally, marketers point out that if they were intentionally giving poor value to customers, they would leave themselves vulnerable to their competitors. Unsatisfied customers will quickly jump ship and find a new supplier if better products are available elsewhere.

Forced Materialism

Some believe that marketing activities cause people to want things that they neither want nor need through exposure to intensive marketing efforts. There is some evidence that materialism ranks high in people's priorities. Consider the recent rise in popularity of 'designer' clothing and accessories, and consider, also, that these preferences extend not only to adults but even to primary school children!

However, marketers contend that they do not have the ability to force people to want things in which they would otherwise have no interest. Marketers point to the very high percentage of new product failures as testimony to their inability to manipulate the public.

Making Ethical Decisions

Changes in the marketing environment have brought increased attention to the issues involving marketing ethics. Ethics pertain to standards of acceptable and unacceptable behaviour, standards that are usually determined by society or by the particular groups involved. Morals are often confused with ethics, though indeed, the two subjects overlap.

Although opinions vary with respect to the distinctions between ethics and morals, we will offer a way of viewing the two that may be helpful. Morality concerns absolute standards that are inviolate; they cannot be changed because they are linked to a higher or divine authority. Ethics involve standards imposed by society and/or one's peers. Frequently, in business, as in other areas of life, ethics and morals overlap.

Let's look at some examples. Should researchers divulge to respondents the true intent of their research if divulging that information will bias the results? This is one question of ethics with respect to acceptable market research practices. However, suppose that a car company builds a car with known defects that eventually causes the deaths of some occupants. Most people would argue that this is an ethical question, but more than that, it is a moral question because it involves the company's culpability in a moral issue – untimely death perpetrated by negligence.

If a salesperson lies to a customer to get an order but knows full well that the order cannot be delivered on time, is this an ethical problem or a moral problem? Or both? In many cases, it is difficult to separate the two. Certainly intentional lying would be viewed by many as a moral issue; the fact that the salesperson cannot deliver to the customer is also an ethical problem.

Other issues have surfaced in recent years that are engendering much discussion. Scientific findings about the pollution of our environment by companies and products indicate that we are doing irrevocable damage to our earth and to each other by our actions. Passive smoking is now recognised as carrying a significant health risk to the individual. Mining operations that have polluted streams and rivers are now being blamed for illnesses caused by chemicals in drinking water.

People develop individual standards of behaviour based on their beliefs; companies similarly develop organisational standards of behaviour based on the consensus of decision makers within the organisation. In many cases these sets of values conflict. How can such conflicts be resolved and avoided?

Professional codes of ethics, such as the one shown in Table 23.1 for the American Marketing Association, may provide one common basis of authority for groups such as marketers, doctors, accountants and lawyers. In other cases, companies issue their own codes of ethics and standards of behaviour, particularly for those in sensitive positions, such as salespeople and purchasing agents.

Yet even people within the same organisation may not always agree on ethical and moral standards. How then do people make ethical decisions? Unfortunately, no one has yet come up with a way for a free society to regulate all the behaviours of its citizens. Nor would we want them to!

One study of marketing professionals found that three factors influenced their ethical judgements:

1 The extent of ethical problems within the organisation.
2 Top management actions on ethics.
3 Organisational role – that is, whether they were top executives, sales managers, marketing researchers, etc.

Interestingly, those who perceived few problems within the organisation were more likely to take a strong stand against all unethical behaviour than did those who perceived many ethical problems. One conclusion that may be drawn from this is that the more ethical the environment, the stronger the impetus for keeping it that way. Such findings could suggest some interesting conclusions for society. This study also showed that top management was key in influencing the behaviour of respondents, indicating once more that the role of leadership is imperative in creating and maintaining a healthy ethical environment.

TABLE 23.1 American Marketing Association Code of Ethics

Members of the American Marketing Association (AMA) are committed to ethical professional conduct. They have joined together in subscribing to this Code of ethics embracing the following topics:

Responsibilities of the Marketer

Marketers must accept responsibility for the consequences of their activitues and make every effort to ensure that their decisions, recommendations, and actions function to identify, serve, and satisfy all relevant publics: customers, organisations, and society. Marketer's professional conduct must be guided by:

1. The basic rule of professional ethics: not knowingly to do harm;
2. The adherence to all applicable laws and regulations;
3. The accurate representation of their education, training and experience; and
4. The active support, practice, and promotion of this Code of Ethics.

Honesty and Fairness

Marketers shall uphold and advance the integrity, honour, and dignity of the marketing profession by:

1. Being honest in serving consumers, clients, employees, suppliers, distributors, and the public;
2. Not knowingly participating in conflict of interest without prior notice to all parties involved; and
3. Establishing equitable fee schedules including the payment or receipt of usual, customary, and/or legal compensation for marketing exchanges.

Rights and Duties of Parties in the Marketing Exchange Process

Participants in the marketing exchange process should be able to expect that:

1. Products and services offered are safe and fit for their intended uses;
2. Communications about offered products and services are not deceptive;
3. All parties tend to discharge their obligations, financial and otherwise, in good faith; and
4. Appropriate internal methods exist for equitable adjustment and/or redress of grievances concerning purchases. It is understood that the above would include, *but is not limited to*, the following responsibilities of the marketers:

In the area of product development and management,
☐ Disclosure of all substantial risks associated with product or service usage;
☐ Identification of any product component substitution that might materially change the product or impact on the buyer's purchase decision;
☐ Identification of extra-cost added features;

In the area of promotion,
☐ Avoidance of false and misleading advertising;
☐ Rejection of high-pressure manipulations or misleading sales tactics;
☐ Avoidance of sales promotions that use deception or manipulation.

In the area of distribution,
☐ Not manipulating the availability of a product for purpose of exploitation;
☐ Not using coercion in the marketing channel;
☐ Not exerting undue influence over the reseller's choice to handle a product.

In the area of pricing,
☐ Not engaging in price fixing
☐ Not practicing predatory pricing;
☐ Disclosing the full price associated with any purchase.

In the area of marketing research,
☐ Prohibiting selling or fundraising under the guise of conducting research;
☐ Maintaining research integrity by avoiding misrepresentation and omission of pertinent research data;
☐ Treating outside clients and suppliers fairly.

Organisational Relationships

Marketers should be aware of how their behavior may influence or impact on the behavior of others in organisational relationships. They should not demand, encourage, or apply coercion to obtain unethical behaviour in their relationships with others, such as employers, suppliers, or customers.

1. Apply confidentiality and anonymity in professional relationships with regard to privileged information;
2. Meet their obligations and responsibilities in contracts and mutual agreements in a timely manner;
3. Avoid taking the work of others, in whole or in part, or represent this work as their own or directly benefit from it without compensation or consent of the originator or owner.
4. Avoid manipulation to take advantage of situations to maximize personal welfare in a way that unfairly deprives or damages their organisation or others.

Any AMA member found to be in violation of any provision of this Code of Ethics may have his or her Association membership suspended or revoked.

Source: Reprinted with permission from 'AMA Adopts New Code of Ethics', *Marketing News* (September 11, 1987), pp. 1, 10, published by the American Marketing Association.

Social Responsibility for Marketers

Social responsibility for marketers is not exactly the same as ethics. Ethics is generally regarded as individual and organisational decisions about right and wrong. Social responsibility has more to do with balancing the various demands of society in a way that minimises a company's negative impact on society. For example, smokers demand their right to smoke; non-smokers demand the right to be free of the harmful effects of secondary smoke. Marketing managers of hotels, restaurants and others in the entertainment/hospitality industries have had to cope with compromise in this area, finding acceptable solutions for both sides.

There are several reasons why firms should attend to socially responsible behaviour. First, avoiding violations of deeply-held public values is in the best long-term interest of the firm. Negative publicity can lead to falling sales and dissatisfied customers. In the long run, socially responsible behaviour can help preserve the firm's positive image. Second, socially responsible behaviour not only protects but can greatly enhance the firm's image. Certainly that goal prompts many companies to support the Olympics or to contribute to local community projects, for example.

Third, by initiating socially responsible behaviour, companies and industries can avoid needless and sometimes unreasonable government regulation. Self-regulation is always in business' best interests because only business is in a position to fully comprehend and explore long-term consequences of various solutions to its problems.

Finally, socially responsible behaviour on the part of the marketing community can help to change and shape public expectations. Such overwhelming issues as pollution, a deteriorating infrastructure and joblessness involve tremendous social costs to confront and solve these problems. Education, for example, in the form of public service announcements concerning the costs as well as the side-effects of dealing with social issues, can assist society in developing effective solutions.

Consumerism

The consumer movement is a result of trends begun in the past. Although great strides have been made in the last 30–40 years to respond to consumer concerns, unacceptable business practices and changing social values have led to a continued backlash against business. Consumerism is a social movement designed to put pressure on government and business to assist consumers with problems and to protect them from unfair exploitation. Of course these demands must be balanced against what business can reasonably provide and still survive. After all, profits are the reason for a company to stay in business.

The most quoted statement of consumer rights was given by President John F. Kennedy in 1962:

1 'The right to choose freely'.
   Consumers should have multiple options and the freedom to evaluate and choose from among those options.

2 'The right to be informed'.
Consumer education along with product/service information should be sufficient to allow customers to make informed, responsible buying decisions.

3 'The right to be heard'.
Consumers should be able to appeal to appropriate parties – sellers, consumer advocates, government offices, etc. – in the event of unreasonable treatment.

4 'The right to be safe'.
Consumers should be able to feel confident that the products and services they purchase are not unsafe or hazardous to their health as long as those products are used according to manufacturers' instructions and under normal conditions.

SUMMARY

Over the years, many criticisms have been levelled at marketing. Some of these include higher prices, deceptive practices, unfair sales tactics, unsafe or poorly-made products, planned obsolescence and forced materialism. In each case, both sides of the argument have some legitimate points. Marketers have tried to address these concerns by emphasising marketing ethics more and more and by trying to become more socially responsible.

Ethical norms are far from standardised in the business community. However, many professional groups as well as individual business organisations have developed ethical standards to which their members/employees must adhere. These standards show a serious attempt on the part of the business community to be accountable and responsive to society.

Socially responsible programmes are another way that businesses have tried to respond to society's concerns. By recognising the impact and the legitimacy of many consumer complaints, these companies have gone beyond merely an economic interest in their communities and have begun taking active roles in promoting community welfare.

FURTHER READING

'A New Sales Pitch: The Environment.' 1989. *Business Week* (24 July): 50.

Boone, Louis E. and Kurtz, David L. 1992. *Contemporary Marketing*, 7th ed. Ft. Worth, Texas: Dryden Press, Chapter 2.

Buchholz, Rogene. 1989. *Business Environment and Public Policy*, 3rd ed. Englewood Cliffs, New Jersey: Prentice Hall.

Lamb, Jr. Charles W., Hair, Jr., Joseph F. and McDaniel, Carl. 1992. *Principles of Marketing*. Cincinnati: South-Western Publishing Co.

Ottman, Jacquelyn. 1990. 'Environment Concerns Open Markets for New Products.' *Marketing News* (19 Mar.):21.

'P&G Tries Hauling Itself Out of America's Trash Heap.' 1990. *Business Week* (23 Apr.): 101.

Pride, William B. and Ferrell, O. C., 1991. *Marketing*, 7th ed. Boston: Houghton Mifflin Co., Chapter 3.

Index